American
English File

Student Book **3**

Clive Oxenden
Christina Latham-Koenig

OXFORD
UNIVERSITY PRESS

Paul Seligson and Clive Oxenden are the
original co-authors of *English File 1* (pub. 1996)
and *English File 2* (pub. 1997).

Contents

Look out for Study Link
This shows you where to find extra material for more practice and review.

G present tenses: simple and continuous, action and non-action verbs
V food and restaurants
P /ʊ/ and /u/, understanding phonetics

Food: fuel or pleasure?

1 READING & SPEAKING

a What kind of food or dishes do you associate with these countries?

The United States	China	France
Italy	Japan	Mexico

b Read the interviews with **Alice** and **Jacqueline**. Match the questions with their answers.

We talk to women around the world about their relationship with food.

1 Is food a pleasure for you?
2 What do you normally eat on a typical day?
3 Do you ever cook?
4 Do you ever eat "unhealthy" food? How do you feel about it?
5 Are you trying to cut down on anything at the moment?
6 Are people's diets in your country getting better or worse?

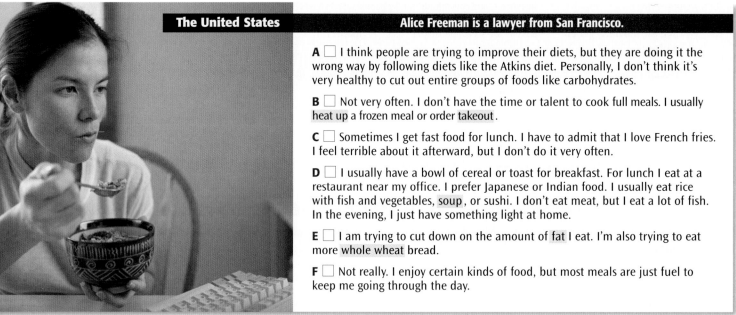

| The United States | Alice Freeman is a lawyer from San Francisco. |

A ☐ I think people are trying to improve their diets, but they are doing it the wrong way by following diets like the Atkins diet. Personally, I don't think it's very healthy to cut out entire groups of foods like carbohydrates.

B ☐ Not very often. I don't have the time or talent to cook full meals. I usually heat up a frozen meal or order takeout.

C ☐ Sometimes I get fast food for lunch. I have to admit that I love French fries. I feel terrible about it afterward, but I don't do it very often.

D ☐ I usually have a bowl of cereal or toast for breakfast. For lunch I eat at a restaurant near my office. I prefer Japanese or Indian food. I usually eat rice with fish and vegetables, soup, or sushi. I don't eat meat, but I eat a lot of fish. In the evening, I just have something light at home.

E ☐ I am trying to cut down on the amount of fat I eat. I'm also trying to eat more whole wheat bread.

F ☐ Not really. I enjoy certain kinds of food, but most meals are just fuel to keep me going through the day.

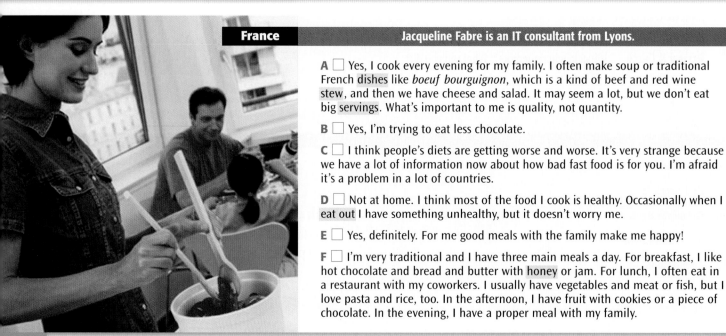

| France | Jacqueline Fabre is an IT consultant from Lyons. |

A ☐ Yes, I cook every evening for my family. I often make soup or traditional French dishes like *boeuf bourguignon*, which is a kind of beef and red wine stew, and then we have cheese and salad. It may seem a lot, but we don't eat big servings. What's important to me is quality, not quantity.

B ☐ Yes, I'm trying to eat less chocolate.

C ☐ I think people's diets are getting worse and worse. It's very strange because we have a lot of information now about how bad fast food is for you. I'm afraid it's a problem in a lot of countries.

D ☐ Not at home. I think most of the food I cook is healthy. Occasionally when I eat out I have something unhealthy, but it doesn't worry me.

E ☐ Yes, definitely. For me good meals with the family make me happy!

F ☐ I'm very traditional and I have three main meals a day. For breakfast, I like hot chocolate and bread and butter with honey or jam. For lunch, I often eat in a restaurant with my coworkers. I usually have vegetables and meat or fish, but I love pasta and rice, too. In the afternoon, I have fruit with cookies or a piece of chocolate. In the evening, I have a proper meal with my family.

c Read the interviews again and answer the questions below. Write **A** (*Alice*), **J** (*Jacqueline*), or **B** (*both of them*).

Who...?

1 often eats in restaurants ____
2 eats quite a lot of sweet things ____
3 eats take-out food ____
4 cooks big meals at home ____
5 enjoys eating ____
6 feels bad when she eats fast food ____
7 is trying to eat less of something ____
8 prefers having good food to having a lot of food ____
9 is negative about eating habits in her country ____

d Match the highlighted words or phrases with the definitions.

1 _____ to have a meal in a restaurant, not at home
2 _____ a sweet, thick liquid made by bees
3 _____ the quantity you eat of a kind of food during a meal
4 _____ to make cold food hot
5 _____ food you buy from a restaurant to eat at home
6 _____ substance from animals or plants used for cooking, e.g., oil, butter, etc.
7 _____ food prepared in a particular way, e.g., sushi, lasagna, etc.
8 _____ made from brown flour
9 _____ a liquid food, often made of vegetables, e.g., tomatoes, onions
10 _____ meat cooked for a long time in liquid, usually with vegetables

e Which of the two women do you think has the healthier diet? Why?

f Now interview each other with the questions from **1b**. How similar are your eating habits?

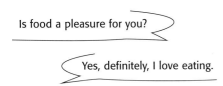

Is food a pleasure for you?

Yes, definitely, I love eating.

2 GRAMMAR present tenses: simple and continuous, action and non-action verbs

Rumiko Yasuda is a magazine editor from Tokyo.	Japan

a 🔊 **1.1** Listen to Rumiko answering questions 2–6 from the interviews. Do you think food is fuel or pleasure for her? Why?

b Listen again and answer the questions.

1 What does she usually have in the morning?
2 Where does she usually have lunch and dinner?
3 Why doesn't she cook very often?
4 Does she eat or drink anything unhealthy?
5 Is she cutting down on anything right now? Why (not)?
6 What's currently happening to the Japanese diet?
7 Does she think this is a completely bad thing?

c Look at some of the things Rumiko said. Circle the correct form. Then compare with a partner and say why the other form is wrong.

1 *I don't usually have* / *I'm not having* breakfast.
2 I used to go to fast-food restaurants, but now *I prefer* / *I am preferring* eating something healthier.
3 *I am drinking* / *I drink* a lot of coffee every day.
4 I think that some Japanese people *get* / *are getting* fatter.
5 *I like* / *I'm liking* the fact that there are more different kinds of food and restaurants now.

d → **p.130 Grammar Bank 1A.** Read the rules and do the exercises.

e Make questions with the simple present or present continuous to ask your partner. Ask for more information.

What / usually have for breakfast?
How many cups of coffee / drink a day?
Where / usually have lunch?
How often / eat out a week?
/ prefer to eat at home or to eat out?
/ need to buy any food today?
/ you hungry? / want something to eat?
/ currently take any vitamins or food supplements?
/ currently try to eat in a healthy way?

3 VOCABULARY food and restaurants

a Take the quiz in pairs.

Food Quiz

Can you think of …?

ONE **red** fruit, ONE yellow fruit, ONE green fruit

TWO things that a strict vegetarian doesn't eat

THREE kinds of food that are made from milk

FOUR things people have for breakfast

FIVE things people eat between meals

SIX vegetables you can put in a salad

SEVEN things that are usually on a table in a restaurant

b 🔿 **p.144 Vocabulary Bank** *Food and restaurants.*

c Ask and answer the questions below with a partner.

Food and eating

1 How often do you eat…?
a take-out food   b frozen meals
c low-fat food   d homemade food

2 What's your favorite…?
a fruit   b vegetable   c snack
d homemade dish

3 What food do you like to eat…?
a when the weather's very cold
b when you're feeling a little depressed
c for Sunday lunch

4 Is there any kind of food you <u>can't</u> eat?

Restaurants

5 What's your favorite…?
a kind of restaurant (French, Italian, etc.)
b restaurant dish   c take-out food

6 How important are these things to you in a restaurant?
Number 1–4 (1 = the most important)
the food ☐   the service ☐
the atmosphere ☐   the price ☐

7 How do you prefer these things to be cooked?
(grilled, boiled, etc.)
chicken   fish   eggs   potatoes

8 If you eat steak, how do you like it cooked?
(rare, medium, well-done)

4 PRONUNCIATION /ʊ/ and /u/, understanding phonetics

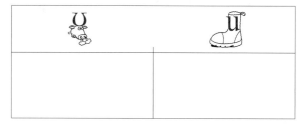

a Look at the sound pictures. How do you pronounce them?

b Put the words in the correct column.

cook	cookies	food	fruit	good
juice	mousse	soup	spoon	sugar

c 🔊 **1.2** Listen and check.

d 🔿 **p.157 Sound Bank.** Look at the typical spellings for /ʊ/ and /u/.

e Look at the information box. How do phonetic symbols in a dictionary help you pronounce words correctly?

> ⚠ **Pronouncing difficult words**
>
> Some words are difficult to pronounce because
> 1 they have a silent syllable or letter, e.g., *vegetables* /ˈvɛdʒtəblz/
> 2 some letters are pronounced in an unusual way e.g., *steak* /steɪk/
> 3 you aren't sure where the stress is, e.g., *dessert* /dɪˈzɜrt/

f 🔊 **1.3** Look at some food words that are difficult to pronounce. Use the phonetics to practice saying them correctly. Then listen and check.

1	knife	/naɪf/
	fruit	/frut/
	salmon	/ˈsæmən/
2	sausage	/ˈsɔsɪdʒ/
	lettuce	/ˈlɛtəs/
	sugar	/ˈʃʊgər/
3	yogurt	/ˈyoʊgərt/
	menu	/ˈmɛnyu/
	diet	/ˈdaɪət/

g 🔊 **1.4** Listen and repeat the sentences.

1 The first course on the menu is lettuce soup.
2 What vegetables would you like with your steak?
3 Do you want yogurt or chocolate mousse for dessert?
4 I take two spoonfuls of sugar in my coffee.
5 Sausage isn't very good for you.
6 Would you like some fruit juice?

5 LISTENING

a Have you ever tried English food? What did you think of it?

b 🔊 **1.5** Kevin Poulter, an English chef, has a restaurant in Santiago, the capital of Chile. Listen to an interview with him and number the photos 1–5 in the order he mentions them.

c Listen again and answer the questions.

1 Why did he decide to open a restaurant in Chile? *New Ideas*
2 Why did he call it Frederick's?
3 Why were Chilean people surprised when he opened his restaurant?
4 What English dishes does he serve in his restaurant? Are they popular?
5 How many women work in his kitchen? Why does he think there are so few women in restaurant kitchens?
6 What is most difficult for him about life in Chile?

d What kinds of restaurants are there in your town? What nationalities do they represent? Which ones do you like?

A

B

D

C

E

6 SPEAKING

a Work in groups of three **A**, **B**, and **C**. First read sentences 1–6 and decide (individually) whether you agree or disagree. Think about examples you can use to support your point of view.

1 Women worry more about their diet than men.
2 Young people today have a worse diet than they did ten years ago.
3 Men cook as a hobby; women cook because they have to.
4 Vegetarians are healthier than people who eat a lot of meat.
5 You can often eat better in cheap restaurants than in expensive ones.
6 Every country thinks that its cooking is the best.

b Now **A** say what you think about sentence 1. **B** and **C** listen and then agree or disagree with **A**. Then **B** say what you think about sentence 2, etc. Try to use the expressions in **Useful language**.

Useful language

For example,…   I agree.   I don't agree.   I think that's true.   I don't think that's true.   (I think) it depends.

G past tenses: simple, continuous, perfect
V sports
P /ɔr/ and /ər/

If you really want to win, cheat

1 GRAMMAR past tenses: simple, continuous, perfect

a In which sports are there the most cases of cheating? How do people cheat in these sports?

b Read the article and find out how the people cheated.

Famous (cheating) moments in sport

Divine intervention?

With a little help from my friends

Dishonischenko!

1 SOCCER

Argentina was playing England in the quarter-finals of the 1986 World Cup in Mexico. In the 52nd minute the Argentinian captain, Diego Maradona, scored a goal. The English players protested, but the referee allowed the goal. However, TV cameras showed that Maradona had scored the goal with his hand! Maradona said the next day, "It was partly the hand of Maradona, and partly the hand of God."

Later in the game Maradona scored another goal and Argentina won 2-1. They went on to win the World Cup.

2 TRACK AND FIELD

Fred Lorz, from New York, won the marathon at the St Louis Olympic Games in 1904. He finished the race in three hours 13 minutes.

After the race, Fred was waiting to get his medal, and the spectators were cheering him loudly. Alice Roosevelt, the daughter of the US President, was in the crowd, and some journalists took a photo of Fred with her. But then suddenly somebody started shouting "cheater" and soon everybody was shouting the same thing. It was true. Fred had traveled 18 of the 42 kilometers in somebody's car! Fred didn't win the gold medal and he was banned from track and field.

3 FENCING

Boris Onischenko, an army officer from the Soviet Union, was competing against Jim Fox from Britain in the 1976 Montreal Olympics. Boris was winning and the electronic scoreboard was showing hit after hit for him. Jim Fox protested to the referee. Fox said that Boris was scoring points without hitting him. Olympic officials examined Boris's sword and they made a shocking discovery. Boris had changed the electronic part of his sword. He could turn on the hit light on the scoreboard even when he hadn't hit Fox. Boris went home the next day, in disgrace. The British newspapers called him "Dishonischenko."

c Look at the highlighted verbs in text 1. What three tenses are they? <u>Underline</u> an example of each tense in the other two texts.

d Which of the three tenses in **c** do we use for…?

  1 completed actions in the past _____
  2 an action in progress at a particular moment in the past _____
  3 an action that happened *before* the past time we are talking about _____

e ⟳ **p.130 Grammar Bank 1B.** Read the rules and do the exercises.

f Cover the texts. In pairs, retell the three stories using the correct tenses.

Text 1	**Text 2**	**Text 3**
England (play) Argentina.	Fred Lorz (win) the marathon in 1904.	Boris Onischenko (compete) against Jim Fox.
Maradona (score) a goal.	He (wait) to get his medal.	Boris (win) but Jim Fox (protest).
The English players (protest) but the referee (allow) the goal.	The spectators (cheer).	The Olympic officials (examine) Boris's sword.
The TV cameras (show) that Maradona (score) the goal with his hand.	Everybody (start) shouting "cheater."	They (discover) that he (change) the electronic part of his sword.
	Fred (travel) 18 km by car!	

2 SPEAKING

a You are going to tell a story. Choose one of the topics below and plan what you are going to say. Ask your teacher for any words you need.

Tell your partner about…

a time you or someone you know cheated (on an exam or in a sport / game)

What were you / was he / she / doing?
Where? When?
Why did you / he / she / cheat? What happened?

a really exciting sports event you saw

Where and when was it?
Who was playing?
What happened?
Why was it so exciting?

a time you had an accident or got a sports injury

What were you doing? How did the accident happen? What part of your body did you hurt? What happened next? How long did it take you to recover?

a time you saw or met a celebrity

Where were you? What was the celebrity doing? What was he / she wearing? Did you speak to him / her? What happened?

b In pairs, tell each other your stories. Ask for more details.

3 LISTENING

a Can you think of two disadvantages of being a professional soccer referee?

b 🔊 **1.6** You're going to hear an interview with a former Champions League referee from Spain. Listen and choose a, b, or c.

Juan Antonio Marín
refereed 200 league and 50 international games

1 What was the most exciting game he ever refereed?
  a His first professional game.
  b He can't choose just one.
  c Real Madrid against Barcelona.

2 Why does he mention Mauro Silva?
  a Because he was the best player he ever saw.
  b Because he was a great person.
  c Because he was a very good player and a good person.

3 The worst experience he ever had as a referee was…
  a when a player hit him during a game.
  b when a woman with a child tried to attack him.
  c when a 16-year-old boy attacked him.

4 Why does he think there is more cheating in soccer today?
  a Because soccer is big business.
  b Because the referees are worse.
  c Because the players are better at cheating.

5 How does he say the players cheat?
  a They fall down when nobody has touched them.
  b They accept money to lose games.
  c They touch the ball with their hands.

6 What's the most difficult thing for him about being a referee?
  a Players who cheat.
  b Making decisions.
  c The rules are too complicated.

7 Does he think fair play still exists?
  a Yes.
  b No.
  c He doesn't say.

c Listen again for more information. Do you agree with him that there is more cheating in soccer (or other sports) than before?

4 VOCABULARY sports

a In pairs, take the quiz.

Sports Quiz

1 How long does a soccer game last?
2 How many referees are there in a basketball game?
3 How many players are there on a volleyball team?
4 How often are the Olympic Games held?
5 How long is a marathon?
6 How many holes are there on a golf course?
7 How long is one lap of a running track?

b ➲ **p.145 Vocabulary Bank** *Sports.*

c In pairs, think of a sports team in your town / country and answer the questions.

- ⚾ What's the name of the team?
- 🎱 What sport do they play?
- 🏀 Where do they play? (in a stadium, arena, etc.)
- ⚽ Who is…?
  a the coach
  b the captain
  c the best player on the team
- 🎾 How many spectators watch their games?
- 🏐 What happened in their last game?

5 PRONUNCIATION /ɔr/ and /ər/

a Write the words in the correct column. Be careful with or (there are two possible pronunciations).

| were | serve | shorts | world | four | girl | hurt |
| score | sport | shirt | warm up | worse | court |

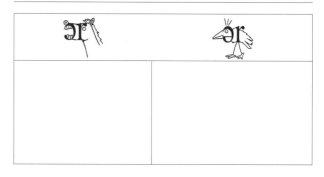

b ◀ **1.7** Listen and check.

c ➲ **p.157 Sound Bank.** Look at the typical spellings for these sounds.

d ◀ **1.8** Practice saying these sentences. Listen and check.

1 I got hurt when I caught the ball.
2 Her serve's worse than the other girl's.
3 It was a tie. The score was 4–4.
4 It's the worst sport in the world.
5 We warmed up on the court.
6 They wore red shirts and white shorts.

6 SPEAKING

In pairs, interview your partner about sports using the questionnaire. Ask for more information.

Do you like sports?

YES

What sport(s) do you play?

Have you ever won a cup or a trophy?

Have you ever been injured playing sports?

Do you prefer playing sports or being a spectator?

Do you prefer watching individual or team sports?

Do you go to watch a local sports team?

Are there good sports facilities in your town?

Is there any sport you'd like to learn to play well?

How many hours do you spend a week watching sports on TV?

NO

What sports do / did you have to play at school?

Do / did you enjoy it?

Do you play any sports in your free time?

Do you think you're in shape?
Would you like to be in better shape?

Do your family and friends like sports?

Is there any sport you don't mind watching on TV?

What sport do you hate watching most on TV?

Have you ever been to a big sports event?

Do you think physical education should be optional at school?

7 READING

When you hear the final whistle

1 *F* One of the hardest things for any professional athlete to do is to know when to retire. Do you retire when you are at your physical peak or do you wait until your body (or your coach) tells you that it's time to go? But even harder is finding the answer to the question "What am I going to do with the rest of my life?"

2 _____. "There's a high risk of depression and people often find adjusting to a new way of life difficult," says Ian Cockerill, a sports psychologist. "For athletes, there's an extra trauma — the loss of status, the loss of recognition, and the loss of the glamour. That's the hardest part." As Eddie Acaro, the US jockey says, "When a jockey retires, he becomes just another little man."

3 _____. Perhaps they just can't stand life without the high of playing professional sports. Michael Jordan, the greatest basketball player of all time, retired three times. He retired once from the Chicago Bulls, made a successful comeback with the Bulls, and then retired again. His second comeback with an inferior team ended in failure, and he retired forever at the age of 40. Jordan said, "There will never be anything I do that will fulfill me as much as competing did."

4 _____. Muhammad Ali needed the money, but his comeback fight, at the age of 39, against Trevor Berbick, was one of the saddest spectacles in modern sports. After losing to Berbick, Ali retired permanently. Three years later, he developed Parkinson's disease.

5 _____. As Jimmy Greaves, a former soccer player for England, said, "I think that a lot of players would prefer to be shot once their career is over." Many of them spend their retirement in a continual battle against depression, alcohol, or drugs.

6 _____. Franz Beckenbauer is a classic example of a soccer player who won everything with his club, Bayern Munich. After retiring, he became a successful coach with Bayern and finally president of the club. John McEnroe, the infamous "bad boy" of tennis, is now a highly respected and highly paid TV commentator. But sadly, for most professional athletes these cases are the exceptions.

Muhammad Ali, former US boxer

Franz Beckenbauer, former German soccer player

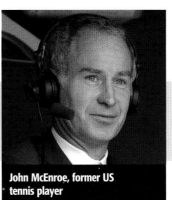

John McEnroe, former US tennis player

Michael Jordan, former US basketball player

a Look at the photos. In pairs, answer the questions.

Have you ever seen any of these people playing sports?
At what age do you think people reach their peak in these sports?
Do you know what these people do now?

b Read the article once. Do most professional athletes find it easy or difficult to retire?

c Complete the article with sentences A–F below.

> **A** For some people the pain of saying good-bye never leaves them.
> **B** Others can't resist the chance of one last "pay day."
> **C** Some athletes go on playing too long.
> **D** But for the lucky few, retirement can mean a successful new career.
> **E** Retirement for people in general is traumatic.
> **F** ~~One of the hardest things for any professional athlete to do is to know when to retire.~~

d Can you remember these words? If not, check with the text. Underline the stressed syllable.

1 adjective: *depressed*   noun: _depression_
2 adjective: *glamorous*   noun: glamor
3 verb: *lose*   noun: loss
4 verb: *recognize*   noun: reconition
5 verb: *fail*   noun: _____
6 verb: *retire*   noun: retirement

e Think of an athlete from your country who has retired. What is he / she doing now? Do you think he / she retired at the right time?

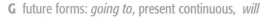

G future forms: *going to*, present continuous, *will*
V family, personality
P prefixes and suffixes

We are family

1 VOCABULARY & SPEAKING family

a Look at the two pictures. Which one do you think shows the typical family of the future?

Read the first paragraph of the article and find out.

Families have a great-great future

Twenty years ago, the typical extended family was "wide." It usually consisted of two or three generations, with many children in each nuclear family. People had lots of aunts and uncles but often didn't know their grandparents. However, according to a new study, the family is changing shape. The family groups of the future will be "long and thin," with three or four small generations.

Here are some of their predictions:

1 Most children will know their great-grandparents (and even great-great-grandparents) because people are living longer.

2 Very few children will have brothers or sisters, and it will be common to be an only child. As a result, future generations will not have many cousins either.

3 Many children will grow up isolated from other children and young adults. This may make them more selfish and introverted.

4 More couples will divorce and remarry, some more than once. They may have children with their new partners, so many children will have a stepmother or stepfather and half-brothers or half-sisters.

5 There will be many "boomerang children." These are children who leave home to get married, but then divorce and return to live with their parents.

6 There will be more single-parent families .

7 Because houses are now so expensive, different generations may decide to live together, so parents, grandparents, and adult children may co-own their houses, and many couples will have to live with their in-laws .

b Now read the whole article. Match the ▢highlighted▢ words with the definitions.

1 _____ your grandparents' parents
2 _____ a child who doesn't have any brothers or sisters
3 _____ families where the mother or father is bringing up the children on his / her own
4 _____ your uncle's or aunt's children
5 _____ the family of your husband / wife
6 _____ all your relatives including aunts, grandparents, etc.
7 _____ your grandparents' grandparents
8 _____ boys who have (for example) the same father but a different mother
9 _____ the new wife of your father
10 _____ two people who are having a relationship

c Read the seven predictions again. In pairs or small groups, answer the questions for each prediction.

1 Is this already happening in your country?
2 Do you think it will happen in the future?
3 Do you think it will be a good thing or a bad thing?

Useful language

I think so.   I don't think so.   Maybe.

Probably.   I'm sure it will.

2 GRAMMAR future forms

a **1.9** Listen to three dialogues between different family members. Who is talking to who (e.g., brother to sister)? What are they talking about?

b Listen again and match two sentences with each dialogue (1–3). Write 1, 2, or 3 in each box.

A I'll make you a cup of tea. ☐1   C Are you going to go to college? ☐1   E I'll be really careful. ☐3
B You'll crash it again. ☐3   D I'm staying at Mom's tonight. ☐2   F It's going to be cold tonight. ☐3

c With a partner, decide which sentence(s) A–F refer(s) to…

a plan or intention   ☐
an arrangement   ☐
a prediction   ☐ ☐
a promise   ☐
an offer   ☐A

d ▶ **p.130 Grammar Bank 1C.** Read the rules and do the exercises.

e Move around the class, ask other students questions, and complete the chart.

Find someone who…	name	more details
is seeing a relative this weekend.		
isn't having dinner with their family tonight.		
is getting married soon.		
is going out with their brother or sister on Saturday night.		
is going to have a new nephew or niece soon.		
is going to leave home in the near future.		
is going to have a big family reunion soon.		
isn't going to go on vacation with their family this year.		

3 READING

a In a family with two children, do you think it's better to be the older or the younger brother or sister? Why?

b You're going to read an article about two sisters, Wendy (the younger sister) and Carnie (the older sister). Before you read, predict the answers to the questions below. Write W (Wendy) or C (Carnie).

Who do you think…?

1 had a more unusual hairstyle
2 admired her sister
3 didn't want to be with her sister
4 followed her sister everywhere
5 tried to compete with her sister
6 wasn't a good student
7 told her parents when her sister did something wrong
8 used to hurt her sister physically
9 was jealous of her sister
10 always defended her sister

c Now read the article and check your answers.

d Look at the highlighted words and phrases. In pairs, choose the right meaning, a or b.

1 a boring
   b fashionable
2 a children
   b adults
3 a age difference
   b the time they weren't together
4 a become friends again
   b stop speaking
5 a kiss
   b hurt with your fingers
6 a say bad things about someone
   b say good things about someone
7 a we got along very well
   b we got along very badly
8 a ask other people for help
   b say that somebody is responsible for something bad

e Do you think their relationship is typical of brothers and sisters?

We are family…

Two sisters tell the truth about themselves – and each other…

Wendy Wilson and her older sister Carnie are the daughters of the Beach Boys founder, Brian Wilson. They formed the band Wilson Philips (with the daughter of Michelle Philips of The Mamas and Papas) and their first album was a worldwide hit. Today they are both married and live in Los Angeles. Here they talk about their relationship.

Wendy

Carnie

Wendy, the younger sister, says:

I always thought Carnie was really [1] cool, especially when she was a teenager and had bright red spiky hair. But, like most older sisters, she wasn't at all interested in her younger sister. I desperately wanted to be with her and her friends. Sometimes I used to follow them, but she hated that.

When we were [2] kids, we both had a lot of material things like toys and clothes, but even then we knew that Mom and Dad weren't happy. We used to talk about it all the time. After a while they separated and we stayed with my Mom. We didn't see Dad for quite a few years, which really hurt us. But it's also the thing that brought me and Carnie closer together. When I was 16 or 17, the one and a half year [3] age gap between us didn't matter anymore, and we started to get along with each other and to write songs together.

Being in a band – or working at anything – with a member of your family can be difficult, but it also has advantages. If we have a big argument about a song, after a while we remember that we are sisters and we [4] make up. Nothing is going to stop us from being sisters.

Carnie, the older sister, says:

I sometimes think that poor Wendy has spent all her life competing with me. She was a very quiet, shy child, while I was incredibly talkative and demanding. I was awful! I wasn't interested in studying. All I wanted to do was go to parties, and Wendy used to tell my parents. So I was horrible to her. I used to [5] pinch her and bite her.

I was very jealous of Wendy also because she was more attractive. But she always defended me when other people [6] criticized me. Sometimes it seemed as if she was the older sister and I was the younger one. Although we were complete opposites, [7] we were also very close and had a lot of fun together. We still do.

I think I suffered a lot because of my father leaving us when we were small, but Wendy helped me to understand that Dad loved us too, but in a different way. She also taught me that you can't [8] blame other people for your problems. You have to look at yourself.

HOW WORDS WORK...

Look at two sentences from the *We are family* text.

"We started to get along with each other ."

"You have to look at yourself ."

- Use *each other* when A does something to B and B does the thing to A
  We love each other = I love you and you love me.
- Use a reflexive pronoun (*myself, yourself, himself, herself, itself, ourselves, yourselves, themselves*) when the subject of the verb is the same as the object.
  I cut myself. She looked at herself in the mirror.
- You can also use a reflexive pronoun for emphasis.
  Nobody helped me. I did it all myself.

Complete the sentences with *each other* or a reflexive pronoun.

1 After the argument, they didn't speak to _____ for a week.
2 This light is automatic. It turns on and off by _____.
3 We built the house _____. It took three years.
4 We only see _____ once a month.
5 They argue a lot. They don't understand _____.
6 I blame _____ for the accident. It was my fault.

4 VOCABULARY   personality

a Can you remember? What do you call a person who…?

  1 talks a lot _____
  2 doesn't talk very much _____
  3 feels uncomfortable and nervous when he / she meets new people _____
  4 thinks someone loves another person more than him / her _____

b ⊙ **p.146 Vocabulary Bank** *Personality.*

c Write down the first **three** personality adjectives that you can remember from the Vocabulary Bank. Don't show them to your partner. Your teacher will tell you what they say about you.

5 PRONUNCIATION   prefixes and suffixes

a Underline the stressed syllable.

  1 jealous   ambitious   generous
  2 sociable   reliable
  3 responsible   sensible
  4 competitive   talkative   aggressive   sensitive
  5 unfriendly   insecure   impatient

b 🔊 **1.10** Listen and check. Are *-ous* / *-able* / *-ible* / *-ive* stressed? Are *un-* / *in-* / *im-* stressed?

c Practice saying the adjectives.

6 LISTENING & SPEAKING

a What's your position in the family? Are you the oldest child, a middle child, the youngest child, or an only child?

b 🔊 **1.11** Listen to a psychologist talking about the influence your position in the family has on your personality. Complete the chart by writing four more personality adjectives in each column.

Oldest children	Middle children	Youngest children	Only children
self-confident	*independent*	*charming*	*spoiled*

c Compare with a partner. Then listen to the four sections again and check your answers. What details can you remember?

d Look at the completed chart above. In pairs, say
  – if you think it is true for you. If not, why not.
  – if you think it is true for your brothers and sisters or your friends.

7 🔊 **1.12** SONG ♫ *We are family*

THE STORY SO FAR

1.13 Listen to the story of Mark and Allie. Mark the sentences T (true) or F (false).

1 Mark met Allie in London two years ago.
2 He's American and she's British.
3 They work for MTV.
4 He invited her to San Francisco for a vacation.
5 They both got jobs in the new Paris office.
6 Mark is going to be Allie's boss.
7 They are both in Paris now.

Mark	_Hi_. I'm Mark Ryder.
Nicole	Ah, you're the new marketing director.
Mark	That's right.
Nicole	I'm Nicole Delacroix. I'm Allie's personal assistant. _welcome_ to Paris!
Mark	Thank you.
Nicole	I'll just tell Allie you're here. Allie? Mark Ryder's here. OK. You're from San Francisco, _are_ you?
Mark	Yes, I am.
Allie	Hello, Mark.
Mark	Allie. It's _good_ to see you again. How are you?
Allie	Very well. Did you have a good _____?
Mark	Yes, fine, no problems.
Allie	Let me _____ you to the team. You've _met_ Nicole, my personal assistant?
Mark	Yes, we've said hello.
Allie	_This_ is Jacques Lemaître, our PR director.
Jacques	How _do_ you do?
Mark	Mark Ryder. How do you do?
Allie	And this is Ben Watts, our designer.
Ben	Hi, Mark.
Mark	Great to _____ you, Ben.
Ben	We've _heard_ a lot about you.
Mark	Really? All good, I hope.
Allie	OK. Shall we go to my office?

MEETING PEOPLE

a **1.14** Cover the dialogue and listen. What do the people in the Paris office do?

Mark

Allie

Jacques

Ben

Nicole

b Read the conversation. In pairs, what do you think the missing words are? **Don't write them in yet.**

c Listen again and complete the conversation.

d Look at the highlighted phrases. Which is the most formal way to greet someone?

e **1.15** Listen and repeat the highlighted phrases. Copy the rhythm.

f Move around the class in pairs, introducing your partner to other students. Use the highlighted phrases.

SOCIAL ENGLISH It's a secret

a **1.16** Listen. What do Mark and Allie want to keep secret?

b Listen again. Answer with **M** (Mark), **A** (Allie), or **B** (both).

_A_ 1 Who thinks it's strange that they're together now? _A_
_B_ 2 Who missed the other person a lot?
_M_ 3 Who thinks Nicole is very friendly?
_B_ 4 Who thinks it's going to be hard to keep their secret?
_M_ 5 Who wants to find an apartment?
_M_ 6 Who's thinking about work?

c **1.17** Complete the USEFUL PHRASES. Listen and check.

d **1.17** Listen again and repeat the phrases. How do you say them in your language?

USEFUL PHRASES

Why d_on't_ we sit down?
I h_ave_ to find an apartment.
Don't worry. It won't t_ake_ you long.
I was w_wondering_ (what kind of a boss…).
W_ell_, you'll find out tomorrow.

  US English _apartment_
UK English _flat_

Study Link MultiROM

a Read the two e-mails once and answer the questions.

  1 Why has Stephanie written to Claudia?

  2 Does Claudia recommend her friend?

b The computer has found <u>five spelling mistakes</u> in Claudia's e-mail. Can you correct them?

c Read Claudia's e-mail again. Then cover it and answer the questions from memory.

  1 Which ⊞ adjectives describe Amanda's personality?

  2 What does she like doing in her free time?

  3 What negative things does Claudia say about Amanda?

d Look at the highlighted expressions we use to modify adjectives. Put them in the right place in the chart.

Anna is	very / _____	messy.
	_____	
	_____	

Useful language: describing a person

He's pretty / very, etc. + adjective
  (e.g., *friendly*, *outgoing*, etc.)

She's a little + negative adjective (e.g., *messy*, *shy*, etc.)

He likes / loves / doesn't mind + verb + *-ing*

He's good at + verb + *-ing*

Imagine you received Stephanie's e-mail asking about a friend of yours.

WRITE an e-mail to answer it.

PLAN what you're going to write using the paragraph summaries below. Use the **Useful language** box and **Vocabulary Bank p.146** *Personality* to help you.

Paragraph 1	age, family, work / study
Paragraph 2	personality (good side)
Paragraph 3	hobbies and interests
Paragraph 4	any negative things?

CHECK the e-mail for mistakes (grammar , punctuation , and spelling).

From: Stephanie
To: Claudia
Subject: Hi from New Jersey

Dear Claudia,

I hope you're doing well.

I just got an e-mail from your friend Amanda. She wants to rent a room in my house this summer. Could you tell me a little about her (age, personality, etc., and what she likes doing) so that I can see if she would fit in with the family? Please be honest!

Send my regards to your family and I hope to hear from you soon.

Best wishes,

Stephanie

From: Claudia
To: Stephanie
Subject: Re: Hi from New Jersey

Hi Stephanie,

Thanks for your e-mail.

Of course I can tell you about Amanda. She's 21, and she's studing law with me.

I think she's pretty extroverted and very sociable – she has lots of freinds. She's also very good with children. She has a young stepbrother and several young cousins, and I know she likes playing with them. She's extremely hardworking and responsable. She passed all her exams last year, which is more than I did!

She likes going out, watching movies, and listenning to music, but not rock or heavy metal – so don't worry about noise! And she's happy to do things on her own. She's very independent, so you won't really have to look after her. Her parents are divorced, and she lives with her mother and stepfather, but she also sees her father regularly.

The only negative things I can think of are that she's a little messy – her room is usualy not very neat – and that her English is, well, not great. But I'm sure she'll learn fast! I think she's really nice and that you and the family will get along well with her.

I hope that's useful. Let me know if you need any more information about her.

Love,
Claudia

P.S. I'm attaching a photo of the two of us.

GRAMMAR

Put the verbs in the correct tense.

A Wow. _Is_ that your new car? (be)

B Yes.

A When [1]_____ it? (you / get)

B I [2]_____ (buy) it last month.
[3]_____ it? (you / like)

A Yes, it's great. What happened to your headlight?

B I [4]_____ (hit) another car when I [5]_____ (drive) to work. I thought the traffic light [6]_____ (change), but it hadn't. Would you like to go for a drive?

A I can't right now because I [7]_will_ (meet) a friend in ten minutes. How about tomorrow evening? It's Wednesday and I usually [8]_____ (finish) work early.

B OK. I [9]_will_ (pick you up) at 7:00. You [10]_love_ (love) it, I know.

A I'm sure I will. See you tomorrow, then.

10

VOCABULARY

a Word groups. <u>Underline</u> the word that is different. Say why.

1 fresh   seafood   frozen   (homemade)
2 fried   chicken   duck   sausage
3 knife   (roast)   fork   spoon
4 referee   coach   captain   (field)
5 pool   track   beat   (court)
6 aggressive   jealous   bossy   (affectionate)
7 charming   sensible   sociable   (moody)
8 cousin   family   mother-in-law   grandfather

b Write words for the definitions.

1 It's an adjective for food that is hot, e.g., curry or chili.
s_____
2 It's what you have before the main course.
a_____.
3 It's when two teams finish a game with the same score.
t_tie_
4 It means to hurt yourself in an accident or playing a sport.
get i_injury_
5 Your mother's second husband is your s_step father_.
6 It's an adjective for a person who always thinks about himself / herself.
s_selfish_
7 It's an adjective. It's the opposite of _generous_.
s_stingry_

c Fill each blank with one word.

1 I always ask _for_ steak when we eat _out_.
2 What do you usually have _for_ lunch?
3 It's a good idea to warm _up_ before you start running.
4 Who do you get _along_ with best in your family?

20

PRONUNCIATION

a <u>Underline</u> the word with a different sound.

1		pool	tuna	fruit	course
2		cook	food	look	good
3		court	short	worse	warm
4		couple	moody	cousin	duck
5		sausage	bossy	frozen	loss

b <u>Un</u>derline the stressed syllable.

menu   referee   impatient   sociable   irresponsible   **10**

CAN YOU UNDERSTAND THIS TEXT?

Jam today, tomorrow, yesterday…

Craig Flatman is every nutritionist's nightmare – a fifteen-year-old who never eats anything except bread and jam but, unbelievably, is perfectly healthy! Although his diet contains hardly any protein and is 60 percent sugar, he is 1.84 meters tall, weighs 69 kilos, and his parents say he has never been seriously ill apart from typical childhood illnesses.

Craig, or "Jam Boy," as his friends have nicknamed him, rejects any form of meat, fish, fresh fruit, or vegetables. The only time he doesn't eat bread and jam is for breakfast, when he has chocolate cereal, and for snacks, when he occasionally has a slice of chocolate cake. He also drinks two pints of low-fat milk a day.

Craig's strange diet started when he was four years old. As a baby he had refused to eat solid food, and rejected everything until his father gave him a sugar sandwich when he was nine months old. He also ate chocolate spread sandwiches, and this, with milk, was his diet until he was four, when he asked to try jam and started an eleven-year obsession.

Craig sometimes craves some variety, but every time he tries something else he feels sick. Doctors believe that his condition may have been caused by choking on solid food when he was a baby. "They tell me I'll grow out of it," says Craig, "but I don't know if I'll ever change." Although Craig's parents eat a normal diet, their family meals are made more difficult by the fact that Craig's sister Amy, 13, is a vegetarian. And every time they go out for a meal together, they have to call in advance – to find out if they can bring jam sandwiches for Craig!

Adapted from a newspaper

a Read the article and mark the sentences T (true), F (false) or DS (doesn't say).

1 Craig doesn't eat any protein. T
2 He eats ten jam sandwiches a day. F
3 The only other things he eats are chocolate cereal and cake. T
4 When he was a baby, he didn't like solid food. T
5 His obsession with jam sandwiches started when he was eleven. F
6 Craig doesn't want to try any other kinds of food. F
7 Doctors have done a lot of tests on Craig. DS
8 They think Craig's diet will change when he gets older. T
9 Craig's family eats out about once a month. DS
10 Craig also has jam sandwiches when his family eats out. T

b Guess what the highlighted words and phrases mean. Check with your teacher or a dictionary.

CAN YOU UNDERSTAND THESE PEOPLE?

a 1.18 Listen and circle the correct answer, a, b, or c.

1 How many people want orange juice?
a two
(b) three
c four
2 Why doesn't the woman want anything to eat?
a Because she's not hungry.
(b) Because she doesn't feel well.
c Because she's on a diet.
3 What does Robertson do now?
a He owns a restaurant.
b He works in Orlando.
(c) He works with young players.
4 Who's coming to lunch?
(a) The man's mother-in-law and his sister.
b The man's mother and his sister-in law.
c The man's mother-in-law and her sister.
5 What are they going to give their granddaughter for her birthday?
a Money.
b Clothes.
(c) They can't decide.

b 1.19 You will hear a man calling to reserve a tennis court. Complete the information on the secretary's form.

Hartford Sports Center
Tennis court reservations:

Name: *Mark* [1] read
Membership number: [2] 040155
Day: [3] Sunday
Time: [4] 6 to 7 PM
Court number: [5] 5

CAN YOU SAY THIS IN ENGLISH?

Can you…? Yes (✓)
☐ talk about your diet
☐ describe a sports event you have been to (where, when, what happened)
☐ describe a member of your family and his / her personality
☐ say how you think families will change in the future

G present perfect and simple past
V money, phrasal verbs
P saying numbers

2A Ka-ching!

1 VOCABULARY & LISTENING money

a **2.1** Listen to a song about money and complete it with these words. What is "Ka-ching?"

<u>afford</u>	blow	broke	credit card	earn
<u>greedy</u>	loan	mall	<u>mortgage</u>	spend

b Now look at words 1–10 in the song and match them with their meanings.

A _____ (verb) to give or pay money for something

B _____ (noun) money that a person or a bank lends you

C _____ (verb) to have enough money to buy something

D _____ (noun) a shopping center

E _____ (adj) having no money (informal)

F _____ (noun) a small plastic card you use to buy things

G _____ (verb) to get money by working

H _____ (adj) wanting more money, etc. than you really need

I _____ (verb) to spend a lot of money on something (informal)

J _____ (noun) the money a bank lends you to buy a house

c Listen again and read the lyrics. What do you think the song is saying?

1 Money always makes people happy.
2 The world has become obsessed with money.
3 The singer would like to have more money.

d ➲ **p.147 Vocabulary Bank** *Money*.

Ka-ching

We live in a ¹_____ little world
that teaches every little boy and girl
to ²_____ as much as they can possibly,
then turn around and spend it foolishly.
We've created us a ³_____ mess,
we ⁴_____ the money that we don't possess.
Our religion is to go and ⁵_____ it all,
so it's shopping every Sunday at the ⁶_____.

Chorus
All we ever want is more,
a lot more than we had before.
So take me to the nearest store.
Can you hear it ring?
It makes you want to sing.
It's such a beautiful thing – Ka-ching!
Lots of diamond rings,
the happiness it brings,
you'll live like a king,
with lots of money and things.

When you're ⁷_____ go and get a ⁸_____.
Take out another ⁹_____ on your home,
consolidate so you can ¹⁰_____
to go and spend some more when you get bored.

Chorus

Ka-ching!

20

2 GRAMMAR present perfect and simple past

a Shelley and Ben are having an argument about money. Read what Shelley says and complete the conversation with Ben's answers from the box below. Then try to guess his last answer.

> We've had it for at least three years. Maybe longer.
> It's old.
> No. What is it?
> Why not?
> ~~Yes. I bought it yesterday.~~
> I can't.

Shelley	Is that a new camera?
Ben	¹ *Yes. I bought it yesterday.*
Shelley	What's wrong with our old camera?
Ben	²_____
Shelley	Old? How long have we had it? A year?
Ben	³_____
Shelley	Three years? I'm sure we bought it last year. Look. We can't afford a new camera.
Ben	⁴_____
Shelley	Have you seen this?
Ben	⁵_____
Shelley	The gas bill. It arrived this morning. And we haven't paid the phone bill yet. Take it back to the store and get your money back.
Ben	⁶_____
Shelley	Why not?
Ben	Because…

b 🔊 **2.2** Listen and check.

c In pairs, read the dialogue again and <u>underline</u> four examples of the present perfect and three examples of the simple past. Then answer the questions.

Which form of the verb do we use for…?
1 a completed action in the past
2 things which started in the past and are true now
3 past actions when we don't say exactly when
4 past actions when we say exactly when

d ➡ **p.132 Grammar Bank 2A.** Read the rules and do the exercises.

3 SPEAKING

In pairs, interview each other with the questionnaire. Ask for more information.

> Have you ever wasted money on something you've never used?

> Yes, I bought an exercise bike.

> Why did you buy it?

The MONEY Questionnaire

Have you ever...?

(waste) money on something you've never used

(sell) anything on the Internet

(lose) a credit card or your wallet

(save) for something for a long time

(win) any money (e.g., in a lottery)

(be) robbed

(lend) money to someone who didn't pay you back

Have you...recently?

(buy) anything on the Internet

(go) to a shopping mall

(buy) anyone a present

(use) a credit card

(take) money out of an ATM

(borrow) money from someone in your family

4 READING

a Which of these sentences best describes your attitude towards money?

1 All I want is enough money to enjoy life.
2 Money is very important to me. I'd like to earn as much as possible.
3 I would be happy to live with less money and fewer possessions.

b You're going to read an article about a woman who lives without money. Why do you think she does it? How do you think she survives? Read the article to find out.

c Read the article and answer the questions.

1 What was Heidemarie's job?
2 What possessions does she have now?
3 How did the experiment start?
4 Where has she lived since the experiment started?
5 Does she still work?
6 What does she do when she needs something?
7 What is she trying to show with her experiment?
8 What did she do with the money she earned from her book?

d Match the highlighted phrasal verbs with their definitions. Write the verbs in the base form.

1 _throw away_   put into the trash
   e.g., *Please ... those candy wrappers.*
2 _____   arrive, appear
   e.g., *I invited 20 people to my party but only 10 will ...*
3 _____   give something to somebody without wanting anything in return
   e.g., *She decided to ... her old clothes to the local hospital.*
4 _____   start a new company or organization
   e.g., *My brother is going to ... a software company.*

e In pairs, answer the questions.

1 Do you agree with Heidemarie that...?
   • all jobs are equally important
   • most people don't like their jobs
   • people judge you according to how much you earn
2 What do you think of Heidemarie? Would you like to have her as a friend?

My life without money

Heidemarie Schwermer, a 63-year-old German woman, has lived without money for the last ten years, and has written a book about her experiences called *My Life Without Money*.

At the age of 54, Heidemarie quit her job as a psychotherapist, gave away all her money and her apartment, and threw away her credit cards. Today, aside from some clothes (three sweaters, two skirts, two pairs of shoes, and a coat) and a few personal belongings, she doesn't own anything.

It all began as a one-year experiment. In her home city of Dortmund, she set up a "swapping circle" where people exchange services without using money, for example, a haircut for a mathematics class. To prove that this could work, she decided to give up using money for a year. But when the year ended, she continued and has not used money since then.

At first she house-sat for friends who were on vacation. She stayed in their houses in return for watering the plants and taking care of their animals. At the moment, she is staying in a student residence where she can sleep, take a shower, or use a computer in return for cooking for the young people who live there. She also "works" as a psychotherapist. "Before I treated very wealthy people but now I help anyone who turns up. Sometimes they give me something in return, but not always."

Heidemarie says, "I can live thanks to my contacts. A lot of people who know me understand what I'm doing and want to help me. When I need a bus ticket, for example, or a new tube of toothpaste I think, 'Who can I ask? What can I give them in return?' If I want to go to the movies, I might offer to take care of somebody's children for the afternoon.

It is one of the mistakes of our society that most people do something they don't like just to earn money and spend it on things they don't need. Many people judge you according to how much you earn. In my opinion, all jobs are equally important. You may not earn a lot of money, but you may be worth a lot as a person. That's my message."

So what did she do with all the money she earned from the sales of *My Life Without Money*?

"I gave it all away..."

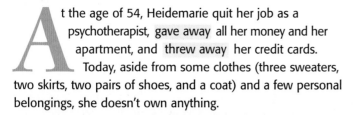

5 VOCABULARY & PRONUNCIATION
saying numbers

a 🔊 **2.3** Write the numbers. Then listen and repeat. Practice saying them.

Numbers	
15	fifteen
50	fifty
100	a hundred / one hundred
750	seven hundred and fifty
1500	one thousand five hundred
7500	seven thousand five hundred
75 000	seventy-five thousand
750 000	seven hundred and fifty thousand
1 000 000	a million / one million
7 500 000	seven and a half million

b 🔊 **2.4** Complete the numbers. Then listen and check.

Money, percentages, decimals and fractions		
$2.50	two *fifty*	
€8.99	eight *euros* and *ninty* *nine* cents	
£3.20	three *pounds* *twenty*	
50%	fifty *percent*	
0.5	zero *point* five	
3.9	*tree* *point* *nine*	
7.35	*seven* *point* three five	
½	a *half* / one *half*	
⅓	a *third* / one *third*	
¼	a *quater* / one *quater*	
¾	three *quaters* / three *quaters*	
6½	six *and* a half	

c In pairs, practice saying these numbers.

⅔ 0.7 1¾ 7.8

30% $90 100%

430 2,800 9,250

€600 £200,000 3,000,000

6 LISTENING & SPEAKING

a 🔊 **2.5** Listen to a news program. How many different news items are there?

b Listen again and answer the questions with a number.
1 How many people were injured in the crash? *17*
2 How fast was the truck going? *85 m./h*
3 How many transit workers have walked off the job? *100*
4 What pay raise do they want? *8.5%*
5 How many more unemployed people are there this year? *138,000*
6 How many are there in total? *6.9*
7 By how much have house prices increased in the last five years? *⅓*
8 How much does an average single-family house cost in the US? *236,000 dollars*

c Answer the questions with a number, percentage, etc. If you don't know the exact number, use *about* or *approximately.*

1 What's the population of…? your country   your town / city
2 What percentage of the people in your country…?
 speak English   have more than two children
 have a dog   smoke
3 How much do these things cost?
 a cup of coffee   a laptop computer   a small apartment downtown
 a newspaper   a DVD   a small car

2 B

G present perfect continuous
V strong adjectives: *exhausted, amazed*, etc.
P sentence stress, strong adjectives

Changing your life

1 LISTENING

a Answer the questions in pairs.

1 If you could spend a year working or studying in another country, which country would you choose? Why?

2 What would you like to do there?

3 What problems do you think you might have?

b Read about Angela and describe what you can see in the photos.

c **2.6** Listen to Angela and answer the questions.

1 Why did she choose Ecuador?

2 Why did she want to take a year off?

3 Where is Angela taking art classes?

4 What is the most difficult thing for Angela in Spanish?

5 How do the students in her art classes feel about having a foreigner in the class?

6 What does Angela like about teaching English?

7 What does she like most about living in Ecuador?

d Compare your answers with a partner. Then listen again to check.

2 GRAMMAR present perfect continuous with *for / since*

a **2.7** Listen and complete these questions and answers from the interview with Angela.

1 How long have you been _____ here?

2 I've been _____ and _____ since I was a child.

3 What have you been _____ here since you arrived?

4 I've been _____ some art classes at the university.

5 I've been _____ for about three months now.

b Look at sentences 1–5 and answer the questions.

1 Are the verbs action or non-action verbs?

2 Do they refer to single actions or continuous / repeated actions?

3 Do they refer to a completed action or one that is still happening?

c ⬤ **p.132 Grammar Bank 2B.** Read the rules for present perfect continuous for unfinished actions. Do exercise **a** only.

"My name's Angela and I'm an elementary school teacher. A few months ago, I decided to change my life. I took a year off and went to live in Ecuador."

3 PRONUNCIATION sentence stress

 An important part of clear communication in English is stressing the words in a sentence that carry the information, and **not** stressing the other ones.

a **2.8** **Dictation.** Listen to five sentences. Try to write down the stressed words. Look at the words and try to remember the whole sentence. Then listen again and write the complete sentences.

b **2.9** Listen and copy the rhythm.

1 I've been living here for two years.
2 How long have you been learning English?
3 She's been working in Italy since October.
4 How long have you been waiting?
5 It's been raining all night.
6 We've been looking for an apartment for ages.

4 SPEAKING

a Look at the circles, and write something in as many as you can.

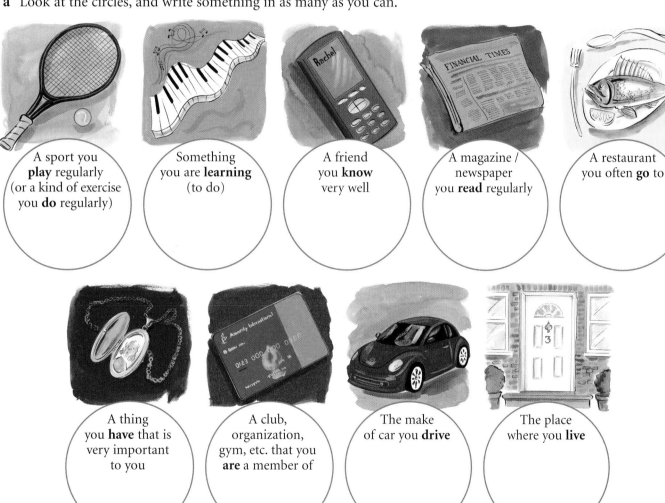

A sport you **play** regularly (or a kind of exercise you **do** regularly)

Something you are **learning** (to do)

A friend you **know** very well

A magazine / newspaper you **read** regularly

A restaurant you often **go** to

A thing you **have** that is very important to you

A club, organization, gym, etc. that you **are** a member of

The make of car you **drive**

The place where you **live**

b Compare circles with a partner. Ask your partner at least three questions about the things they've written. One question must be *How long have you…?*

 Remember after *How long…?* with **action** verbs, e.g., *play*, use the present perfect continuous, with **non-action** verbs, e.g., *know*, use the present perfect simple.

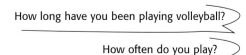

How long have you been playing volleyball?

Since I was about 15.

How often do you play?

5 READING

a Can you think of one way that a vacation could change your life for the better?

b You're going to read an article about two people whose lives were changed by a vacation. Work in pairs. **A** read about Victoria, **B** about Sally.

c In pairs, take turns telling each other about the two women. Answer these questions.

What is she doing now?
What was she doing before?
What made her change her life?
How does she feel now?

d Read the text that you didn't read before. Did your partner leave out any important information?

e In pairs, try to guess the meaning of the highlighted words. Then match them with their definitions below.

First text
1　of little importance　_trivial_
2　crazy　_insane_
3　a person who looks after animals (e.g., in a zoo)　_keeper_
4　animals like large monkeys　_apes_
5　not looked after well　_____

Second text
6　the London subway　_the tube_
7　very good-tasting　_delicious_
8　asked for (in writing)　_Ap ~ for_
9　burning brightly　_blazing_
10　very small　_tiny_

f Whose life do you think has changed the most? Which of the two vacations would you choose?

It was just a vacation, but it changed my life

Vacations can be good for your health. You lie on a beach and relax, and tensions disappear. But sometimes a vacation can change your life completely, which is what happened two years ago to Victoria Smith and Sally Gook.

Victoria Smith, six years ago, was working as a manager at a chain store. Then she went on vacation to Borneo...

"It was a working vacation," said Victoria, "where you could study orangutans in the wild. I have always been interested in apes, so I thought it would be fun." The vacation was wonderful, and when Victoria came home she found it very difficult to return to her old life. "Suddenly the problems in the store just seemed so trivial." Although everybody told her she was insane, she decided to go back to college and study biology. Four years later she became a chimpanzee keeper.

For the last two years Victoria has been working at Monkey World, a center that takes care of apes that have been mistreated. Many have been rescued from laboratories and circuses all over the world. She works

long hours, and the pay isn't very good, but she loves it. "Apes are like a big family, each with their own personality."

"I'm really happy now. Since I started working here, I feel that I've been doing something important, not just wasting my life."

"I feel that I've been doing something important."

"Suddenly I knew there was a different life waiting for me."

Sally Gook wakes up every morning to a deep blue sky and blazing sun. For the last two years she has been living on the tiny Greek island of Lipsi, which is only 16 square kilometers in size and has a population of just 650.

But until a few years ago she lived in London. "I was working for a large financial services company and I had a good social life and made a lot of money. But I had to get up very early every morning, often in horrible weather, and get a train and the Tube to work."

Then one day she and a friend decided they needed a relaxing vacation, and they came to Lipsi. "I loved it – the people, the mountains, the sun, and the delicious food. Suddenly I knew there was a different life waiting for me here." A few months later she applied for a job at the travel company that had organized her vacation.

Since then she has been living on Lipsi and working as a tourist guide. Her boyfriend, who is Greek, is a farmer. Sally said, "I've only been back to London once, and I can't imagine ever living there again."

Adapted from a newspaper

6 VOCABULARY & PRONUNCIATION strong adjectives

a Write synonyms for the strong adjectives.

Strong adjectives	Normal adjectives
1 The island's **tiny** – only 16 square kilometers.	= very _small_
2 The food in Lipsi was **delicious**.	= very _good-tasting_
3 Her father's **furious**. She crashed his car.	= very _mad_
4 I'm **terrified** of flying. I never travel by plane.	= very _afraid_
5 I've been working all day. I'm **exhausted**.	= very _tired_
6 It's going to be **boiling** tomorrow – about 40ºC!	= very _hot_
7 Can I have a sandwich? I'm **starving**.	= very _hungry_
8 The apartment's **enormous**. It has five bedrooms.	= very _big_
9 I'm not going to swim. The water's **freezing**.	= very _cold_
10 Your car's **filthy**. Why don't you wash it?	= very _dirty_
11 That's a **great** idea! Let's do it.	= very _good-idea_
12 This book's **awful**. I can't finish it.	= very _____

b Cover **a**. Complete the responses with a strong adjective.

1 Are you hungry?	Yes, I'm _starving_.
2 Was your mother angry?	Yes, she was _furious_.
3 Is her apartment small?	Yes, it's _tiny_.
4 Are you tired?	Yes, I'm _exhaust_.
5 Is the floor dirty?	Yes, it's _filthy_.
6 Are you afraid of spiders?	Yes, I'm _terrific_ of them.

c 🔊 **2.10** Listen and check. Are the strong adjectives stressed? Listen again and repeat.

d ➡ **Communication** *Are you hungry? Yes, I'm starving!* A p.116 B p.119.

7 GRAMMAR present perfect continuous (for recent continuous actions)

a Look at the pictures. How do the people look? What do you think has been happening?

b 🔊 **2.11** Listen and check. What have they been doing? Complete the sentences.

1 Sharon and Kenny _Arguing_.
2 The man _reading on the sun_.
3 The man and woman _worn out_ and _tired_.

c ➡ **p.132 Grammar Bank 2B.** Read the rules for the present perfect continuous for recent continuous actions. Do **b**.

d Look at the adjectives and imagine that you are *exhausted*, *filthy*, etc. Think of an explanation for each one. Then in pairs, invent a short conversation using each adjective.

exhausted	filthy	furious
very stressed	very red	

Hi. You look exhausted. What have you been doing?

I've been working in the backyard.

2 C

G comparatives and superlatives
V transportation and travel
P stress in compound nouns

Race to the sun

1 READING

a In pairs, ask and answer the questions.

1 When was the last time you traveled…?
by train   by car   by plane
Where did you go?
How long did your trip take?
Did you have a good trip?

2 In general, which of the three forms
of transportation do you prefer? Why?

b Read the introduction to the article, *Race to the sun*. Answer the questions
with *by car*, *by train*, or *by plane*.

Which trip do you think was…?

the quickest _____   the most comfortable _____

the cheapest _____   the most convenient _____

c You're going to read about the first **two** trips, but the paragraphs
are not in the right order. Find the first paragraph for the plane trip,
and then the other three. Do the same for the train trip. Then compare
with a partner.

The plane   **The train**

1 _____ 2 _____ 3 _____ 4 _____   1 _____ 2 _____ 3 _____ 4 _____

d Now read about the two trips again carefully in the right order.
Answer the questions with T (the train) or P (the plane).

On which trip…?

1 did the traveler have to get up earlier ☐
2 could the traveler have something to eat or drink ☐
3 was the traveler more stressed ☐
4 could the traveler see beautiful scenery ☐
5 did the traveler have a meal when he arrived ☐
6 did the traveler arrive earlier than expected ☐

Which trip was…?

7 quicker ☐
8 cheaper ☐
9 more comfortable ☐
10 more convenient ☐

HOW WORDS WORK…

The bus took 45 minutes.

It took me just 30 minutes from home.

How long does it take you to get to school?

Use *take* (+ person) + time (+ *to get to*)… to talk about the duration
of a trip.

Ask and answer the questions in pairs.

How long does it take you to get to work / school?
How long does it take to get downtown from your house?
a by car   **b** by bus   **c** by subway   **d** on foot

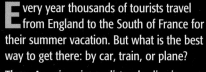

Every year thousands of tourists travel from England to the South of France for their summer vacation. But what is the best way to get there: by car, train, or plane?

Three American journalists who live in England decided to find out. They traveled from their homes in London to Avignon.

All three travelers set off one Saturday morning in July.

Charles went by train (the Eurostar).

Rosemary flew with a discount airline.

Martin traveled by car.

A When I got to security, I saw that there was a really long line. I began to worry that I might miss my flight because you have to board 40 minutes before take-off. I had to run to gate 48 and I arrived completely out of breath.

B I arrived on time! I picked up my suitcase and followed the Exit signs. It was great not to have to wait for my luggage or to worry about getting a bus or taxi downtown.

C We boarded. Because there are no seat numbers on these flights, everybody tries to get on as quickly as they can. I sat next to a friendly Frenchman. We took off and soon I was looking down on London. There was no meal, not even coffee, but we landed 10 minutes ahead of schedule.

D At 4:15 a.m. a taxi picked me up and took me 32 miles to Stansted airport. Although it was early morning, there was a lot of traffic and I arrived later than I had planned. I took my luggage to check-in and asked for a window seat, but the woman said there were no seat numbers.

E At 7:10 a.m. I arrived at Waterloo station by taxi. It took me just 30 minutes from home. I bought a newspaper and walked to the platform. I got on and found my seat. As soon as we started moving, I went to find the dining car and had a cup of coffee.

F Just outside the station I looked up and saw the medieval walls of Avignon's historic city center. It was 2:20* in the afternoon and I was just in time for a late lunch! My ticket cost £65.80, and I gave the trip 8/10 for comfort and 9/10 for convenience.

G I only had to wait 20 minutes for my luggage. Then I walked outside into bright sunshine and waited for the bus to Avignon, about 40 kilometers away. I didn't have to wait long and the bus took 45 minutes. It was only 11:00* and I had the whole day in front of me. My ticket cost £63, and I gave the trip 5/10 for comfort and 5/10 for convenience.

H I looked out of the window. Although we were moving at 340 kilometers an hour, the trip was smooth and relatively quiet. The part where we traveled under the English Channel took just 22 minutes. Soon I was looking at the fields and farmhouses of France. The sun was shining. I closed my eyes and went to sleep.

* France is one hour ahead of the UK.

2 LISTENING

a 2.12 Listen to Martin talking about his trip from London to Avignon by car. Number the pictures 1–7.

b Listen again. Mark the sentences T (true) or F (false).

1 There's a lot of traffic in London on Saturday mornings.
2 Gas is more expensive in Britain than in France.
3 There are two ways to cross the English Channel by car.
4 You can't drive through the Channel Tunnel.
5 The trip through the tunnel takes an hour.
6 Drivers must sit in their car when they go through the tunnel.
7 The speed limit on French highways is 120 km/h.
8 French highways aren't free.
9 It's 970 kilometers from Calais to Avignon.

c 2.13 Listen to Martin talking about his trip and fill in the **By car** column in the chart. Now compare the information with your answers in **1a**.

London to Avignon	By plane	By train	By car
How long did it take? (from home)	5 hours 45 mins	6 hours 40 mins	
How much did it cost?	£63	£65.80	
Comfort /10	5	8	
Convenience /10	5	9	

d Think of a town / city in your country. How many different ways are there of getting there? Which do you think is the best? Why?

3 GRAMMAR comparatives and superlatives

a Read the sentences. Read the highlighted phrases. Mark them right (✔) or wrong (✘). Correct the wrong sentences.

1 What's the quicker way to get to the South of France?

2 Driving is more boring than going by train.

3 Gas isn't as cheap in Britain than in France.

4 Does the plane cost the same as the train?

5 Going by train is less expensive as flying.

6 It was the more comfortable hotel I've ever stayed in.

7 The worst month to travel through France is August.

8 Do the British drive more carefully than the French?

b ⊃ **p.132 Grammar Bank 2C.** Read the rules and do the exercises.

c With a partner compare the experiences below using the **bold** adjectives.

> 1 **safe, exciting, healthy**
> traveling by motorcycle
> traveling by car
> traveling by bike
>
> 2 **enjoyable, dangerous, relaxing**
> traveling by yourself
> traveling with friends
> traveling with your family
>
> 3 **difficult, expensive**
> learning to drive
> learning to ride a bike
> learning to fly a plane

4 VOCABULARY transportation and travel

a Put the words into the correct column.

dining car	check in	gate	highway
platform	rush hour	speed limit	
station	take off		

train	car	plane
——	——	——
——	——	——
——	——	——

b ⊃ **p.148 Vocabulary Bank** *Transportation and travel.*

5 PRONUNCIATION & SPEAKING stress in compound nouns

a [2.14] Listen and repeat the compound nouns. Which word is usually stressed more?

traffic light	pedestrian area
boarding pass	gas station
parking lot	rush hour
car crash	seat belt
bike lane	traffic radar
parking ticket	speed limit
traffic jam	ticket office

b Ask and answer the questions in pairs.

In your town / city...

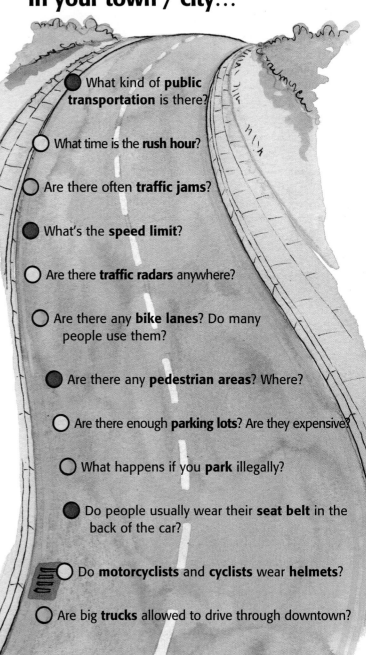

● What kind of **public transportation** is there?

○ What time is the **rush hour**?

○ Are there often **traffic jams**?

● What's the **speed limit**?

○ Are there **traffic radars** anywhere?

○ Are there any **bike lanes**? Do many people use them?

● Are there any **pedestrian areas**? Where?

○ Are there enough **parking lots**? Are they expensive?

○ What happens if you **park** illegally?

● Do people usually wear their **seat belt** in the back of the car?

○ Do **motorcyclists** and **cyclists** wear **helmets**?

○ Are big **trucks** allowed to drive through downtown?

6 LISTENING & SPEAKING

a Read the beginning of a newspaper article and then talk to a partner:

1 Do you (or your family) ever do any of these things while driving a car?

2 Which three do you think are the most dangerous? Number them 1–3 (1 = the most dangerous).

Which of these things is the most dangerous when you're driving a car?

- making a call on your cell phone
- listening to your favorite music
- listening to music you don't know
- opening a bag of chips or a can of soda
- picking up a specific CD from the passenger seat
- talking to other passengers

A car magazine tested car drivers in a driving simulator. The drivers had to "drive" in the simulator and at the same time do the things in the list above. The results of the tests were surprising (and worrying).

b **2.15** Now listen to a road safety expert talking about the tests. Number the activities 1–6. Were your top three right?

c Listen again and answer the questions.

1 What should you do when you are driving?

2 Why is opening a bag of chips or a can of soda so dangerous?

3 What do people often do when they pick up a CD?

4 What gets worse when drivers are talking on the phone?

5 How do people drive when they are listening to their favorite music?

6 What happens if the music is fast and heavy?

7 What's the main problem when drivers talk to other passengers?

8 Why is listening to music you don't know the least dangerous?

d Look at the statements below and decide whether you agree or disagree. Put a ✔ next to the ones you agree with and an ✘ next to the ones you disagree with. Think about your reasons.

Drivers should not use any kind of phone when they are driving.

The minimum age for riding a motorcycle should be 25.

People who drink and drive should lose their license for life.

The speed limit on highways should be 100 kilometers an hour.

Cyclists are just as dangerous as car drivers.

Police traffic radars do not stop speeding.

People over 70 are more dangerous drivers than young people.

e In groups, give your opinions on each sentence. Do you agree?

REQUESTS AND PERMISSION

a (2.16) Cover the conversation and listen. Answer the questions.

  1 What does Jacques ask Mark to do?

  2 What does Mark ask Ben to do?

  3 What does Nicole ask Allie?

b Read the conversation. In pairs, what do you think the missing words are? **Don't write them in yet.**

c Listen again and complete the conversation.

Jacques	Mark? Would you mind _sending_ me those concert dates?
Mark	Of _course_ not. Ben, are you busy?
Ben	Me? Never.
Mark	_Are_ you help me? I can't open this document.
Ben	_Sure_.
Mark	Thanks.

....

Allie	Hi, Nicole.
Nicole	Could you sign these, please?
Allie	Sure.
Nicole	Is it _OK_ if I take tomorrow afternoon off?
Allie	I'm _sorry_, but tomorrow's really difficult.
Nicole	What about Friday afternoon?
Allie	Friday? That's fine. Do you _think_ you could _you_ me the request by e-mail?
Nicole	Uh, yes, of _course_.
Allie	Hello? Hi, Mark. Could you hold a moment, Mark? Thank you, Nicole. _Can_ you come and see me when you have a moment?

d (2.17) Listen and repeat the highlighted phrases. Copy the rhythm.

e Look at the highlighted phrases in the dialogue. Complete the chart.

Request	Response
Would you mind…?	Of course not
Are you help me	sure
is't ok if I take tomorrow aftern	I'm sorry, but tomorrow really difficult
Permission	
	✓

f ➲ **Communication** *Requests* page 119.

SOCIAL ENGLISH   Office gossip

a (2.18) Listen. Who do Mark and Nicole talk about?

b Listen again and mark the sentences T (true) or F (false).

  T 1 Mark hasn't found an apartment yet.

  T 2 Mark likes Ben and Jacques.

  F 3 Jacques's wife is a lawyer.

  F 4 Nicole likes the way Allie dresses.

  F 5 She thinks Allie is friendly.

  T 6 Allie orders a soda.

c (2.19) Complete the USEFUL PHRASES. Listen and check.

d Listen again and repeat the phrases. How do you say them in your language?

USEFUL PHRASES

Have you started l _looking_ for an apartment?

I haven't had time y _et_ .

J _ust_ a minute.

H _ow_ do you like (the office)?

Have you h _eard_ of (Isabelle)?

L _et_ me get you (a drink).

Thanks. I'll h _ave_ a (Diet Coke™).

Nightmare trips

We asked you to tell us about your nightmare trips. Rita from California wrote to us about hers...

A nightmare trip I remember was three years ago ¹____ I was going to the airport with my friend. We were going to Hawaii on vacation and we had to be at Los Angeles airport two hours before the flight.

We leaved home with plenty of time, ²____ when we got to the freeway there was a huge traffic jam! The traffic wasn't moving at all. We didn't knew what to do. It was too late to go another way, ³____ we just sat in the car getting more and more stressed. ⁴____ ten minutes, the traffic started moving slowly. We decided to leave the freeway and try to found another way to the airport, ⁵____ I wasn't sure of the way and we got completely lost. We was sure we were going to miss the flight. We finally arrived at the airport just thirty minutes before the plane was going to leave. The woman at the check-in counter said we couldn't to check in our luggage ⁶____ it was too late, ⁷____ we had to run with all our suitcases to the departure gate.

⁸____ my friend felt down and hurt her leg, we managed to get to the gate in time and ⁹____ we caught our flight.

a Read the story once. What happened in the end? Then correct the six grammar mistakes with the verbs (wrong tense or wrong form).

b Read the story again and complete with a connecting word or phrase.

after	although	because	but (x2)	in the end	so (x2)	when

c Look at the list of possible travel problems in the **Useful language** box below. Mark them C if they refer to a trip by car and P if they refer to a trip by plane.

Useful language: travel problems

the flight was delayed	there was a traffic jam
your car broke down	you got a flat tire
you got lost	you forgot your passport
you missed your flight	your flight was overbooked

WRITE about a nightmare trip you've had (or invent one).

PLAN what you're going to write using the paragraph summaries below: Use the **Useful language** box and **Vocabulary Bank p.148** *Transportation and travel* to help you.

Paragraph 1   When was the trip? Where were you going? Who with? Why?

Paragraph 2   What went wrong? What happened?

Paragraph 3   What happened in the end?

CHECK the story for mistakes (grammar , punctuation , and spelling).

GRAMMAR

a Complete the sentences with one word.

1 **A** Would you like to watch the movie?

   B No. I've [1]_____ seen it three times.

2 **A** How [2] _long_ have you lived here?

   B [3]_____ 2004.

3 **A** [4]_____ you read this novel?

   B No. Is it good?

   A I haven't finished it [5]_____.

b Complete the second sentence so that it means the same as the first.

1 I started to work here three years ago.

   I've _____ _____ here for three years.

2 I bought this camera in 2006.

   I've _____ this camera _____ 2006.

3 The train is cheaper than the plane.

   The plane is _____ _____ than the train.

4 Women drive more carefully than men.

   Men don't drive as _____ _____ women.

5 None of the other sofas is as comfortable as this one.

   This sofa is _____ _____ comfortable one.

`10`

VOCABULARY

a Word groups. Underline the word that is different. Say why.

1 coin	check	bank	bill
2 save	waste	mortgage	owe
3 exhausted	terrified	hungry	furious
4 delicious	wonderful	great	awful
5 flight	journey	trip	travel
6 bus	van	helmet	truck
7 bike lane	train station	speed limit	traffic jam

b Write words for the definitions.

1 It's an adjective. It means "very dirty." **f**_____

2 It's a noun. It's money that you pay to the government.
   t_____

3 It's a noun. It's the time of day when buses and trains are full.
   r_____ **h**_____

4 It's a verb. To give someone money that they must later pay back.
   l_____

5 It's a noun. It's the place in a train station where you get on or off a train.
   p_____

6 It's a verb. It means to receive money from a relative after their death.
   i_____

7 It's a noun. It's the piece of paper you need to get on a plane.
   b_____ **p**_____ or **c**_____

8 It's an adjective. It means "very small." **t**_____

c Complete the sentences with one word.

1 What time did the plane take _____?

2 She got some money _____ the ATM.

3 Who paid _____ the meal last night?

4 When can you pay me _____ the money you owe me?

5 Can I pay _____ credit card?

`20`

PRONUNCIATION

a <u>Underline</u> the word with a different sound.

1		afford	board	card	enormous
2		tiny	pick up	traffic	ticket
3		crash	station	rush	charge
4		coin	check	cyclist	car
5		seat	earn	speed	greedy

b <u>Un</u>derline the stressed syllable.

invest   security   luggage   pedestrian   terrified   `10`

CAN YOU UNDERSTAND THIS TEXT?

Why I didn't want to be a millionaire

When Lydia Nash appeared on the TV show *Who Wants to be a Millionaire?* and was fortunate enough to win £16,000, she decided to give all the money away. This wouldn't have been surprising if she had been rich or famous, but Lydia was a 19-year-old then.

Lydia gave all the money to a charity that helps orphaned children in Thailand and where she had also worked as a volunteer for the previous three years. "I first visited the orphanage when I was seventeen, and I felt very depressed by what I saw. When I got back to England, I felt angry. Looking around, all I could see were people who were obsessed with money. That convinced me to return to Thailand the following year."

After she won the money, some of her friends at the university thought that maybe she had made the wrong decision. "Some people said I should have saved it for a down payment on a house or to pay back my student loan." Lydia said. "That really annoyed me. Students seem to live in an unreal world, where they constantly complain about being poor. But there's an enormous difference between our situation and that of people who have absolutely no money."

With the help of the money Lydia gave them, the charity has just finished building Rainbow House, a new facility that will house 50 young children and where they will live until they are adopted.

If Lydia had won a million pounds and not only £16,000, would she still have given away all the money? She said, "Before going on the show, I thought a lot about what it would be like to have a lot of money, and I realized that I wouldn't like it at all. And then, of course, as I had been to the orphanage and had seen all the work that needed to be done, I knew how useful that money could be. It was far more important for the charity than it could ever be for me. I definitely think I got more enjoyment out of giving the money away than if I had kept it for myself."

Adapted from a newspaper

a Read the article once. Then read it again and choose a, b, or c.

1 People were surprised that Lydia gave away the money she won because _____.
   a she was young and not very wealthy
   b she already had a lot of money of her own
   c she had won a lot of money

2 Before winning the money, Lydia had been to the orphanage in Thailand _____.
   a once   b twice   c several times

3 Lydia thinks that students today _____.
   a are broke all the time
   b have a lot of money
   c are not as poor as they think

4 The charity has used the money to _____.
   a build a new house for the teachers
   b adopt more children
   c build a new residence for children

5 Lydia _____.
   a wouldn't mind being rich
   b wouldn't like to be rich
   c would like to be a little bit richer

b Look at the highlighted words and phrases. Can you guess what they mean?

CAN YOU UNDERSTAND THESE PEOPLE?

a 2.20 Listen and circle the correct answer, a, b, or c.

1 Where did the woman probably lose her credit card?
   a In the gas station.
   b In the flower shop.
   c In the restaurant.

2 How long has he been working as a teacher?
   a 1½ years   b 2½ years   c 3½ years

3 How can people travel today?
   a By road.   b By train.   c By air.

4 How are they getting to Buffalo?
   a Route 17   b the Thruway   c Route 80

5 Who is working at the moment?
   a Her brother.
   b Her brother's wife.
   c Her brother and his wife.

b 2.21 Listen to a conversation between a bank manager and a client. Complete the sentences with a number.

¹Ms. Stevens wants to borrow $_____.
²The period of the loan will be _____ years.
³The monthly payments will be $_____.
⁴The interest rate is _____ %.
⁵The first payment will be on _____.

CAN YOU SAY THIS IN ENGLISH?

Can you...? Yes (✓)

☐ talk about different things you can do with money
☐ say how long you've been living in this town and learning English
☐ compare traveling by car, train, and plane in your country

35

G *must, have to, should* (obligation)
V cell phones
P sentence stress

3 A Modern manners

1 VOCABULARY & SPEAKING cell phones

a Match the word with the country. How do you
say *cell phone* in your language? Which name
do you like best?

1	France	a	cell phone
2	Germany	b	telefonino
3	Italy	c	celular
4	the US	d	movil
5	the UK	e	portable
6	Spain	f	mobile
7	Argentina	g	Handy

b **3.1** Listen and match the sentences with
the sounds.

A ☐ He's **dialing** a number.
B ☐ She's **texting** a friend.
C ☐ He just **hung up**.
D ☐ She's choosing a new **ring tone**.
E ☐ He's **calling back**.
F ☐ She **left a message** on his **voice mail**.
G ☐ The line's **busy**.

c Use the questionnaire to interview another student.
Ask for more information.

Cell phone questionnaire

Do you have a cell phone?

If so, how long have you had it?

If not, are you thinking of getting one?

How many of your friends or family have cell phones?

What kind of ring tones do they have?

What do they use their cell phones for (aside
from talking)?

Where or when should people turn off their cell phones?

Have you ever...?

...seen someone using a "hands-free" phone

...forgotten to turn your phone off (with embarrassing
consequences)

...used a cell phone while you were driving

2 GRAMMAR *must, have to, should* (obligation)

a In pairs, look at the picture and answer the questions.

1 What's the man doing? Does it annoy you when people do this?
2 Does this happen a lot in your country?
3 What other things do people do with cell phones that annoy you?

b **3.2** Listen to five people talking about things that annoy them about cell phones. Match the speakers with what they say.

Who…?

A says talking on your cell phone can be dangerous ☐
B complains about people who are very impatient to use their cell phones ☐
C complains about people using cell phones on social occasions ☐
D hates having to listen to other people's conversations ☐
E complains about people who interrupt a conversation to answer the phone ☐

c Match these sentences from the dialogues with their meaning.

1 **You shouldn't** answer the phone if you're talking to a salesperson. ☐
2 **You have to** turn off your cell when you fly. ☐
3 **You must not** use your phone until you get off the plane. ☐
4 **You don't have to** shout. The other person can hear you. ☐
5 **You should** talk quietly if you are in a public place. ☐

A You don't need to do this. It isn't necessary.
B Don't do this. It isn't allowed / permitted.
C Do this because it's a rule or the law.
D I think it's a bad thing to do this.
E I think it's a good thing to do this.

d ➲ **p.134 Grammar Bank 3A.** Read the rules and do the exercises.

3 PRONUNCIATION & SPEAKING sentence stress

a **3.3** Listen and repeat the sentences. Copy the rhythm.

1 You <u>must</u> <u>not</u> <u>use</u> your <u>phone</u> on a <u>plane</u>.
2 I <u>don't</u> <u>have</u> to <u>go</u> to <u>work</u> <u>tomorrow</u>.
3 We <u>have</u> to <u>take</u> an <u>exam</u> in <u>June</u>.
4 You should <u>turn</u> <u>off</u> your <u>cell</u> <u>phone</u> in <u>class</u>.
5 You <u>shouldn't</u> <u>talk</u> <u>loudly</u> on a <u>cell</u> <u>phone</u>.
6 I <u>must</u> <u>go</u> to the <u>bank</u> this <u>morning</u>.

b Read the definition of manners. Then look at phrases 1–8. Are these laws (or against the law) or just good / bad manners? Mark M (manners) or L (law).

> **manners** [pl noun] a way of behaving that is considered to be polite in a society or culture

Manners or the law?

1 Play noisy games on a cell phone in public
2 Send text messages when your car is stopped at a traffic light
3 Turn off your cell phone on a plane
4 Turn off your cell phone in class
5 Talk loudly on a cell phone on public transportation
6 Use a handheld cell phone while driving a car
7 Make very personal calls in public
8 Use your cell phone at a gas station

c Compare with a partner. Then make sentences with…

You should / shouldn't …(for manners)
You have to / can't / must not …(for the law)

4 READING

a What does the expression <u>culture shock</u> mean? Have you ever had culture shock?

b Read the article and check (✔) the sentence which says what the article is about.

☐ The English have very good manners.   ☐ The English and Russian ideas of good manners are different.

☐ The English are polite but insincere.   ☐ Russians are very rude and unfriendly.

Culture shock

Good manners are always good manners – anywhere in the world. That's what Miranda Ingram, who is English, thought until she married Alexander, who is Russian.

When I first met Alexander and he said to me, in Russian, "*Nalei mnye chai* – pour me some tea," I got angry and answered, "Pour it yourself." Translated into English, without a *Could you…?* and a *please*, it sounded really rude to me. But in Russian it was fine. You don't have to add any polite words.

However, when I took Alexander home to meet my parents, I had to give him an intensive course in *pleases* and *thank yous* (which he thought were completely unnecessary), and to teach him to say *sorry* even if someone else stepped on his toe, and to smile, smile, smile.

Another thing that Alexander just couldn't understand was why people said things like, "Would you mind passing me the salt, please?" He said, "It's only the salt, for goodness sake! What do you say in English if you want a *real* favor?"

He also watched in amazement when, at a dinner party, we swallowed some really disgusting food and I said, "Mmm…delicious." In Russia, people are much more direct. The first time Alexander's mother came to our house for dinner in Moscow, she told me that my soup needed more seasoning. Afterward, when we argued about it, my husband said, "Do you prefer your dinner guests to lie?"

Alexander complained that in England he felt "like the village idiot" because in Russia if you smile all the time, people think that you are crazy. In fact, this is exactly what my husband's friends thought of me the first time I went to Russia because I smiled at everyone, and translated every *please* and *thank you* from English into Russian!

At home we now have an agreement. If we're speaking Russian, he can say "Pour me some tea," and just make a noise like a grunt when I give it to him. But when we're speaking English, he has to add a *please*, a *thank you*, and a smile.

Adapted from a newspaper

c Read the article again and mark the sentences T (true) or F (false). Correct the wrong sentences.

1 Miranda got angry because her husband asked her to make the tea.
2 Miranda had to teach him to say "sorry" when something wasn't his fault.
3 Her husband thinks English people are too polite.
4 Alexander wasn't surprised when people said they liked the food at the dinner party.
5 The food was delicious.
6 Miranda didn't mind when her mother-in-law criticized her cooking.
7 Alexander thought his mother was right.
8 In Russia it isn't normal to smile all the time when you speak to someone.
9 His Russian friends thought Miranda was very friendly because she smiled a lot.
10 Alexander never says "thank you" for his tea when he and Miranda are speaking in Russian.

d Now cover the text. Can you complete the phrases with the missing verbs?

1 _____ on someone's foot or toe (by accident)
2 _____ some water into a glass or tea into a cup
3 _____ a noise, like a grunt
4 _____ food (so that it goes from your mouth to your stomach)
5 _____ a word from English into Russian

e Are people in your country more like Miranda or Alexander?

5 LISTENING

a **3.4** Listen to four people answering the question, "Are Americans polite?" Do they answer "yes" or "no"?

1	Clare, a student from Ireland	Yes/No
2	Paul, an American business man in China	Yes/No
3	Andrea, an American from Chicago	Yes/No
4	Marcos, an economist from Latin America	Yes/No

"Have a nice day! Have a nice day! Have a nice day! Have a nice day! Have a . . ."

b Listen again and answer the questions.

1 Why do some foreigners find the expression "Have a nice day" annoying?
2 Does Clare disagree?
3 What do some Chinese people call the Americans?
4 How does Paul's friend explain this?
5 What three reasons are given for people being ruder now?
6 What do some American tourists do that shows they don't respect local customs?
7 Does Marcos feel that all American tourists are like this?

6 SPEAKING

Look at the five situations. In groups, discuss…

Do people do these things in your country?
Do you think it's good or bad manners to do these things, or does it not matter?

> In my country, we don't kiss people when we meet them for the first time.

Good manners?
Bad manners?
Does it matter?

Greeting people
- kiss people on both cheeks when you meet them for the first time
- call older people by their first names
- use more formal language when speaking to an older person

In a restaurant
- let your children run around and be noisy
- be very affectionate to your boyfriend or girlfriend
- talk on your cell phone

Driving
- always stop at a pedestrian crossing
- honk at someone who's driving slowly
- drive with the windows down and your music playing loudly

Men and women – a man's role
- pay for a woman on the first date
- wait for a woman to go through the door first
- make sure a woman gets home safely at night

Visiting people
- take a present if you're invited to dinner at someone's house
- arrive more than 10 minutes late for a lunch or dinner
- smoke in a house where the owners don't smoke

3 B

G *must, may, might, can't* (deduction)
V describing people
P *-eigh, -aigh, -igh*

Judging by appearances

1 READING

a Answer the questions in pairs.

1 How many documents do you have that have your photo on them?

2 Where was your passport or ID card photo taken?

  a in a photo booth   **b** at home
  c at a photo studio

3 Do you think the photo looks like you?

4 Do you like the photo? Why (not)?

b Look at the three people and their passport photos. Do they look like their passport photos?

c Read the first paragraph of the article and answer the questions.

1 Why is our passport or ID card photo important?

2 Which nationality is the least happy with their passport photo?

3 Which is the happiest?

4 Which nationality is the vainest?

d Now read the rest of the article. Who is happy with their photo? Who isn't? Why?

e Look at the highlighted words in the text and choose the correct meaning.

1 a a study
  b a book

2 a feeling uncomfortable
  b feeling happy

3 a journalists
  b famous people

4 a feeling pleased with yourself
  b feeling unhappy with yourself

5 a very beautiful
  b very ugly

6 a without hair
  b with a lot of hair

7 a a kind of document
  b false hair

Do I really look like this?

Our passport or ID photos are the photos we show to the largest number of different people during our lives. But how happy are we with our passport photo? Do we make an effort to get a good one? According to [1] research done by the US printer company Lexmark, the answer varies according to nationalities. It seems that the Italians are the most [2] embarrassed about their passport photo (21% said they didn't like showing it to other people). On the other hand, 98% of Norwegians said they were happy with their photos. And the French spend the most time trying to get the perfect photo (sometimes spending an hour in the photo booth!). We asked three [3] celebrities how they felt about their passport photos…

Michael Winner
movie director

"I used to be very [4] proud of my passport photo," said Michael Winner. "For more than forty years I looked like an elegant movie director." But recently Michael renewed his passport and took a new photo in a photo booth. "Now I look like a drug dealer," he says.

Ruth England
TV host

Ruth England spends her life traveling and showing her passport photo to passport officials around the world. She confessed, "Once I had a passport photo where I looked really [5] hideous and so I deliberately 'lost' my passport and got a new one. For my latest passport, I took several photos and I chose the best one. It's pretty good. I've had much worse ones."

Toby Young
author and journalist

Toby Young said, "I'm often stopped when I go through immigration because I don't look like my passport photo at all. In my photo I had a lot more hair but now I'm [6] bald. No one believes it is me. So, now I have two possibilities: take a [7] wig with me every time I travel or get a new passport photo!"

Adapted from a newspaper

HOW WORDS WORK...

Look at two sentences from the text:

Once I had a passport photo where I looked really hideous.

I looked like an elegant movie director.

You can use the verbs *look* and *look like* to talk about a person's appearance.

- Use *look* + adjective (or an age).
- Use *look like* + a noun or pronoun.

Complete the sentences with *look* or *look like* in the correct form.

1 This photo doesn't _like_ you at all. When was it taken?
2 You _look_ very young in this photo. How old were you?
3 Your brother _looks_ a football player. He's huge.
4 You _look_ tired. Why don't you go to bed?

2 VOCABULARY describing people

a ⊙ p.149 Vocabulary Bank *Describing people*.

b (3.5) Look at the four men and listen. Which one is the bank robber?

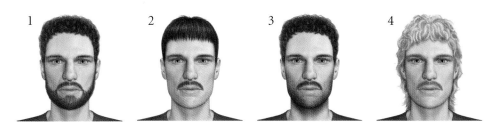

3 PRONUNCIATION -eigh, -aigh, -igh

a Look at the pink letters in the words below. Are they pronounced /eɪ/ or /aɪ/? Put the words in the correct column.

| bright | height | high | in his eighties | light brown |
| might | neighbor | overweight | sight | straight | weigh |

b (3.6) Listen and check.

c How is *-igh* always pronounced? How is *-eigh* usually pronounced? Which word is an exception here?

d (3.7) Practice saying the sentences. Listen and check.

1 She has light brown hair. It's short and straight.
2 He's medium height and slightly overweight.
3 He's in his eighties, but his eyesight's very good.
4 She likes wearing tight straight-leg jeans.

4 GRAMMAR *must, may, might, can't* (deduction)

a Look at the photo of the three women. Who do you think is who? Match texts A–C with the photos.

Judging by appearances

Millionaire's daughter?

Managing director?

Policewoman?

Who do you think is who?

b Read the texts again. In pairs, answer the questions.

1 Which two women feel they are judged because of their appearance? How?
2 Which woman thinks she is judged because of her name? How?

c Look at the highlighted phrases in the texts and answer the questions.

1 Which phrase means *it's impossible*? _____
2 Which phrase means *it's certain*? _____
3 Which phrase means *it's possible*? _____

d ○ **p.134 Grammar Bank 3B.** Read the rules and do the exercises.

e ○ **Communication** *Who do you think they are? p.116* Match more people with their jobs.

A

Laura Day, policewoman

When people first meet me, they think I might be a teacher or a hairdresser. When I'm not wearing my uniform, they never believe me that I'm a policewoman. When I tell people what I do, the typical reaction is, "You can't be a policewoman, you're too small!" I'm only 5 feet 4 inches* tall. People always think that policewomen are big and masculine. Often people only believe me when I show them my police identity card.

* = 1.6 meters

B

Sam Roddick, daughter of Anita Roddick (the millionaire founder of Body Shop)

When I introduce myself to people and say my name, they often say, "Oh you must be the Body Shop woman's daughter." Later they can't remember my name. I'm very proud of my mother, but I would never say, "My mom's Anita Roddick." I don't know if I am very different from the typical "rich kid" because I don't know any. My friends never mention my background or money and neither do I.

C

Thea Callan, managing director of *Nails Inc.* (a chain of nail salons*)

People often ask me who my boss is. They think, "She can't be the managing director – she's a woman." They're expecting to see an older man in a suit. Or when people speak to me on the phone and hear that I am a woman, then they think that I must be a 50-year-old woman who wears pant suits and is very unfeminine. They're very surprised when they see me. I'm not like that at all. In the office I just wear jeans and tennis shoes.

* = salons where you can have manicures and pedicures

5 LISTENING

a In pairs, look at the man in the photo and answer the questions. Use *must, may, might, can't be*. Say why.

1 Where do you think he's from?
   the US   Sweden   Spain
2 How old do you think he is?
   in his 20s   in his 30s   in his 40s
3 What do you think his job is?
   priest   musician   accountant

b **3.8** Listen to the first part of a radio interview with him and check your answers. Were you right?

c Listen again and make notes under the headings below. Compare with a partner.

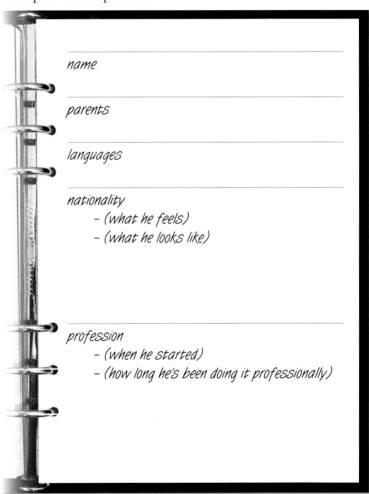

> name
>
> parents
>
> languages
>
> nationality
>   – (what he feels)
>   – (what he looks like)
>
> profession
>   – (when he started)
>   – (how long he's been doing it professionally)

d **3.9** Now listen to the second part of the interview and answer the questions.

1 In which of the two countries is it easier for him to make a living?
2 In what other countries is there a lot of interest in his job?
3 What is the stereotype of someone doing his job?
4 In which of the two countries does he think people judge him by his appearance?

e How important is appearance in your country? Do people in *your* country judge by appearances?

3 C

G *can, could, be able to* (ability and possibility)
V *-ed / -ing* adjectives
P sentence stress

If at first you don't succeed, ...

1 GRAMMAR *can, could, be able to*

a Look at the title of the lesson, which is the first half of a well-known saying. Look at the different second halves below. Which do you think is the real saying? Which do you think is the best advice?

...ask for advice.	...leave it until tomorrow.
...give up.	...pay someone else to do it for you.
...have a cup of coffee.	...try, try again.

b Look at the definition of *be able to*. What other verb is it similar to?

> **be able to do sth** to have the ability, opportunity, time, etc.
> to do something, e.g., *Will you be able to come to the meeting next week?*

c Read the article about people who have tried (but failed) to learn something. Complete the text with these phrases.

A	I've never been able to say
B	I was able to learn
C	you'll never be able to speak
D	I just wasn't able to do it
E	I hate not being able to communicate
F	I would suddenly be able to do it
G	all my friends are able to do

I'm a failure! I've never been able to...

...pass my driving test

I started taking driving lessons when I was 17. Although I'm normally a fast learner, ¹_____. After 18 months I failed my first test. I was really disappointed. Since then I've taken the test again three times, but I've always failed – usually on reversing or parking. The problem is I get so nervous during the tests that I can't drive very well. It's so embarrassing to admit that I can't learn to do something that ²_____!

Amanda, Dallas

...learn to dance

I've always wanted to be able to dance salsa, and when I was working in Ecuador there were free classes, so I joined. But the art of salsa is to keep your arms still and move your hips, and I just couldn't do it. When I hear music, my arms start moving but my hips don't. After about ten hours of classes, ³_____ the steps, but I was dancing like a robot! I didn't give up, but soon everyone in the class was dancing and I was just slowly moving from side to side and counting out loud "one, two, three, four." I was sure that one day ⁴_____ – but that never happened. I can still remember the first two steps, though, and I still try to dance when I hear a salsa tune, as long as nobody is watching.

John, Tampa

...speak a foreign language

I've started learning English at least ten times. I've been to classes, I've had a private teacher, I've used a self-study course, but ⁵_____ anything in English. I even had an American girlfriend once, but she learned Portuguese before I managed to improve my English, so we always spoke in Portuguese. I travel a lot for my job and ⁶_____. It's so frustrating. I'm 32 now and I think if you don't learn a language when you're a child, or go and live in the country, ⁷_____ it well.

*Guilherme, Brasília ***

* translated from Portuguese

d Look at phrases A–G. What tense or form of *be able to* are they?

e ○ **p.134 Grammar Bank 3C.** Read the rules and do the exercises.

f ○ **Communication** *Guess the sentence A p.116 B p.119.*

2 PRONUNCIATION   sentence stress

a [3.10] **Dictation.** Listen and write six sentences with *can / can't* or *could / couldn't*.

b [3.11] Listen and repeat the sentences. Copy the rhythm.

1 I'd <u>love</u> to be <u>able</u> to <u>ski</u>.
2 We <u>won't</u> be <u>able</u> to <u>come</u>.
3 I've <u>never</u> been <u>able</u> to <u>dance</u>.
4 She <u>hates</u> <u>not</u> being <u>able</u> to <u>drive</u>.

c [3.12] Listen and make new sentences with the verbs you hear.

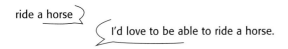

ride a <u>horse</u>

I'd love to be able to ride a horse.

HOW WORDS WORK...

1 Look at the two uses of *so*. Match them with their uses.

1 It's so frustrating!
2 The classes were free, so I joined.

☐ to emphasize an adjective or an adverb
☐ to connect a cause and a result

2 Look at the sentences below. Is *so* use number 1 or use number 2?

A I love Paris. It's so beautiful. ☐
B The bus didn't come, so I walked home. ☐
C Why does he talk so much? ☐
D I was so tired that I went to bed at 9:00. ☐
E I was tired, so I went to bed. ☐

3 SPEAKING

Interview your partner with the chart.

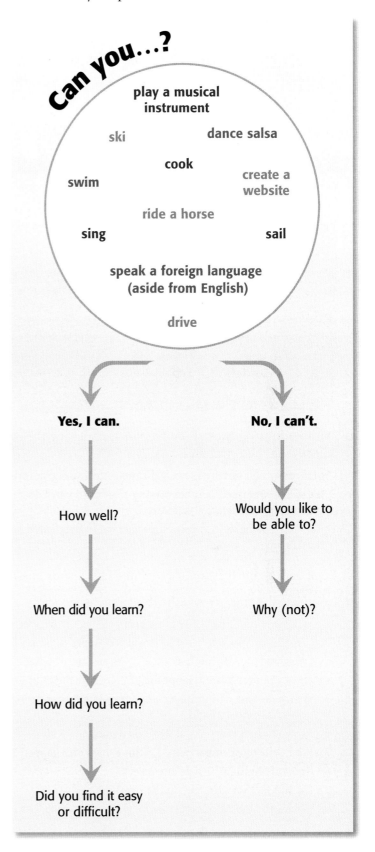

Can you...?

play a musical instrument

ski   dance salsa

cook

swim   create a website

ride a horse

sing   sail

speak a foreign language (aside from English)

drive

Yes, I can.   **No, I can't.**

How well?   Would you like to be able to?

When did you learn?   Why (not)?

How did you learn?

Did you find it easy or difficult?

4 VOCABULARY *-ed / -ing* adjectives

a Look at the picture.

1 Which person is bored? Which person is boring?
2 Which person is embarrassed? Which person is embarrassing?

b Without looking back at the texts in 1, <u>underline</u> the correct adjective in these sentences.

1 I failed my first test. I was really **disappointed / disappointing**.
2 It's so **embarrassed / embarrassing** to admit I can't do something that all my friends are able to do.
3 I hate not being able to communicate. It's so **frustrated / frustrating**.

c Look back at the texts on page 44 and check your answers.

d Complete the adjectives with *-ed* or *-ing*.

1 What do you think is the most **excit**_____ sport to watch?
2 What music do you listen to if you feel **depress**_____?
3 What was the last **interest**_____ TV show you watched?
4 Have you ever been **disappoint**_____ by a birthday present?
5 Which do you find more **tir**_____, traveling by car or by public transportation?
6 Are you often **bor**_____ at work or school?
7 What's the most **embarrass**_____ thing that's ever happened to you?
8 Are you **frighten**_____ of any insects?
9 Do you feel very **tir**_____ in the morning?
10 What's the most **bor**_____ movie you've ever seen?

e Ask and answer the questions in pairs. Ask for more information.

5 LISTENING

a You're going to hear a psychologist talking about how to succeed at learning to do something new. Before you listen, match these phrasal verbs with their meanings.

1 I want to **take up** scuba diving.
2 I'm going to **give up** learning Japanese. It's too difficult.
3 If I like the music, I'll **keep on** dancing.
    ☐ a stop, abandon
    ☐ b continue
    ☐ c start something new

b **3.13** Read these seven tips. Now listen to the program. Check (✔) the five things the psychologist says.

1 ☐ Be realistic about what you choose.
2 ☐ Always take up a new activity at the beginning of the year.
3 ☐ Don't think you'll be bad at all sports just because you're not good at one.
4 ☐ Don't give up an activity before you've given it a good chance.
5 ☐ If you're learning something new, don't think you're going to become the best in the world at it.
6 ☐ Always take up a new activity with a friend.
7 ☐ Learning something new is a good way of meeting people.

c Listen again. What examples does she give for each point you've checked?

6 READING

a Can you think of anyone you know or a famous person who has been successful in very difficult circumstances?

b Work in pairs. **A** read about Natalie; **B** read about Bethany. Complete the chart.

	Natalie	Bethany
1 How did she lose a limb?		
2 When did she start her sport again?		
3 How did she feel?		
4 What has she achieved since then?		
5 How does she see her future?		

c **A** use the chart to tell **B** about Natalie. **B** complete the chart. Then change roles.

d Now read the other article. <u>Underline</u> five words / phrases in either article that you want to remember.

e What do the two women have in common? What's different about them?

Never give up

Natalie, the swimmer who lost a leg

Natalie du Toit, the South African swimmer, was only seventeen when she lost her leg in a car accident. She was going to a training session at the swimming pool on her motorcycle when a car hit her. Her leg had to be amputated at the knee. At the time, she was one of South Africa's most promising young swimmers. Everybody thought that she would never be able to swim competitively again.

But Natalie was determined to persevere. She went back into the pool only three months after the accident. And just one year later, at the Commonwealth Games in Manchester, she swam 800 meters in 9 minutes 11.38 seconds and qualified for the final – but not for disabled swimmers, for able-bodied ones! Although she didn't win a medal, she still made history.

"I remember how thrilled I was the first time that I swam after recovering from the operation. It felt like my leg was there. It still does," says Natalie. "The water is the gift that gives me back my leg. I'm still the same person I was before the accident. I believe everything happens in life for a reason. You can't go back and change anything. Swimming was my life and still is. My dream is to swim faster than I did before the accident."

Bethany, the surfer who lost an arm

Bethany Hamilton was the best girl surfer of her age when she lost an arm in a shark attack. She was only thirteen years old and was surfing in Hawaii when a tiger shark attacked her and tore off her left arm. It happened so fast she didn't even scream.

But Bethany was determined to get back on a surfboard as soon as possible. As soon as she left the hospital, she began practicing her surfing exercises on the beach. Everyone was amazed to see her surfing so soon after her accident. Incredibly, she finished 5th at the National Surfing Championships.

"The first time I went back into the water, I was so happy I cried," she said. "It was easier than I thought. But obviously it's much more difficult than with both arms, and I have to accept I'll probably never be world champion, which used to be my dream."

Since then, Bethany has signed a contract with Rip Curl and has written a book about her experience, which has been made into a movie. "I always dream of the ocean," she says. "When you surf a wave, it's like walking on water, and when you're in the air, it's like flying."

7 🔊 3.14 **SONG** ♫ *You can get it if you really want*

HOW TO GET THERE

a (3.15) Cover the conversation and listen. Where is the apartment that Mark is going to see? What's the best way to get there? How is Mark going to get there?

b Read the conversation. In pairs, what do you think the missing words are? **Don't fill them in yet.**

Mark	Where _exactly_ is it? I'm sorry, I didn't catch that. OK. _How_ far is it? OK, OK. Merci. Au revoir.
Jacques	Any luck?
Mark	I think I've found an apartment. How do I _get_ to Belleville?
Jacques	The easiest _way_ is to get the metro at Pyramides. Take Line 14 and _change_ at Châtelet.
Mark	OK.
Jacques	Then take Line 11 _towards_ Mairie des Lilas.
Mark	Where do I _get_ off?
Jacques	At Belleville.
Mark	How many _stops_ is it?
Jacques	Six, I think.
Mark	Oh right, I've found it on the map. How long does it _take_ to get there?
Jacques	About half an hour.
Nicole	Have you found a flat?
Mark	Yes, in Belleville this time.
Nicole	When are you going to see it?
Mark	This afternoon.
Nicole	If you can wait till six, I'll _give_ you a lift. I live near Belleville so I'm driving that way.
Mark	That's great. Thanks.

c Listen again and complete the conversation.

d (3.16) Listen and repeat the highlighted phrases. Copy the rhythm.

e In pairs, try to remember the questions for these answers.
  1 The easiest way is to get the metro.
  2 At Belleville.
  3 Six, I think.
  4 About half an hour.

f ○ **Communication** *How do I get there? A p.117 B p.120.*

SOCIAL ENGLISH   What's going on?

a (3.17) Listen. Does Mark decide to rent the apartment?

b Listen again and answer the questions.
  1 What are the main advantages and disadvantages of the apartment?
  2 What two lies does Mark tell? Why? Do you think Nicole believes him?

c (3.18) Complete the USEFUL PHRASES. Listen and check.

d Listen again and repeat the phrases. How do you say them in your language?

USEFUL PHRASES

So, what do you t_hink_?	I can't w_ait_ (to see it)!
It's a long w_ay_ from (the station).	Are you on your o_wn_?
What's it l_ike_?	I'll call you b_ack_.

Amanda went to the US and stayed with Stephanie and David in New Jersey. After she had gone home, she wrote to thank them.

a Look at the list of things she says in her letter. Number them in a logical order 1–7.

A ☐ She suggests the best time to come to Mexico.

B ☐ She thanks them for inviting her.

C ☐ She talks about what she's been doing recently.

D ☐ She apologizes for not writing earlier.

E ☐ She mentions two really good experiences in the US.

F ☐ She thanks them again and invites them to stay.

G ☐ She talks in general about the nice things that happened in the US.

b Now read Amanda's letter and check your answers to **a**.

c Find and correct five punctuation and capitalization mistakes in the second paragraph.

d Look back at the e-mails on page 17. What difference is there in style between an informal letter and an e-mail?

Useful language: informal letters / e-mails

Beginnings

Dear + name (**e-mail:** Dear or Hi)

Sorry for not writing earlier but…

Thank you / Thanks (so much) for (your letter, inviting me, etc.).

It was great to hear from you…

Endings

That's all for now.

Hope to hear from you soon. / Looking forward to hearing from you.

(Give my) regards / love to…

Best wishes / Love (from)

PS I enclose a photo of the three of us (**e-mail:** I'm attaching…)

Imagine you have some American friends in the US, and you stayed with them for a week last month.

WRITE a letter to thank them.

PLAN what you're going to say. Use 1–7 above and the **Useful language** box to help you.

CHECK the letter for mistakes (grammar , punctuation , and spelling).

Ave. Gustavo Baz 179
46800 Puerto Vallarta
Mexico
August 25

Dear Stephanie and David,

Sorry for not writing earlier but I've been incredibly busy since I got back!

Im writing to thank you for inviting me to stay with you in july I had a fantastic time. The weather was perfect and I really think my english got better. i hope you think so too!

It was very nice to meet Claire and Emma. There were a lot of memorable days, but I'll never forget the rock concert we went to – it was amazing – or the visit to New York.

For the last three weeks I've been very busy organizing everything for my next year at college. I have to register for all my subjects and choose the electives I want to take. I've also been exercising a lot as I put on three kilos while I was in New Jersey! I've been going swimming every day and playing volleyball with my friends. Talking of sports, I was sorry to see that the Mets lost on Saturday. Let's hope they play better next week.

Anyway, that's all for now. Thanks again for everything. Don't forget my invitation to come to Mexico. My family would love to meet you. Spring would be a great time as it's not too warm or too crowded.

Give my love to Claire and Emma.

Best wishes,

Amanda

P.S. I enclose a photo I took of the girls in New York.

GRAMMAR

Complete the second sentence with **two words** so that it means the same as the first. Contracted forms, e.g., *isn't*, count as one word.

I really think it's important for you to learn to drive.

You really *must* *learn* to drive.

1 Why don't you join a tennis club? It would be good for you.

  I think you *shouldn't* ___ a tennis club.

2 I'm sure she's not American. She doesn't have an American accent.

  She ___ ___ American, she doesn't have an American accent.

3 I can't go out tonight.

  I won't ___ ___ to go out tonight.

4 It's prohibited to take photos there.

  You *must* *not* take photos there.

5 I'm not sure if she'll like her present.

  She *may not* like her present.

6 Wearing a uniform is not mandatory.

  You ___ ___ to wear a uniform.

7 The lights are on, so I'm sure he's at home.

  The lights are on, so he *must be* at home.

8 I think this is probably their house.

  This *might be* their house.

9 Paying in advance is obligatory at this school.

  You *have to* pay in advance at this school.

10 Drinking a lot of coffee isn't a good idea.

  You *shouldn't* a lot of coffee.

10

VOCABULARY

a Complete the description.

My cousin Ann is very attractive. She's in her [1] m_edle_ -twenties – 24 or 25 I think. She's blond, with shoulder-[2] l_____ hair. It's completely [3] s_____, not curly at all. Her [4] b_angs_ are very long and get in her eyes. She's very near-sighted, but she [5] w_ears_ contact lenses.

b Complete with an adjective from the **bold** verb.

1 Are you _interes___ in sports?   **interest**
2 I was very _frustated_ when I failed the test.   **depress**
3 This book is really _____. I can't finish it.   **bore**
4 I completely forgot his name. It was so _____!   **embarrass**
5 I felt very _____ because I just couldn't do it.   **frustrate**

c Complete with one word.

1 Please turn _____ your cell phone. You can't use it here.
2 John's not here. Can you call _____ later?
3 I can't believe it! He hung _____ in the middle of our conversation!
4 She looks _____ her mother. They both have big eyes.
5 He's _in_ his late forties.

15

PRONUNCIATION

a <u>Underline</u> the word with a different sound.

1	🚲 aɪ	dial	might	(fifties)	frightened
2	🚂 eɪ	weight	(height)	straight	engaged
3	🪚	bald	long	(brown)	tall
4	🧒	gray	ugly	glasses	(change)
5	🕯	check	(mustache)	watch	choose

b <u>Underline</u> the stressed syllable.

disappointed   embarrassing   interested   frustrated   overweight

10

CAN YOU UNDERSTAND THIS TEXT?

Good News— Bad News

One of the best days of my life was the day one of my professors called to say that I had been accepted to study for a year at the University of the Sorbonne in Paris. I had never traveled much, and I didn't think I would ever have the chance to go to Europe. The news came one afternoon in May of 1993. I was just 19 years old and I was in my room at college. Just before the call, a friend of mine came into my room, threw herself into a chair, and burst into tears . She had had plans to get married in June, but her boyfriend had just broken up with her! At that very moment the phone rang. So there I was listening to the best news of my life, while my friend was crying over the worst news in hers. My professor said, "What's the matter? Aren't you excited?" I said, "Yes, I am, but I'll tell you about it later." I did my best to console my friend, but it was really hard for me to be sympathetic while I was so happy about my news.

Finally I couldn't stand it anymore. I said to my friend, "Stay here. I have to go out for a few minutes." I went out and got a big pizza, a quart of chocolate ice cream, and a big bottle of soda. "You and I are going to have a feast," I said, and then I told her my news. That friend was a much happier person when she left. I went to France and had a wonderful year. I studied hard, became fluent in French, traveled, and met many wonderful people. When I came back, I ran into my friend. Although she'd been deeply hurt by the break up with her boyfriend, she had also had a good year at school and was about to leave for graduate school. We laughed together over that "famous" day in my room, possibly the best and worst day of our lives.

a Read the article and choose a, b, or c.

1 In 1993, the writer was ___ about the chances of ever traveling to Europe.
a optimistic b pessimistic c worried

2 When her professor called, she felt that she ___ celebrate the news.
a shouldn't b had to c could

3 Her professor couldn't understand ___.
a why she was crying b what she was saying
c why she didn't sound happy

4 In the end, the writer's friend ___.
a felt better b felt worse c left early

5 When the friends met again a year later, they ___ that "famous" day.
a felt sorry about b enjoyed remembering
c didn't talk about

b Look at the highlighted words and phrases. Can you guess what they mean?

CAN YOU UNDERSTAND THESE PEOPLE?

a 3.19 Listen and circle the correct answer, a, b, or c.

1 Where's the girl's cell phone?
a In the cafe. b In her pocket. c In her bag.

2 How late are their friends?
a Less than 15 minutes. b 15 minutes.
c More than 15 minutes.

3 Which photo does the man like?
a The woman's. b His own. c Neither of them.

4 The girl's new boyfriend is…
a tall and with long dark hair.
b tall with short dark hair.
c short with short dark hair.

5 How many times has the woman failed her driving test?
a One. b Two. c Three.

b 3.20 Listen and complete the form with the missing information.

The Language School

Name:	1 _____
Last Name:	2 _____
Nationality:	3 _____
Student wants to take the 4 _____ level.	
Student has been to 5 _____.	

CAN YOU SAY THIS IN ENGLISH?

Can you…? Yes (✓)

☐ talk about bad cell phone manners, and what you think people should do

☐ describe yourself and other people

☐ talk about something you've tried to learn but weren't able to and say why

G first conditional and future time clauses + *when*, *until*, etc.
V education
P /ʌ/ or /yu/?

4A Back to school, age 35

1 VOCABULARY education

a Answer the questions in pairs.

> 1 When did the Second World War end?
> 2 What is the capital of Colombia?
> 3 Who wrote *Don Quixote*?
> 4 How many kilobytes are there in a megabyte?
> 5 Who invented the theory of relativity?
> 6 What's 5×18÷4?
> 7 How many legs does an insect have?
> 8 What is water made of?

b Match the questions with these school subjects.

chemistry   5
geography   2
history   1
information technology   ☐
literature   3
math   6
physics   ☐
biology   8

c ➡ **p.150 Vocabulary Bank** *Education*.

2 PRONUNCIATION & SPEAKING /ʌ/ or /yu/?

⚠ The letter *u* between consonants or at the beginning of a word is usually pronounced /ʌ/ or /yu/.

a Put the words in the correct column.

computer   lunch   fun   usually   result
study   subject   uniform   university

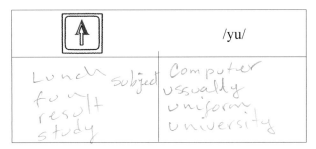

↑	/yu/
Lunch fun result study subject	Computer ussually uniform university

b 🔊 **4.1** Listen and check. Practice saying the words. Why do we say *a university* but *an umbrella*?

c 🔊 **4.2** Practice saying these sentences. Listen and check.

1 What subjects did you study in high school?
2 Do students at that school wear uniforms?
3 Most students have lunch in the cafeteria.
4 We usually have fun in our music class.

d Interview your partner using the questionnaire. Ask for more information.

Your education

What kind of high school / you go to?

/ you like it?

How many students / there in each class?

How much homework / you have?

/ you have to wear a uniform?

/ discipline very strict?

/ students behave well?

Which subjects / you good and bad at?

Which / your best and worst subjects?

So school these days is easy? Think again.

People and politicians complain that school is getting easier. Damian Whitworth, a 35-year-old journalist, decided to see for himself. He spent a week as a student at a British secondary school, Brentwood County High School. It's a large public school and has about 1,800 students, girls and boys, ages between 11 and 18.

3 READING

a Look at the photo above. What's unusual about one of the students?

b Read the introduction. Why did Damian Whitworth go back to school? What kind of school did he go to?

c Read Damian's diary for one of the days he spent back at school. Does he think school is easier or harder now?

d Read the text again and put the phrases A–H in the correct places.

A A crowd of students is watching.

B However, the students are totally involved.

C He's friendly with the students but not *too* friendly.

D When I was the same age as these kids, I had never used a computer.

E It's a magical moment and the most effective class I have seen.

F "Are you really in our class?"

G One boy says he has fries every day.

H Phones that ring in class are confiscated until the end of the week.

e In pairs, look at the highlighted words and phrases. Try to guess what they mean from the context. Then check a dictionary.

f In pairs, look at each heading and say if what happens is the same, similar, or different from the high school you went (or go) to.

French

My first lesson is French. I am in a class of thirteen-year-olds. Outside the classroom some girls start interrogating me. [1] *"Are you really in our class?"* "How old are you?" "How old do you think I am?" I reply.
"Well… you're not 13!"
First we have a listening test that I find difficult. I get 14 out of 20. Not bad. Then we make review lists on the computer. [2]_____. Now every student has one.

Math

As we wait outside the math classroom a teacher tells me to button my shirt all the way up. The math teacher uses an interactive whiteboard that has graphics and video, but the students don't look very interested in the lesson. A cell phone rings and the owner hurries to turn it off. [3]_____

History

Mr. Fishleigh is the history teacher. He doesn't have any problems controlling the noise level. (Other teachers do.) [4]_____. He talks to them as if they were adults and gets their attention in return .

Lunch

In the cafeteria we can choose between traditional and fast food. Burgers and fries are the most popular meal. [5]_____

Information and communication technology

We are designing spreadsheets for cell phone sales and I cannot imagine a more boring lesson. [6]_____.

Most students have Internet access at home and the school has a website where parents can see what homework their children have and when they have to hand it in .

Religious education

The teacher introduces us to meditation. We sit cross-legged and try to fill our minds with blackness and think positively about people who we have been thinking negatively about. For 15 minutes the students sit, eyes closed, in total silence. When they leave the class they are slightly dazed :
"Incredible!"
"Amazing!"
"We should do this in math!"

[7]_____

The bell rings. End of school for the day.

As we leave there is a fight at the school gates. [8]_____ "If anyone hits anyone, I'll call the police," says a teacher.

So has school gotten easier?

It's difficult to say if school has become harder or easier since I was a child because teaching methods have changed so much. All I can say is that during my working life I have had many tiring experiences. Being back at school for a week was as tiring as any of them. Being a student today is very, very hard work.

4 GRAMMAR   first conditional and future time clauses

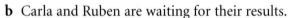

a In pairs, answer the questions.

1 When was the last time you took a test? Did you pass or fail?
2 What's the next test you are going to take? How do you feel about it?
3 How do you usually feel before you take a test?
4 What do you usually do the night before a test?
5 Have you ever failed an important test you thought you had passed
   (or vice versa)?

b Carla and Ruben are waiting for their results.
   4.3 Listen to Carla and answer questions 1–5. **4.4** Then do the same for Ruben.

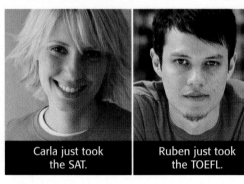

Carla just took
the SAT.

Ruben just took
the TOEFL.

1 Was the test difficult?
2 When and how will you get the results of the test?
3 How will you celebrate if you get a high score?
4 What will you do if you don't get the score you need?

c **4.5** Listen and complete the sentences.

1 They probably won't admit me **unless**
   _____.

2 **As soon as** _____, I'll look up my
   scores!

3 I don't want to plan any celebrations **until**
   _____.

4 **If** I don't get into college, _____.

5 **When** _____, they'll mail the results.

d **○ p.136 Grammar Bank 4A.** Read the rules
and do the exercises.

e Choose **five** sentence beginnings from the
list below and make true sentences about
yourself. Then tell your partner.

I won't stop studying English until I…	I'll have a big party if…
I'd like to retire when…	I'll always live here unless…
I'll leave home as soon as…	I'll have more free time when…
I'll be really annoyed if…	I'll have something to eat as soon as…
I don't want to have children before…	I won't get married until…

f **4.6** Listen to Carla and Ruben. Did they get the results they needed? What
scores did they get? What are they going to do?

5 LISTENING

a Look at this extract from a TV guide and the photo. Answer the questions.

8:00 That'll Teach 'Em

Final part of the six-part series following a group of modern 16-year-old students in a 1950s boarding school.

1 What do you think the idea of the program was?
2 Which of these things do you think the students hated most?

the food	wearing a uniform
not being able to watch TV	going for cross-country runs
having a lot of homework	taking cold showers
not being able to use cell phones	

3 What do you think the discipline was like? How do you think the students were punished if they behaved badly?
4 Do you think the students did well or badly when they took 1950s exams?

b **4.7** Listen to a TV critic talking about the program *That'll Teach 'Em*. Check your answers to **a**. Were you surprised?

c Listen again and mark the sentences T (true) or F (false).

1 Sixteen teenagers took part in the experiment.
2 They didn't have to sleep at school.
3 The uniforms were not very comfortable.
4 They had to stay inside the school grounds all the time.
5 The students weren't allowed to talk during the classes.
6 They really missed being able to use computers and calculators.
7 They thought the classes were boring.
8 The students failed because they weren't intelligent enough.
9 School subjects today are easier than in the 1950s.
10 Most of the teenagers enjoyed the experiment.

d Do you think school subjects in your country are easier than they used to be?

6 SPEAKING

a In groups, each person chooses a different statement from the list below. Decide if you agree or disagree with your statement, and write down at least three reasons.

Private schools are usually better than public schools.

All schools should let children wear whatever they want to at school.

Cooking and housekeeping should be taught at all schools.

Physical education should be optional.

Girls study better without boys in the class.

Summer vacation should be shorter.

Boys study better in a mixed class.

b Explain to the rest of your group what you think about your topic. The others in the group should listen and say if they agree or disagree with you and why.

Useful language

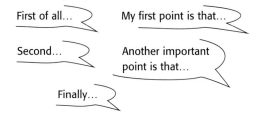

First of all…

My first point is that…

Second…

Another important point is that…

Finally…

4 B

G second conditional
V houses
P sentence stress

In an ideal world...

Getting personal

Our weekly questionnaire. This week we ask the actress and model Isabella Rossellini and dancer Joaquín Cortés...

1 If you could live in another period of time for its fashion, when would you choose and why?

2 If you could come back in another life, who (or what) would you like to be?

3 If you could ban one article of clothing, what would it be?

4 What would you wear if you were invited on a date by someone you really liked?

5 What would you eat for your last meal and who (dead or alive) would you share it with?

Adapted from a newspaper

1 GRAMMAR second conditional

a Look at the two photos on page 56 and describe the people. Do you know anything about them?

b Read the questions in *Getting personal* and match two answers with each question. Try to guess which answers are Isabella Rossellini's and which are Joaquín Cortés's.

A ☐ *A fly on the wall, so I could watch people.*

B ☐ *Either the thirties, for its elegance, or the seventies, for its hippy clothes and great music.*

C ☐ 4 *Jeans and a shirt.*

D ☐ 3 *Very high heels on shoes.*

E ☐ 5 *With a fabulous woman. I wouldn't really care about the food.*

F ☐ 2 *Vertical-striped pants with horizontal-striped jackets.*

G ☐ 1 *Some super comfortable French pajamas that everyone thinks are clothes.*

H ☐ 2 *A bird.*

I ☐ 5 *I would have pasta with my dog, Macaroni. It's what she has wanted her whole life.*

J ☐ 1 *I'd choose today or any time after the end of the corset.*

c Look at *Getting personal* again, and answer these questions.

1 In questions 1–4, what tense is the verb in the *if* clause?
2 What tense is the other verb?
3 How is question 5 different?
4 Do the questions refer to real or imaginary situations?

d ⮕ **p.136 Grammar Bank 4B.** Read the rules and do the exercises.

e ⮕ **Communication** *What would you do if...? A p.117 B p.120.*

2 PRONUNCIATION & SPEAKING sentence stress

a Match the sentence halves.

1 I <u>wouldn't</u> <u>wear</u> that <u>hat</u>   ☐   A if she <u>practiced</u> <u>more</u>.
2 If you <u>exercised</u> more,   ☐   B I'm <u>sure</u> she'd <u>understand</u> you.
3 If it <u>weren't</u> so <u>expensive</u>,   ☐   C if I could <u>find</u> the <u>right</u> <u>person</u>.
4 I'd <u>get</u> <u>married</u> <u>tomorrow</u>   ☐   D you'd <u>feel</u> <u>much</u> <u>better</u>.
5 She'd <u>play</u> <u>better</u>   ☐   E I'd <u>buy</u> it.
6 If you <u>talked</u> to her,   ☐   F if <u>I</u> were <u>you</u>.

b ▶ **4.8** Listen and check.

c Listen again and repeat. <u>Copy</u> the <u>rhythm</u>. Then cover A–F and try to remember the sentences.

d Choose three of the sentence beginnings below and complete them in a way which is true for you. Tell a partner and say why.

If I won a "dream vacation" in a contest, I'd go...

If I could choose any car I liked, I'd have a...

If I could be very good at a sport, I'd choose...

If I could choose my ideal job, I'd...

If I had more time, I'd learn...

If I could buy a house in another country, I'd buy...

3 VOCABULARY houses

a Look at the cover of the magazine. Which room is it? How many things in the room can you name?

b ◯ p.151 Vocabulary Bank *Houses.*

c In pairs, ask and answer the questions.

Where do you live?

What do you like about the area where you live?

What don't you like?

What do you like about your house / apartment?

What would you change?

4 LISTENING & SPEAKING

a 4.9 Listen to four people describing their "dream house." Match the speakers 1–4 to the pictures.

A

B

C

D

b Listen again and match the people with what they say.

Which speaker…?
☐ would not like to have other people living nearby
☐ would like to live somewhere that was partly old and partly modern
☐ would not spend much time inside their dream house
☐ doesn't think they will ever get their dream house

c Think for a few minutes about what your dream house would be like and write down notes. Use **Vocabulary Bank** *Houses* to help you.

Where would it be?
What kind of house or apartment would it be?
What special features would it have?

d In groups, describe your houses. Whose do you like best?

5 READING

a Have you ever visited the house where a famous person was born or lived? Where was it? What do you especially remember about it?

b Read the article about Casa Azul. Which part of the house are these things connected to? Why are they mentioned?

two giant statues
Leon Trotsky
a yellow floor
a monkey and a parrot
a pair of shoes
a cupboard with a glass door
July 7, 1910
1929–1954

c Match the highlighted words with their meaning.

1 _China cabinets_ a piece of furniture with cupboards at the bottom and shelves above, to hold cups and plates, etc.

2 _glass_ material that you can see through

3 _entrance_ the door, gate, or opening where you go into a place

4 _Gallery_ a room where paintings are hung

5 _upstair_ the floor above where you are

6 _airy_ with a lot of fresh air inside

7 _shutters_ wooden or metal covers that are attached to windows

8 _patio_ an area, usually behind a house, where people can sit and eat outside

d What did you find out about Frida Kahlo and her life? Would you like to visit her house?

6 4.10 SONG ♫ *Our house*

Houses you'll never forget
Casa Azul (The Blue House)

On the corner of Londres and Allende Street in Coyoacán, an old residential area of Mexico City, there is a house with bright blue walls, tall windows and green shutters, surrounded by trees. It is one of the most extraordinary places in Mexico, the home of the surrealist painter Frida Kahlo, who died in 1954, when she was only 47.

The entrance is guarded by two giant statues nearly seven meters tall. As you walk past them, you enter a garden with tropical plants and fountains. When you go inside the house, the first room is the spacious and airy living room. Here Frida and her husband, the painter Diego Rivera, entertained their famous friends, including the millionaire Nelson Rockefeller, the composer George Gershwin, and the political leader Leon Trotsky. Now the room is a gallery where some of Frida's paintings can be seen.

The first thing you notice when you go into the kitchen is the floor – painted bright yellow to stop insects from coming in. There is a long yellow table where Frida and Diego often had lunch parties, and a yellow china cabinet holding traditional green and brown Mexican dishes. Here, their guests often found themselves in the company of Frida's pets, Fulang Chang, a beloved monkey, or Bonito the parrot, who used to perform tricks at the table in return for butter!

Everywhere in the house you can feel the spirit of Frida and Diego. Upstairs Frida's palette and brushes are still on the worktable in her studio, as if she had just put them down. In Diego's bedroom you can see his stetson hat and a huge pair of shoes – he had enormous feet. In another bedroom there is a cupboard with a glass door that contains one of the colorful Mexican dresses that Frida loved to wear.

Above the cupboard, in Spanish, are painted these words: "Frida Kahlo was born here on July 7, 1910." In fact, she was born three years earlier (July 6, 1907), but she changed her birth date to the year of the Mexican Revolution. On the walls of the patio is another inscription "Frida and Diego lived in this house from 1929–1954." Again, this is not entirely true. She and her husband lived in separate houses for five years during that period, and they divorced in 1939, though they remarried a year later. The house, like Frida's life, is full of contradictions.

4
C

G *usually* and *used to*
V friendship
P /s/ or /z/?

Still friends?

1 VOCABULARY & SPEAKING friendship

a Complete the text with the phrases below.

argue   close friend   coworker   get along very well
have a lot in common   keep in touch   known
lost touch   met

I have a _close friend_ named Irene. I've ¹_____
her for about 15 years now. We ²_____ at work.
She was a ³_____ of mine at the company
where I used to work, and we used to have our coffee
breaks at the same time.

We ⁴_____, although we don't ⁵_____.
We have pretty different interests. We don't work
together anymore, and when I changed jobs, we
⁶_____ for a couple of years. But now we
⁷_____ regularly. We call each other once
a week, and we see each other about twice a month.
We don't ⁸_____ very often, only sometimes
about movies, as we have completely different tastes!

b Think of a close friend of yours. In pairs, ask and
answer the questions.

How long have you known him / her?

  Where did you meet?

   Why do you get along well?

   What do you have in common?

Do you ever argue? What about?

  How often do you see each other?

   How do you keep in touch the rest of the time?

   Have you ever lost touch? Why? When?

Do you think you'll stay friends?

2 GRAMMAR usually and used to

a Have you ever tried to get in touch with an old friend?
Why? Did you succeed?

b Read about the *Friends Reunited* website and answer
the questions.

  1 What's it for?
  2 How do you use it?

Friends Reunited is a website that helps you find
old friends and lets you read what people you've lost touch
with are doing now.

How does it work?

New visitors find their old schools or workplaces, which
are usually listed on the web page, and then add their
names to the list of people already registered. They can
also post photos and information about what they are
doing now. When they want to contact another member,
Friends Reunited forwards the message. Communication
takes place without revealing personal e-mail addresses or
contact details until members decide they want to do so.

c Now read about two people who registered on the
website. Who did they want to meet? Why?

d Complete the texts with the sentences below.

  he used to go to   I used to know   I used to live
  used to come   we used to go out

e Look at the two texts again. When do we use *used to*?
How do you make negatives and questions?

f ⟳ p.136 Grammar Bank 4C. Read the rules and
do the exercises.

Friends Reunited?

Carol, 52, from Miami

When I was 15, I fell in love with a boy called Robert. I was at school and he was in his first year of college.
[1]_____ in secret because my parents didn't like him at all. Robert was a long-haired hippy who played the guitar. But after a year, I broke up with him because my parents were making my life impossible. Robert was very angry, and we completely lost touch. But I always wondered what had happened to him, and when I heard about *Friends Reunited* I decided to try to get in touch again. I'm divorced now, and I thought "you never know…".
I remembered the name of the school that [2]_____ and I went to their web page on *Friends Reunited* and there was his name! I sent him an e-mail and two days later I got a reply…

Alex, 24, from Chicago

[3]_____ in Chicago but when I was eighteen, my family moved to Los Angeles. Two years ago I had a really bad motorcycle accident. I was in a coma for two weeks and in the hospital for six months. I completely lost my memory, not just of the crash itself but also of my past. While I was in the hospital, my family [4]_____ every day and play my favorite music and show me photos. Little by little, I began to remember who I was and who my family was. But I still couldn't remember anything about the rest of my life. Then my sister had the idea of contacting *Friends Reunited*. Through them she contacted people [5]_____ in Chicago when I was at school. She arranged a reunion at a restaurant and I traveled to Chicago in search of my past.

3 LISTENING

a **4.11** Read the text about Carol again. Now listen to her talking about what happened next. Was the meeting a success?

b Listen again and answer questions 1–5.
  1 Why was Carol surprised at Robert's choice of job?
  2 What happened when she got to the restaurant?
  3 What do Carol and Robert look like now?
  4 What did Carol realize as soon as she saw Robert?
  5 How had Robert changed?

c **4.12** Read the text about Alex again. Now listen to him talking about what happened next. Was the meeting a success?

d Listen again and answer questions 6–10.
  6 Did he recognize any of the people?
  7 How did he feel?
  8 What did they talk to him about?
  9 What did he remember when he saw the photos?
  10 Who is Anna? What does he think of her now?

4 PRONUNCIATION & SPEAKING /s/ or /z/?

a **4.13** Listen to the sentences. Is the se in the verbs pronounced /s/ or /z/? Write s or z in the box. Which pronunciation is more common?
  1 I used to live in New York. ☐
  2 I used my credit card to pay. ☐
  3 Excuse me. Can you help me? ☐
  4 We won't win; we'll lose. ☐
  5 They advertise on TV. ☐
  6 They promised to keep in touch. ☐
  7 Could you close the window? ☐

b Now practice saying the sentences.

c In pairs, tell each other about three of the following. Give as much information as you can.

A machine you used to use a lot but don't anymore

A friend you used to have but that you've lost touch with

A teacher at school you used to hate

A sport you used to play but don't anymore

A singer you used to listen to a lot and that you still like

A food or drink you didn't use to like but like now

An actor you used to like a lot but don't anymore

5 READING

a How often do you see your really good friends? Would you like to see them more often? Do you spend much time with people you don't really like?

b Now read the magazine article. What does "edit your friends" mean?

Do you need to "edit your friends ?"

Is your cell phone directory full of phone numbers of people you don't really want to talk to? Do you go out with people from work or school more often than with your <u>real</u> friends? Do you say *yes* to invitations because you think you should, not because you want to? If you answered *yes* to at least two of these questions, then maybe it's time to "edit your friends?"

Nowadays people tend to spend a lot of time socializing with coworkers or classmates. The result is that we don't have enough time to see our real, close friends. As our lives get busier, it becomes more important to spend the little free time we have with people we really want to see, people we love and who really love us.

Who are the friends you need to edit? A few years ago, I read a book about how to get rid of unnecessary possessions.

It said you should ask yourself about each thing you have: Is it useful? Do I really like it? Do I feel better every time I look at it? If the answer is *no* to any one of those questions, you should throw it away. Maybe we should ask similar questions about our friends.

What kind of friends will you probably need to edit? Sometimes it's an old friend — somebody that you used to have a lot in common with, but who, when you meet now, you have very little or nothing to say to. Or it might be a new friend that you get along pretty well with, but who is taking up too much of your time. Next time one of these people calls you and suggests a meeting, think, "Do I <u>really</u> want to see this person?" and if the answer is *no*, say *no*, and make an excuse. That way you'll have more time to spend with your real friends.

Adapted from a magazine

c Now read the article again. Choose the best summary of each paragraph, a, b, or c.

1 People need to "edit" their friends if…
  a they have moved to a different area.
  b all their friends are people from work or school.
  c they are spending a lot of time with people who are not real friends.

2 People today are often very busy, so…
  a they should see their friends less.
  b they should think carefully about how they spend their free time.
  c they should try to make friends with people from work / school.

3 The writer says that…
  a we should ask ourselves who our real friends are.
  b most of our friends are unnecessary.
  c we shouldn't treat friends as possessions.

4 The kind of friends we probably need to "edit" are…
  a old friends who don't talk very much.
  b new friends who talk too much.
  c friends that we don't really want to see anymore.

d Read the article again. <u>Underline</u> five new words or phrases you want to learn.

e Do you agree with the article? Do you need to "edit your friends?"

HOW WORDS WORK...

1 Look at these expressions with *get* that have appeared in this lesson.
Match them with their meanings A–G.

1 ...a book about how to get rid of unnecessary objects ☐   A make contact with somebody

2 ...a new friend that you get along pretty well with ☐   B have a good relationship with

3 ...I sort of relaxed and felt I was getting to know them again ☐   C become

4 ...I got to the restaurant late ☐   D know somebody (or something) little by little

5 ...I decided to try to get in touch ☐   E receive

6 ...and two days later I got a reply ☐   F throw away

7 ...I got really excited ☐   G arrive at / in

2 Complete the questions with *get* or an expression with *get*.
Ask and answer the questions in pairs.

1 Who do you _____ best in your family?

2 Does it take you long to _____ new people?

3 Do you _____ more e-mails from friends than from coworkers?

4 How do you normally _____ with your friends (by text, phone, etc.)?

5 How often do you _____ things (e.g., clothes) that you don't use anymore?

6 LISTENING & SPEAKING

a **4.14** Read sentences A–F below. Now listen to three people talking.
Which sentences are they talking about? Write 1, 2, or 3 next to the sentence.

A Men keep their friends longer than women.

B It's more difficult to keep in touch with friends now than it used to be.

C It's impossible to stay "good friends" with an ex-boyfriend or girlfriend.

D You should never criticize your friend's boyfriend or girlfriend.

E You should never lend money to a friend.

F You can only have two or three close friends.

b Listen again. Do they agree or disagree with the statements?
What are their reasons? What examples do they give?

c Now look at the sentences and mark them with a (✔) or (✘)
to say if you agree or disagree. Think about your reasons.

d In groups, compare opinions. Try to give real examples
from your own experience or of people you know.
Use the phrases below to help you.

Useful language

Agreeing

I agree with that.   I think that's true.

Disagreeing

I don't agree with that (at all).   I don't think that's true.

Giving examples

For example, I have a friend who...

"Sorry, Frank, but I can no longer go on with
this charade. Not only am I not your best friend,
I'm not even sure I like you at all."

MAKING SUGGESTIONS

a (4.15) Cover the conversation and listen. What's the problem? Where do Mark and Allie decide to take Scarlett?

b Read the conversation. In pairs, what do you think the missing words are? **Don't write them in yet.**

Allie	I got a message this morning. It's from Jacques. (*Allie plays the message.*)
Allie	You've met Scarlett Scarpino, haven't you, Ben?
Ben	The punk princess? Yeah, I met her in London last year.
Allie	What's she like?
Ben	Let's say she's a bit ... difficult.
Allie	What are we going to _do_ with her?
Mark	Why _don't_ you show her around Paris?
Allie	I have a _better_ idea. Why don't *you* show her around Paris?
Mark	What, me? I'm new here!
Allie	You can't leave me to do this on my own.
Mark	OK, why _don't_ we take her to Notre Dame? I mean, it's her first time in Paris, isn't it?
Ben	I don't think churches are really her thing.
Mark	How _about_ taking her on a boat trip?
Allie	Brilliant!
Mark	And then we could go up the Eiffel Tower.
Allie	_that's_ a good idea. I'm sure she'll love the view.
Ben	And she might fall off!
Mark	Thanks for your help, Ben. Shall we have lunch after that?
Allie	_Let's_ go somewhere really nice. Do you have any recommendations, Ben?
Ben	_What_ about La Renaissance? It's Jacques's favorite.
Allie	That sounds perfect. Uh, Ben, do you want to come, too?
Ben	Sorry, Allie. I'm really busy. But I'm sure you'll have an unforgettable meal.

c Listen again and complete the conversation.

d (4.16) Listen and repeat the highlighted phrases.

e Look at the highlighted phrases again. Then cover the conversation. Try to remember the missing words for making suggestions.

Making suggestions

Why _don't_ _we_ take her to Notre Dame?
what _about_ taking her on a boat trip?
Let's go somewhere really nice.
what _about_ La Renaissance?

f Imagine you are going to go out with the other students next Saturday. In small groups, ask and answer the questions.

1 What time and where should we meet?
2 Where should we have dinner?
3 What should we do after dinner?

SOCIAL ENGLISH   An unforgettable meal

a (4.17) Listen. What does Scarlett have for lunch?

b Listen again and mark the sentences T (true) or F (false).

1 Scarlett isn't hungry. F
2 She doesn't eat meat or fish. T
3 She's allergic to seafood. F
4 She didn't enjoy the boat trip. T
5 They went up the Eiffel Tower. F
6 Allie doesn't like Scarlett. F
7 Mark guesses what Scarlett would like to eat. T

c (4.18) Complete the USEFUL PHRASES. Listen and check.

d Listen again and repeat the phrases. How do you say them in your language?

USEFUL PHRASES

What w_ould_ you like?
Aren't you h_ungry_?
(The seafood) l_ooks_ good.
I'm a_llergic_ to (mushrooms, strawberries, nuts, etc.)
No, h_olden_ on. I have an idea.
Do you think you could p_ossible_ do me a favor?

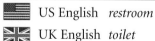
US English *restroom*
UK English *toilet*

Would you like to stay in this beautiful house in the heart of the Canadian Rocky Mountains?

It's a spacious house with four bedrooms, a living room, a large kitchen, two bathrooms, and plenty of storage. There are breathtaking views of the mountains from all the windows. It has a large balcony, which is ideal for eating outside in the summer. The house has wooden floors, a jacuzzi™, cable television, and Internet.

It's a quiet, safe neighborhood and the neighbors are very warm and friendly. The house is within walking distance from stores and restaurants in the local town and a short drive from areas with excellent skiing and hiking. In the area around the house; you can see amazing wildlife such as bears, wolves, deer, and mountain goats.

This house is perfect for families or two couples. It's a non-smoking property and, sorry, no pets.

Four-bedroom house, Alberta, Canada

Rent this *nice* superb two-bedroom apartment. It's perfectly located between 43rd Street and 8th Avenue, five minutes from Time Square and most of the theaters, and a fifteen-minute walk from Central Park.

It's a *nice* 150-square-meter apartment on the19th floor of a new building. It has two bedrooms, a *nice* living room with a huge balcony, a kitchen/dining room, and two bathrooms. The apartment has very big windows, so during the day it's very light and at night you have a *nice* view of midtown Manhattan, especially on the 4th of July, when you can see all the fireworks!

The neighborhood is colorful, and it's *nice* for people who like eating out or going to the theater and clubs. There's a subway station on the corner, and it's a ten-minute walk to Grand Central station. JFK airport is about half an hour away by taxi.

This apartment is *nice* for couples. Sorry, no children or pets and definitely no smoking.

Two-bedroom apartment, Manhattan, New York City

a Read the two ads from a website. Which one would you prefer to rent for a two-week vacation? Why?

b Read about the house in Canada again. Highlight any adjectives which help to "sell" the house.

c Now read about the New York apartment again. Improve the description by replacing the word *nice* with one of the adjectives below. Often there is more than one possibility.

breathtaking   ideal   magnificent   perfect   spacious   ~~superb~~

Useful language: describing location

It's | perfectly located…
| within walking distance from…
| a (fifteen-minute) walk from…
| a short drive from…

The neighborhood is (safe, friendly, etc.)
It's a (beautiful) area…

WRITE a description of a house / an apartment (real or imaginary) for a website.

PLAN what you're going to write. Use the **Useful language** box and **Vocabulary Bank p.151** *Houses* to help you.

Paragraph 1   A brief introduction. What kind of house / apartment is it? Where is it exactly?

Paragraph 2   Describe the house / apartment. What rooms does it have? Does it have any special characteristics?

Paragraph 3   Describe the neighborhood. How far is it from places of interest, public transportation, etc.?

Paragraph 4   Say who the house / apartment is suitable for. Are there any restrictions?

CHECK the description for mistakes (grammar , punctuation , and spelling).

GRAMMAR

a Complete the sentences with the right form of the verb in parentheses.

1 If I don't pass the exam, I _____ it again in January. (take)
2 You'd sleep better if you _____ less coffee. (drink)
3 Don't buy it unless you _____ sure you like it. (be)
4 If I could ban a piece of clothing, I _____ big hats. (ban)
5 As soon as he _____, we can have dinner. (arrive)

b Choose a, b, or c.

1 Where _____ if you took the job in Boston?
   a will you live   b did you live
   c would you live
2 I used _____ with that man over there.
   a going out   b to go out   c go out
3 I _____ enjoy flying, but now I love it.
   a not used to   b didn't used to
   c didn't use to
4 In the summer I _____ to the country.
   a usually go   b use to go
   c usually to go
5 _____ to wear glasses?
   a She used   b Does she use
   c Did she use

10

VOCABULARY

a Word groups. <u>Underline</u> the word that is different. Say why.

1 cottage   village   apartment   house
2 sink   dishwasher   refrigerator   shower
3 elementary   uniform   private   public
4 cheat   pass   exam   fail
5 classmate   friendship   coworker   close friend

b Complete the sentences.

1 Math, physics, and geography are **s**_____.
2 A school year is often divided into two **s**_____.
3 A school where you have to pay is a **p**_____ school.
4 A senior university teacher is a **p**_____.
5 The area outside the central part of a city is called the **s**_____.
6 Smoke goes up and out the **c**_____.
7 The part that covers the top of a house is the **r**_____.
8 The "door" of a yard is the **g**_____.

c Fill each blank with one word.

1 They often argue _____ politics.
2 Do you keep _____ touch _____ old school friends?
3 They live _____ the suburbs.
4 Do you get _____ well with the people in the office?
5 My son is _____ the university.
6 We don't have very much _____ common.

20

PRONUNCIATION

a Underline the word with a different sound.

1	⬆	touch	study	student	subject
2	/yu/	punish	music	argue	university
3	☎	close	cosy	country	stone
4	🐱	ban	cottage	balcony	math
5	⏰	common	copy	modern	homework

b <u>Underline the stressed syllable.</u>

uniform   exam   secondary   residential   coworker

10

We don't need no education...
or do we?

The children who sang on *Another Brick in the Wall* by the British group Pink Floyd have changed their tune since 1979. Twenty-five years later, they are trying to take the group to court because of unpaid royalties.

The song, which was a number 1 hit in the UK and abroad, was an attack on school and education and it had the famous chorus, "We don't need no education, we don't need no thought control... teacher, leave those kids alone!" The chorus was sung by thirteen schoolchildren from Islington Green School in London, who were taken to the Britannia Row record studios to sing on the recording by their music teacher. They never met the group and were not paid for their work. When the principal of the school heard the song with its anti-school lyrics, she banned the children from receiving any publicity or from appearing on TV.

Peter Rowan, a royalty expert from Edinburgh, has spent two years trying to find the children, now adults, and he intends to help them make a legal claim for royalties. Mr. Rowan said, "They probably won't get more than a few hundred pounds each, but this is about recognition. They deserve to have their work recognized even if it has taken 25 years."

Ian Abbott, 40, was one of the children who sang on the record. He said, "Now I don't agree that 'We don't need no education.' Education is so important. I really regret that I didn't study more at school. I would like to go to university now and get a degree. But work gets in the way when you get older. Sometimes I say to my nieces, 'You must study harder,' and they say, 'But why? Look at what you sang on that song.'"

Mirabai Narayan, another one of the children, now works as a teacher herself. She said, "I sometimes wonder if the song influenced my career. My job now is to help kids with learning difficulties."

CAN YOU UNDERSTAND THIS TEXT?

a Read the article and mark the sentences T (true), F (false), or DS (doesn't say).

1 *Another Brick in the Wall* was also successful outside the UK.
2 The children got a little money for singing on the record.
3 The music teacher was a friend of the group Pink Floyd.
4 The principal of the school wasn't happy about the song.
5 Peter Rowan was one of the thirteen children.
6 He thinks the children will get a lot of money.
7 Ian Abbott is sorry that he didn't work harder at school.
8 He doesn't have any children of his own.
9 Mirabai Narayan is sure the song made her become a teacher.

b Look at the highlighted words and phrases. Can you guess what they mean?

CAN YOU UNDERSTAND THESE PEOPLE?

a 🔊 **4.19** Listen and circle the correct answer, a, b, or c.

1 What problem does the teacher want to discuss?
  a A girl copied from John.   b John cheated on an exam.
  c John is lazy.
2 The woman in the restaurant is...
  a slim with blond hair.   b tall and dark.
  c short and heavy.
3 Which house are they going to buy?
  a The house with a yard.   b The townhouse.
  c They haven't decided.
4 When did Dennis graduate?
  a 1977   b 1981   c 1988
5 When are they going to have lunch?
  a Thursday 2:00   b Thursday 12:30   c Tuesday 1:00

b 🔊 **4.20** Listen to two men talking about an apartment share. Complete the missing information.

Apartment share

1 _____ Elm Street.
Rent: $2 _____ a month + 3 _____ bills
Room available 4 _____
5 _____ permit costs $60 a year

CAN YOU SAY THIS IN ENGLISH?

Can you...? Yes (✓)

☐ talk about a school you used to go to (or go to now)
☐ describe your ideal house
☐ talk about a close friend (where and when you met, how often you meet, etc.)

5 A

G quantifiers
V noun formation
P -ough and -augh

Slow down, you move too fast

1 GRAMMAR quantifiers

a Answer the questions and compare with a partner.

How much time (approximately) do you spend on a **weekday**...?

- sleeping
- having meals (breakfast, lunch, etc.)
- working (or studying)
- cooking
- doing housework or shopping
- relaxing, exercising, or seeing friends

b Read the article *Are you happy with your work–life balance?* Which situation is most typical in your country?

c Read the article again and <u>underline</u> the correct phrases.

d ⬤ **p.138 Grammar Bank 5A.** Read the rules and do the exercises.

e Talk in small groups about the things below. Are you happy with your work–life balance?

How much time do you have...?
for yourself
to exercise
to see friends
to be with your family

How much...do you have?
work
school / college work
English homework
energy

Dan, project manager, software company, Boston, US

1 I'm not happy with my work–life balance at all. I work at least 50 or 60 hours a week, so I don't have ¹*any time* / *no time* at all for myself or my children. I communicate with my wife by leaving messages on the fridge. We hardly ever see each other because we work different hours and I never have time to see my friends or keep in shape. Also, I eat very badly because my lunch "hour" (about 10 minutes!) isn't ²*enough long* / *long enough* for me to have a proper meal. OK, I earn ³*a lot of* / *a lot* money but I don't have ⁴*enough time* / *time enough*. Is it worth it?

2 I didn't use to have ⁵*much time / many time* for anything because I was working ⁶*too much / too many* hours – 45 or more a week. But then I decided to stop working overtime and to use my time at work more efficiently. Nowadays I have ⁷*plenty of / plenty* time for myself. I play tennis two evenings a week, and I don't take work home on weekends. I am much happier. I think when you have time to enjoy your personal life, you work much better.

3 Yes, I am happy with it because I've chosen a lifestyle that I like and that gives me ⁸*a lot of / a lot* free time. But my father, on the other hand, works more than 70 hours a week for a car company, which I think is crazy. ⁹*Lots of / Much* Japanese people do the same. There's an expression in Japanese, *karoshi*, which means "dying because you work ¹⁰*too hard / too much hard*." A lot of people in Japan get sick or die because they work ¹¹*too / too much*. I think my generation is different. We don't want our lives to be ruled by work. I work ¹²*a few / a little* hours a day in a store – that gives me enough money to live. I spend the rest of my time seeing my friends and playing baseball.

2 PRONUNCIATION   *-ough* and *-augh*

> ⚠ Be careful with the letters *ough* and *augh*. They can be pronounced in different ways.

a Write the words in the list in the correct column.

although	bought	brought	caught	daughter
enough	laugh	thought	through	tough

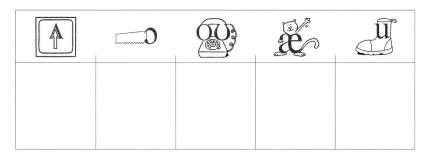

b 🔊 **5.1** Listen and check. Which is the most common sound? Which three words end with the sound /f/?

c 🔊 **5.2** Practice saying the sentences. Then listen and check.

1 I bought some steak, but it was very tough.
2 Although it was dark, we walked through the tunnel.
3 I thought I'd brought enough money with me.
4 I laughed when my daughter caught the ball.

3 LISTENING

a 🔊 **5.3** You are going to hear an expert telling us five ways in which we can slow down in our daily lives. Listen once and complete **Tips** 1–5 with two words.

Tips	Why?
1 Eat breakfast _____ _____.	
2 Forget the _____. Do _____ instead.	
3 Go for a _____ _____.	
4 Spend 10 minutes each day _____ _____.	
5 Take a _____, not a _____.	

b Listen again and write down any other information you can in the **Why?** column. Compare with a partner.

c Which do you think are the best two tips? Do you already do any of them?

4 READING & VOCABULARY

a Read the leaflet and match the verbs with their meanings.

We promise to...	
increase	teachers' salaries
reduce	unemployment
promote	national products abroad
encourage	people to get more exercise
protect	wildlife
ban	smoking in streets and parks

1 _____ influence somebody in a positive way, e.g., *I ... my children to play sports.*

2 _____ to make something bigger, e.g., *The boss is going to ... my salary.*

3 _____ to say something is not allowed, often by law, e.g., *We want to ... smoking everywhere.*

4 _____ to help something to happen or develop, e.g., *The meeting helped to ... better relations.*

5 _____ to make something smaller, e.g., *... the noise, the number of cars.*

6 _____ to defend somebody or something, or keep them safe, e.g., *We need to ... these birds as they are becoming extinct.*

b Read the introduction to the article. What is the "counterrevolution?"

c Work in pairs, **A** and **B**.

A read **Do you eat "slow food"?** and find the answers to these questions.
1 Who started the Slow Food movement? Why?
2 What did he think was wrong with today's world?
3 What are the aims of the Slow Food movement?
4 How big is the Slow Food movement now?

B read **Would you like to live in a "slow city"?** and find the answers to these questions.
1 How did the Slow City movement start?
2 What are the aims of the Slow City movement?
3 Where has it spread to?
4 What do the people of Aylsham in the UK think about living in a Slow City?

d Cover the article. **A** tell **B** about the Slow Food movement. **B** tell **A** about the Slow City movement.

e Do you think these movements are a good idea?

Slow down, you move too fast

The clock rules our lives. The more we try to save time, the less time we seem to have. In every area of our lives, we are doing things faster. And many of us live in towns and cities that are getting noisier and more stressful as each day passes.

But now a worldwide movement, whose aim is to slow life down, has started a counterrevolution. Its supporters are people who believe that a happier and healthier way of life is possible...

Slow Food®

Do you eat "slow food"?

The Slow Food movement was founded the day that an Italian journalist, Carlo Petrini, saw that a fast-food restaurant had opened in Piazza di Spagna, the beautiful square in Rome. He thought it was tragic that many people today live too quickly to sit down for a proper meal and only eat mass-produced fast food. He decided that he had to try to do something about it and so he started the Slow Food movement. Although he didn't succeed in banning the fast-food restaurant from Piazza di Spagna, Slow Food has become a global organization and now has more than 80,000 members in 100 countries.

"Each meal," says William Rubel of Slow Food, California, "should be a special occasion."

Slow Food also encourages people to eat local and regional food, to use local shops and markets, to eat out in small family restaurants, and to cook with traditional recipes. As member Jon Winge says, "I think it's such a cool idea. You support the people who produce beautiful products for you."

Would you like to live in a "slow city"?

The idea of "cittaslow" or "slow cities" was inspired by the Slow Food movement, and it was started by the mayor of the small Italian town of Greve in Chianti. The aim of slow cities is to make our towns places where people enjoy living and working, and where they value and protect the things that make the town different. Towns that want to become a Slow City have to reduce traffic and noise, increase the number of green areas, plant trees, build pedestrian areas, and promote local businesses and traditions.

Many other small towns in Italy have joined the movement, and it has spread to other countries all over the world. Aylsham in the UK recently became a slow city, and most people are delighted.

"Slow cities are about having a community life in the town, so people don't come home from work, shut their doors and that's it," said a local resident. "It is not 'slow' as in 'stupid.' It is 'slow' as in the opposite of 'frantic' and 'stressful.' It is about quality of life."

But not everybody in Aylsham is happy. For teenagers, who have to go 25 kilometers to Norwich, the nearest city, to buy tennis shoes or CDs, living in a slow city is not very attractive. "It's all right here," says Lewis Cook, 16. "But if you want excitement, you have to go to Norwich. We need more things here for young people."

5 VOCABULARY   noun formation

> ⚠ Nouns are often formed:
> from verbs, by adding -*ment*, -*ion*, -*ation*, and -*al*
> from adjectives by adding -*ness* or -*ity*

a Form nouns from the verbs and adjectives below and write them in the chart.

crazy	discuss	govern	happy	move	organize
possible	propose	react	relax	similar	survive

-ment	-ation	-ion

-al	-ness	-ity

b 🔊 **5.4** Listen and check. Underline the stressed syllable in each word. Which ending has a stressed syllable?

6 SPEAKING

a Imagine that your town is thinking of becoming a "slow city" and is planning to do the following things:
- Ban all fast-food restaurants.
- Promote small family restaurants.
- Ban cars from downtown.
- Create more pedestrian areas.
- Create more green areas and plant more trees.
- Reduce the speed limit in the town to 30 km/h.
- Use speed bumps and traffic radars to control speed.
- Move all big supermarkets outside the city.
- Encourage local shops and ban multinational chain stores.
- Ban loud music in bars and clubs.

Mark the sentences with a (✔) or (✘) to say if you agree or disagree.

b Work in groups. Have a "meeting" to discuss each proposal and then vote for or against it.

Useful language

> I'm for / against (banning...)

> I think / I don't think it would be a good idea (to create...)

> The problem with (reducing...) is that...

> I don't think that would work.

> That would really make a difference.

c Compare with other groups. Which proposals are the most popular?

5 B

G articles: *a / an*, *the*, no article
V verbs and adjectives + prepositions
P sentence stress, *the*, /θ/ or /ð/?

Same planet, different worlds

1 GRAMMAR articles: *a / an*, *the*, no article

a Read the text and complete it with *a / an*, *the*, or – (no article).
Do you agree with the text?

Five things you don't usually hear a woman say to a man

1 "No thanks. I don't like _____ chocolate."
2 "I know it's our anniversary _____ next Saturday, but let's not go out. Let's stay in and watch _____ the baseball game on TV."
3 "I want to buy _____ new car – I really like _____ new BMW. It has fuel injection and does 180 kilometers _____ hour."
4 "I'm glad you like _____ junk food. I love _____ men with _____ fat stomachs. I find them very attractive."
5 "Don't worry, I wasn't expecting _____ present. I don't like _____ presents anyway."

b ⟳ p.138 Grammar Bank 5B. Read the rules and do the exercises.

c Read the text and complete it with *a / an*, *the*, or – (no article).
Do you agree with the text?

Five things you don't usually hear a man say to a woman

1 "I see Brad Pitt has _____ new movie out. Would you like to go to _____ movies tonight and see it?"
2 "I'm completely lost, so I'll stop and ask _____ woman over there for directions."
3 "I thought _____ sheets needed changing, so I put them in _____ washing machine."
4 "I think _____ red dress looks nice, but take your time. There are lots of other stores we can try."
5 "I really admire the way you can go to _____ work, run _____ house, and raise _____ children so well!"

2 PRONUNCIATION sentence stress, *the*, /θ/ or /ð/?

a (5.5) **Dictation.** Listen and write six sentences. Practice saying them with the correct rhythm. Are articles normally stressed?

b (5.6) Listen and repeat the phrases. When is *the* pronounced /ðə/? How is it pronounced in the other phrases?

the store	the address	the owner	the sun	the engineer	the world

> ⚠ Remember *th* can be 🐻 e.g., *the*, or ✊ e.g. *think*.

c (5.7) Listen and circle *th* when it is pronounced /ð/. Then repeat the sentences.

1 That man over there is very wealthy.
2 June is the sixth month of the year.
3 There are three things you have to remember.
4 I threw it away the other day.
5 We have math in the third year.
6 The athletes run through that gate.

3 READING & SPEAKING

a In pairs, look at the list of subjects below. Who do you think talks about them more, men or women? Write **M** or **W**.

sports ___ work ___ clothes ___ health ___
family ___ movies ___ politics ___ cars ___
their house ___ the opposite sex ___

b Read the first paragraph of *Gossiping with the girls?* Does the writer agree with you? Who talks about most topics?

Gossiping with the girls?

Women are experts at gossiping, and they always talk about trivial things, or at least that's what men have always thought. However, some new research suggests that when women talk to women, their conversations are far from frivolous, and cover many more topics (up to 40 subjects) than when men talk to other men. Women's conversations range from health to their houses, from politics to fashion, from movies to family, from education to relationship problems. Sports are notably absent. Men tend to have a more limited range of subjects, the most popular being work, sports, jokes, cars, and women.

According to Professor Petra Boynton, a psychologist who interviewed over 1,000 women, women also tend to move quickly from one subject to another in conversation, while men usually stick to one subject for longer periods of time.

At work, this difference can be an advantage for men, as they can put other matters aside and concentrate fully on the topic being discussed. On the other hand, it also means that they sometimes find it hard to concentrate when several things have to be discussed at the same time in a meeting.

Professor Boynton also says that men and women talk for different reasons. In social situations women use conversation to solve problems and reduce stress while men talk with each other to laugh or to compare opinions.

Adapted from a newspaper

c Now read the whole article. What does the writer say? Choose a, b, or c.

1 When women talk to each other they generally talk about _____.
   a unimportant things
   b very serious things
   c many different things
2 Men _____ as women.
   a don't talk as much
   b don't talk about as many things
   c don't work as much
3 In conversation women _____ than men.
   a talk more quickly
   b change the subject more often
   c talk more about work
4 At work, if there is a meeting that focuses on one subject, _____.
   a men will probably concentrate better than women
   b women will probably concentrate better than men
   c men and women will both concentrate well
5 One of the reasons why women talk to each other is _____.
   a to relax
   b to exchange ideas
   c to tell jokes

d Now prove that the article is wrong! Work in pairs or small groups.

If you're a woman, try to talk for two minutes about:
sports   cars   computers

If you're a man, try to talk for two minutes about:
fashion   shopping   losing weight / dieting

HOW WORDS WORK...

1 Look at the highlighted words and phrases in *Gossiping with the girls?* Which one(s) do we use…?
   1 to compare and contrast two facts or opinions *while*
   2 to introduce an opposite point of view _____ _____
   3 to introduce some extra information _____
   4 to explain who says or believes something _____

2 Complete the sentences with one of the words or phrases. Sometimes there are two possibilities.
   1 My sister plays tennis and she _____ goes swimming once a week.
   2 Traveling by yourself can be fun. _____, it is often more dangerous.
   3 _____ doctors, we shouldn't drink too much coffee.
   4 Dogs are very affectionate, _____ cats are more independent.
   5 New technology makes our lives easier. _____, it can be difficult to learn to use.

4 LISTENING

a Have you ever been to a spa? If yes, did you enjoy it? If no, would you like to go? Why (not)?

b Read the introduction to the article. Why did the journalists go to the spa?
Which treatment do you think a) Joanna and b) Stephen will like best?

Spas – women love them. Can men enjoy them, too?

Two reporters, Joanna Duckworth and Stephen Bleach, decided to find out. They spent a day together at a health spa that offers thermal baths, saunas and steam rooms, an outdoor swimming pool, and a wide variety of massages and treatments.

These are some of the treatments they had:

Banana, papaya and strawberry body polish
– a treatment that will smooth and hydrate your skin, with a head massage – 40 minutes.

Kanebo Kai Zen facial
– a deep intensive cleansing, with face and neck massage – 1 hour 40 minutes.

Elemis foot treatment
– a foot bath, pedicure and foot massage – 55 minutes.

c Listen to the two journalists talking after the first treatment and write the information in the chart.
Listen again to check. Repeat for the second and third treatments.

	Stephen		Joanna	
	points out of 10	reasons	points out of 10	reasons
1 The body polish 5.8	0	uncomfortable hot st	10 o 10	wanderfull relaxing smal so good.
2 The facial 5.9	0 4	horrible, hot fuel streaky	9 to 10	
3 The foot treatment 5.10	9 at 10		9 to 10	

d 5.11 Listen to five extracts from the recording. Try to write down the missing word.
How do you think you spell it? What do you think it means?

1 It was hot and _steaty_ and extremely uncomfortable.
2 The head massage was _fantastic_!
3 My face feels different – much _smother_.
4 I just use _soop_ and water.
5 I love the color they painted my _neals_!

e Which of the treatments would *you* choose to have?

5 SPEAKING

Look at *A man thing or a woman thing?* Talk in small groups. In your country who does these things more, men or women? Why do you think this is?

Useful language

Generally speaking / In general, I think women go to spas more than men…

I think it's more common for men to watch sports…

I think women tend to read novels more than men…

⚠ Remember not to use an article when you generalize, e.g., I think men… NOT ~~the men~~

A man thing or a woman thing?

- Going shopping
- Going to spas
- Going to the gym
- Going to the movies
- Reading novels
- Going to sports events
- Doing housework
- Learning languages
- Going to restaurants
- Playing games (e.g., cards, chess)

6 VOCABULARY verbs and adjectives + prepositions

Men think that women always **talk about** trivial things.
In fact, they cover more topics than when men **talk to** men.

a Complete the **prepositions** column.

Verbs	Prepositions
1 Do you often **talk** _to_ a friend _about_ your problems?	to about
2 Do you often **think** ___ the future?	about
3 Do you often have to **wait** ___ a bus or train?	for
4 Do you **agree** _with_ your friends about politics?	
5 What dish or dishes do you usually **ask** ___ in a restaurant?	
6 Have you ever **borrowed** money ___ your family?	from
7 Do you often **write** e-mails ___ English-speaking people?	to
8 How often do you **listen** ___ classical music?	to
9 Do you think a man should **pay** ___ dinner on a first date?	for
10 Do you know anyone who **works** ___ a multinational company?	for at
11 Do you know anyone who **works** ___ a DJ?	as
12 Are you going to **apply** ___ a job soon?	for

Adjectives	Prepositions
13 Are you **good** ___ sports?	at
14 Are you **bad** ___ remembering birthdays?	at
15 Are men's hobbies very **different** ___ women's hobbies?	from
16 Are you **afraid** ___ any insects?	of
17 Are you **interested** ___ fashion?	in
18 Are you **worried** ___ anything at the moment?	about

b Cover the prepositions column. Work in pairs. **A** ask **B** the first question. **B** ask **A** the second question. Continue with the rest of the questions.

Then change roles.

7 ♩ 5.12 SONG ♪ *Sk8er Boi*

G gerunds and infinitives
V work
P word stress

5 C

Job swap

1 VOCABULARY work

a Look at the picture story and match a sentence with each picture.

A But he was happy because he had a good **salary** and a company car. ☐ 5
B He **applied for** a job with a food **company**, and sent in his **résumé**. ☐ 2
C He **was fired**. Jake was unemployed again… ☐ 8
D After six months, he **got promoted**. ☐ 6
E Jake was **unemployed** and was looking for **a job**. ☐ ·
F He had to work very hard and **work overtime**. ☐
G But then he had an argument with his **boss**. ☐ 7
H He **had an interview**, and he **got the job**. ☐ 3

b Cover the sentences and look at the pictures. Tell the story from memory.

c ➲ **p.152 Vocabulary Bank** *Work.*

2 PRONUNCIATION & SPEAKING
word stress

a Underline the stressed syllable in each word. Use the phonetics to help you.

1 apply /əˈplaɪ/
2 contract /ˈkɑntrækt/
3 employee /ɛmˈplɔii/
4 experience /ɪkˈspɪriəns/
5 overtime /ˈoʊvərtaɪm/
6 permanent /ˈpərmənənt/
7 qualifications /kwɑləfəˈkeɪʃnz/
8 quit /kwɪt/
9 retire /rɪˈtaɪər/
10 temporary /ˈtɛmpərɛri/

b **5.13** Listen and check. Practice saying the words.

c Talk to a partner.

Do you know anybody who…

• is applying for a job? What kind of job?
• just retired? How old is he / she?
• was promoted recently? What to?
• works a lot of overtime? Why?
• was fired from his / her job? Why?
• is self-employed? What does he / she do?
• is doing a temporary job? What?
• has a part-time job? What hours does he / she work?

3 GRAMMAR gerunds and infinitives

a Complete sentences 1–16 in the questionnaire. Put the verbs in the gerund, e.g., *working*, or the infinitive, e.g., *to work*.

b Read the sentences and check (✔) **only** the ones that you **strongly** agree with. Compare your answers with another student.

c Now see in which group(s) you have most checks. Read the paragraphs on the right to find out which jobs would suit you. Would you like to do any of them?

d Look at the sentences in the questionnaire. Complete the rules with **the gerund** or **infinitive**.

1 After some verbs,
   e.g., *enjoy, don't mind* use… _____
2 After some verbs,
   e.g., *want, would like* use… _____
3 After adjectives, use… _____
4 After prepositions, use… _____
5 As the subject of
   a phrase or sentence, use… _____

e ⊙ **p.138 Grammar Bank 5C.** Read the rules and do the exercises.

The right job for you
– match your personality to the job

1 I am good at *listening* to people.	listen
2 I enjoy Helping people with their problems.	help
3 I don't mind not earning a very large salary.	not earn
4 I'd like working as part of a team.	work

If you have most checks in 1–4, the best job for you would be in the "caring professions." If you are good at science, you could think of a career in medicine, for example, as a doctor or nurse. Also, teaching or social work are areas that would suit your personality.

5 I am good at _____ quick decisions.	make
6 _____ risks doesn't stress me out.	take
7 I don't find it difficult _____ by myself.	work
8 I'm not afraid of _____ large amounts of money.	manage

If you have most checks in 5–8, you should consider a job in the world of business, for example sales or marketing. Other possibilities include accounting or working in the stock market.

9 I am good at _____ myself.	express
10 I always try _____ my instincts.	follow
11 It's important for me improving creative.	be
12 I enjoy doing.	improvise

If you have most checks in 9–12, you need a creative job. Depending on your specific talents, you might enjoy a job in the world of music, art, or literature. Areas that would suit you include publishing, journalism, graphic design, fashion, or the music industry.

13 _____ complex calculations is not difficult for me.	do
14 I enjoy solving logical problems.	solve
15 I find it easy understanding theoretical principles.	understand
16 I am able calculate space and distance.	calculate

If you have most checks in 13–16, you have an analytical mind. A job in computer science or engineering would suit you. You also have good spatial sense, which would make architecture and related jobs another possibility.

f Choose **five** of the topics below and tell your partner about them.

- somewhere you**'d like to go** this weekend
- somebody you find **difficult to talk to**
- something you found **easy to learn**
- something you **prefer doing** by yourself
- something you've **decided to do** soon
- something you **enjoy doing** on Sunday mornings
- something you **regret buying**
- something you often **forget to do**
- something you're **afraid of doing**
- a job **you'd love to be able to do** (but think you couldn't)

4 READING

a Read the title of the article. What kind of personality do you think you need to be a good political reporter?

b Read the text and put these headings in the right place.

The challenge	The contestant
The teachers	The training
~~The program~~	

c In pairs, find the following words in the text:

1 A person who takes part in a competition
   contestant

2 A group of people chosen to discuss or decide something _the challenges_

3 A person who writes about the news in a newspaper or speaks about it on TV
   The program

4 A person who decides how criminals should be punished or who decides the result or winner of a competition
   The training

5 A person who collects, writes or publishes news in the media (newspapers, magazines, TV, or radio)
   _____

6 A person whose job is concerned with politics _Teachers_

d ⬅ **Communication** *Test your memory A p.117 B p.120.*
Who can remember most about the program?

e Do you think Jessica will pass the test? Why (not)? _NO_

From librarian to political reporter... In a month!

How Jessica went from working in a local library to interviewing politicians on TV in just 28 days

1 _The program_

The Pretenders is a very successful and popular TV series. In each program there is a contestant who has just four weeks to learn to do a completely new job. At the end of the month the contestant has to take a "test," where he or she has to do the new job together with three other real professionals. A panel of three judges has to decide which of the four people is pretending to be a professional. Sometimes they can tell who is pretending, but sometimes they can't!

2 _contestant_

Jessica Winters is a 26-year-old librarian. She studied English Literature at a university before getting a job at her local library. She didn't know it, but two of her friends sent her name to the TV company to take part in *The Pretenders*. "When someone from the program called me, I thought it was a joke," said Jessica. "First, I said no, but they asked me to think about it. In the end my friends and family persuaded me to say yes."

3 _challenge_

Jessica had four weeks to turn from a quiet, shy, librarian into a confident TV reporter. At the end of the month, she had to take her final test. This was a live TV interview with the secretary of education. She had to try to make the judges think that she really was a professional reporter.

4 _Teacher_

An experienced political journalist, Adam Bowles, and politician Sally Lynch had the job of transforming Jessica. When they first met her, they were not very optimistic. "Jessica needs to be a lot tougher. She's too sweet and shy," said Adam. "Politicians will eat her alive." They had just 28 days to teach her to be a reporter…

5 _____

Jessica had to spend the month in Washington. She was completely isolated from her family and friends – she could only talk to them on the phone. The training was very hard work. She had to learn how to interview people, how to look more confident, how to speak clearly. She also had to learn about the world of politics. "I'm feeling really nervous," said Jessica. "I'm terrified of being on TV. Also I've never been interested in politics – I don't know anything about it. I didn't even vote in the last election."

5 LISTENING

You're going to hear Jessica and her teacher Adam talking about how she did in her four weeks on *The Pretenders*. Listen to each week and answer the questions in pairs.

Week 1 5.14

1 What did Adam and Sally think of Jessica? *shy*
2 According to Adam, what two problems did Jessica have? *She not*
3 What three things did Jessica have to do this week?
4 How did she feel at the end of the week?

Week 2 5.15

5 How did Jessica change her image?
6 What did she learn to do this week?
7 What did she have to do at the airport?
8 Was she successful? Why (not)?

Week 3 5.16

9 What did Adam think about Jessica?
10 What did she have to do this week?
11 What mistake did she make?
12 What did Adam say that Jessica needed to do?

Week 4 5.17

13 What was Jessica's final test? How did she feel about it?
14 Did the interview go well for Jessica? Why (not)?
15 Did the judges realize that Jessica wasn't a professional reporter?
16 Would Jessica like to become a reporter? Why (not)?

6 SPEAKING

Talk to a partner. Imagine you were asked to appear on the program. Look at the list of jobs that other contestants were trained to do. Which ones would / wouldn't you like to learn to do? Why?

soccer coach	dog trainer	rock singer	mechanic	TV director	stuntman	chef	DJ	car salesman

Useful language

I wouldn't like...

I wouldn't mind...

I think I'd enjoy...

I think I'd be (pretty) good at...

I'd be terrible at...

GIVING OPINIONS

a 🔊 5.18 Cover the conversation. Listen to Allie, Mark, and Jacques discussing promotion for Scarlett's CD. Who has the best idea? What is it?

b Read the conversation. In pairs, what do you think the missing words are? **Don't write them in yet.**

Allie	That was a great concert last night, Scarlett.
Scarlett	Thanks.
Allie	As we know, Scarlett's got a new CD coming out soon. So let's have a look at the best way we can promote it in France.
Mark	OK, well I think Scarlett *shue* visit the major music stores. In my *opwiir*, that's the best way to meet her fans.
Allie	I'm not so *thuk*. What do you *think*, Jacques?
Jacques	Actually, I don't *agree* with Mark. Scarlett isn't commercial in that way.
Allie	Scarlett? Scarlett?
Scarlett	I agree *the* Jacques. I don't have a commercial image. It isn't my style.
Mark	OK, but Scarlett needs more publicity. What about a series of TV and radio interviews? *Are* you agree?
Allie	Yes, but that's what everybody does. What we want is something different.
Jacques	*Persorally*, I think Scarlett should tour clubs and summer festivals. She can DJ, play her favorite music, play the new CD, and meet her fans, too.
Allie	Yes, *Absolut*! That's a much better idea. Mark?
Mark	OK, why not?
Allie	Scarlett?
Scarlett	I think that's a *good* idea. Thank you, Jacques.

c Listen again and complete the conversation.

d 🔊 5.19 Listen and repeat the highlighted phrases. Copy the <u>rhythm</u>.

e Look at the highlighted phrases in the conversation. Put them in the right column in the chart.

Asking people what they think	Saying what *you* think	Agreeing / Disagreeing
What do you think?	*I think…*	*I'm not so sure.*
Dou't you agree	*I'm dou thiks*	*I dou think so*
In my opinco	*I'm not sure*	*Accually*
Personality	*I dou*	*I dou't agre*

f ➡ **Communication** *What do you think? A p.117 B p.120.* In small groups, give your opinion.

SOCIAL ENGLISH   Why is she smiling?

a 🔊 5.20 Listen. Who do they see in the Louvre?

b Listen again and answer the questions.

1 Has Mark been to the Louvre before?
2 Why isn't he very happy?
3 What does Allie say about the meeting?
4 What two theories about the Mona Lisa does Allie mention?
5 What's Mark's theory?
6 Why do they leave in a hurry?

c 🔊 5.21 Complete the USEFUL PHRASES. Listen and check.

d Listen again and repeat the phrases. How do you say them in your language?

USEFUL PHRASES

What's the m*atter*?
It's not a big d*eal*.
You're k*idding*.
Now, I don't know much a*bout* (art)…
That's really un*fair*!
Don't t*urn* around!
Let's g*et* out of here.

a Look at the job advertisement. Which job could <u>you</u> apply for?

b Complete the résumé with headings from the list.

> Work experience   Computer skills
> Education   Languages

c Read the cover letter. Circle the more formal phrase in each pair.

Lucas Méndez

Address	Avenida América 50
	Cartago, Costa Rica
Telephone	Home: 506-555-6389
	Cell: 506-555-6742
E-mail	lmendez@cronline.net
Nationality:	Costa Rican

1 _____

2007–	Assistant physical therapist at a rehabilitation center in Cartago
	I work mainly with patients who need rehabilitation after an operation. In my free time, I also work as a physical therapist for the local soccer team.

2 _____

2002–2006	Degree in physical therapy, University of Costa Rica
1998–2002	Colegio LaSalle (high school)

3 _____

English (TOEFL: 600)
I have a good level of written and spoken English.

I have been studying English at a private language school for the last three years.

German (fluent). My mother is German.

4 _____

Windows Vista /Advanced word processing

The Olympic Committee is looking for dedicated, enthusiastic, and energetic people to work in different areas for the forthcoming Olympic Games. There are vacancies in the following areas:

- Administration
- Hospitality and catering
- Translation and language services
- Medical support

All applicants must be appropriately qualified and a good level of English is essential. Send your résumé and a cover letter (in English) to:
Job applications: The Olympic Committee, PO Box 2456

Avenida América 50
Cartago, Costa Rica
April 30

Olympic Committee
PO Box 2456

Dear Sir / Madam:

[1]*I am writing / I'm writing* to apply for a job with the medical support staff in the forthcoming Olympic Games.

I am a qualified physical therapist and [2]*I've been working / I have been working* at a rehabilitation center here since January 2006. I have a good level of English, and [3]*my German is great / I speak German fluently.*

[4]*I enclose / I'm sending you* my résumé as requested.

[5]*Hope to hear from you soon. / I look forward to hearing from you.*

[6]*Best wishes / Yours truly*

Lucas Méndez
Lucas Méndez

---

d Complete the **Useful language** box with *Sincerely* and *Yours truly*.

Useful language: a formal letter

Formal letters	Greeting	Closing
You don't know the person's name	Dear Sir / Madam	_____
You know the person's last name	Dear Mr. / Ms. / Mrs. García	_____

Layout / style
- Put your address in the top right-hand corner with the date underneath.
- Put the name and address of the person you are writing to on the left.
- Don't use contractions.
- Write your full name under your signature.
- Put *I look forward to hearing from you* if you would like a reply.

WRITE your résumé and a cover letter to apply for a job in the Olympics.

PLAN what you're going to write. Use the **Useful language** box and **Vocabulary Bank p.152** *Work* to help you.

CHECK the letter for mistakes (grammar , punctuation , and spelling).

GRAMMAR

a Choose a, b, or c.

1 I'm not very good at _the_ sports.
   a the   b a   c –

2 He always gets _to_ late on Fridays.
   a to home   b to the home   c home

3 There are _a_ people in this class.
   a too many   b too much   c too

4 _c_ is one of the best forms of exercise.
   a Swim   b Swimming   c Swims

5 I bought a laptop _a_ when I'm traveling.
   a for use   b for to use   c to use

b Complete the second sentence with **two words** so that it means the same as the first.

I really think it's important for you to learn to drive.
You _must_ _learn_ to drive.

1 When they left, they didn't lock the door.
   They left _unlock the_ the door.

2 There aren't very many trees on our street.
   There are only _so many_ trees on our street.

3 It takes him a long time to get up in the morning.
   He spends a long time _a wake_ in the morning.

4 Renting a house is very difficult here.
   It's very difficult _renten out_ a house here.

5 This house is too small for us.
   This house isn't _very big_ for us.

10

VOCABULARY

a Complete with a noun formed from the **bold** word.

1 I think the _govern_ will lose the next election.   **govern**
2 What was his _react_? Was he angry?   **react**
3 My _result_ depends on you.   **happy**
4 They said on the radio that there's a _possible_ of snow tonight.   **possible**
5 You don't need any special _qualify_ to do this job.   **qualify**

b Complete with a preposition.

1 I've applied _____ a job with an airline.
2 Don't worry _for_ anything!
3 I really don't agree _with_ you.
4 Are you good _a_ science?
5 Are you still _in_ the university or have you graduated?
6 She works _____ a flight attendant.

c Complete the missing words.

1 I have to work a lot of **o**_vertime_ in my new job. Sometimes I don't finish until 9 p.m.
2 Could I have a day **o**_ff_ next Friday? It's my cousin's wedding.
3 He argued with his boss and he was **f**_ired_. Now he's unemployed.
4 If you work hard, you may get **p**_____ to manager.
5 She has a good job and gets a very high **s**_alary_.
6 It's a temporary job. I only have a six-month **c**_____.
7 I'm going to **a**_pply_ for a job in a bookstore. I hope I get it!
8 I'm **s**_hort_-**e**_arn_. I work at home as a translator.
9 If he doesn't like his job, he'll **q**_uit_ after the first six months.

20

PRONUNCIATION

a Underline the word with a different sound.

1	↑	enough	company	much	movement
2		afraid	retire	overtime	apply
3		many	temporary	regret	prefer
4		work	short	permanent	earn
5		résumé	boss	salary	works

b Underline the stressed syllable.

employee   unemployed   responsible   temporary   experience

10

CAN YOU UNDERSTAND THIS TEXT?

The secret to a long and happy life is... being lazy!

Joggers who get up early and run through the park, executives who try to work off stress with a game of squash, and people who do bodybuilding may all be shortening their lives. According to Peter Axt, a German researcher and ex-marathon runner, laziness is good for you.

"No top sportsman," says Axt, "has lived to a very advanced age." Among the examples of athletes who have died young, he mentions Jim Fixx, the author of *The Complete Book of Running*, and the man who almost single-handedly launched the American fitness revolution. He died at the age of 52. As Axt says, "Better not to start."

With his daughter Michaela, a doctor, he has written a book called *The Joy of Laziness*. It says that there are three keys to long life: to exercise less, to reduce stress, and to eat less food. He gives the example of an Italian village with an unusually high number of centenarians that seems to owe its communal good health to following the Axt principles. No one runs, siestas stretch though the afternoon from 1p.m. to 4 p.m., and the main activity seems to be sitting in the shade or gossiping.

The Axts' ideas are based on research which argues that animals have only a limited amount of energy. Those who use up energy quickly live for a shorter time than those who conserve energy. So an executive who wants to compensate for a stressful day by going to the gym is in fact multiplying his problems.

However, Peter Axt believes that *light* exercise is beneficial. "I jog gently for 20 minutes three or four times a week," he said, "but I have no time for men over 50 who insist on running several kilometers a day."

a Read the article and mark the sentences T (true), F (false), or DS (doesn't say).

1 Peter Axt regularly runs marathons.
2 He says that people who exercise too much will probably die younger.
3 Jim Fixx got Americans to exercise more.
4 *The Joy of Laziness* is a bestseller.
5 The book says that the only important thing to help you live longer is to exercise less.
6 In the Italian village, people are very healthy but not very active.
7 The book's ideas are based on five years' research.
8 He thinks that if you've had a very tiring day at work, you shouldn't do physical exercise.
9 Axt runs several kilometers a day.

b Look at the highlighted words and phrases. Can you guess what they mean?

CAN YOU UNDERSTAND THESE PEOPLE?

a **5.22** Listen and circle the correct answer, a, b, or c.

1 How many bookstores are there in the town?
  a None b One c Two
2 Where are the women going to have lunch?
  a Roberto's b Trattoria Marco
  c Garibaldi's
3 Who's going to choose the movie?
  a The man. b The woman.
  c The man and the woman.
4 The man has...
  a the right education but little experience.
  b experience but little education.
  c experience and the right education.
5 The girl thinks she wants to...
  a do research. b be a doctor.
  c be a biologist.

b **5.23** You will hear a man and a woman talking about buying a car. Mark the sentences T (True) or F (False).

1 The woman says she prefers the SUV.
2 The man thinks the sedan is too small.
3 The woman damaged their car when she was trying to park.
4 The SUV is cheaper than the sedan.
5 In the end, the man and the woman can't decide what to buy.

CAN YOU SAY THIS IN ENGLISH?

Can you...? Yes (✓)

☐ talk about your town and its facilities
☐ talk about your work–life balance
☐ say what men and women usually talk about
☐ talk about a member of your family's job, and about the job you have or would like to have

6A

G reported speech: statements, questions, and commands
V shopping
P consonant sounds: /g/, /dʒ/, /k/, /ʃ/, /tʃ/

Love in the supermarket

1 GRAMMAR reported speech: statements and questions

a Read the short story and look at the pictures. In pairs, guess the last word.

Love in the supermarket

They met next to the laundry detergent. By the cereal, they told each other their life stories. By the vegetables, he told her that he was falling in love with her. In front of the frozen food, he asked her if she would marry him and she said *yes*. But in the candy aisle, they had their first argument. When they were waiting in line to pay, they decided that it was all _____.

b Now complete the speech bubbles with A–K.

A Will you marry me?

B I'll see you around. Bye.

C Yes, I will.

D I work in advertising.

E I don't think you're really my type.

F ~~Do you need any help?~~

G Do you know how many calories there are in a bar of chocolate?

H Thanks. My name's Olga.

I I'm a student. What do you do?

J Olga, I'm falling in love with you.

K Are you saying I'm fat?

c **6.1** Listen and check.

d Write the sentence and question below in reported speech. Then look at the short story to check your answer.

"I'm falling in love with you."
He told her (that) _____.

"Will you marry me?"
He asked her if _____.

e ○ **p.140 Grammar Bank 6A.** Read the rules for reported speech: statements and questions, and do exercise **a** only.

f Look at pictures 1–6. Tell the story in reported speech.

He asked her if she needed any help…

2 VOCABULARY shopping

a In pairs, say if you think these are the same or different and why.

1 a supermarket and a market
2 a drugstore and a pharmacy
3 a shopping mall and a department store
4 a library and a bookstore

b What are the last three stores you have been to? What kind of stores are they? What did you buy?

c ● p.153 **Vocabulary Bank** *Shopping.*

3 PRONUNCIATION consonant sounds: /g/, /dʒ/, /k/, /ʃ/, /tʃ/

a 6.2 Listen and cross out the word with a different sound.

1	g	bargain	travel agent	argument	drugstore
2	dʒ	vegetables	manager	change	gift shop
3	k	discount	bakery	quit	receipt
4	ʃ	shoe store	stationery store	cereal	cash
5	tʃ	lunch	schedule	cheese	choose

b 6.3 Listen and repeat the sentences. Practice saying them.

1 You can't choose your own schedule!
2 I had an argument with the manager of the gift shop.
3 The bakery gave us a discount.
4 Could you give me the receipt for the shoes, please?
5 My new green jacket was a bargain.

c ● p.159 **Sound Bank.** Look at the typical spellings for these sounds.

4 SPEAKING

Interview another student with the questionnaire. Ask for more information.

The shopping QUESTIONNAIRE

Stores

● What kind of small stores are there near where you live?

● What kind of stores do you like to go to most?

● What are your favorite stores for...?
 a clothes c books and music
 b shoes d presents

● Do you ever shop at...?
 a farmers' markets
 b supermarkets
 c shopping malls

Shopping

● How often do you go shopping?

● Do you prefer shopping by yourself or with somebody?

● What do you enjoy buying?

● What do you hate buying?

● Do you like to shop at sales? What do you usually buy?

● Where do you go if you want to find a bargain?

● Do you ever shop online? What for?

5 READING

Making a complaint – is it worth it?

A ☐ As the machine was no longer under guarantee, Mr. Jones called a local repairman. He charged Mr. Jones $45 to look at it and then told him that he would need to spend $650 plus tax for a new part. Then Mr. Jones took the laptop to a well-known computer retailer – and they told him to buy a new one!

B ☐ Another customer's experience shows that it's worth complaining to the top people of a company if the local company staff are unhelpful.

C ☐ "Four days later, someone called me to say the DVD player / recorder was waiting for me and I could select 10 recordable DVD discs to compensate for my wasted time," he says. "When I picked them up I was treated like a real VIP."

D ☐ Mark Olsen wanted to buy a DVD player / recorder. At his local branch of a chain store that sells electronic goods, they told him that they didn't have the one he wanted in stock, but that they were expecting a delivery "soon." However, when he went back, it still hadn't arrived.

E ☐ 1 Is it really worth complaining when goods or services are not satisfactory? According to a new report from a consumer magazine, it certainly is. As they point out, the old saying "if you don't ask, you don't get" is true for many situations, but particularly so when it comes to compensation. Take the case of Mike Jones. He bought a laptop computer, but just three years later he found that it was getting slower and slower.

F ☐ He returned twice over the following weeks, but each time they told him to come back in a week. He started calling about the machine instead. But after several weeks of calling unsuccessfully, Mr. Olsen lost patience and wrote to the managing director of the store.

G ☐ However, Mr. Jones still felt that his computer should not be out of date after just three years. He decided to write a letter of complaint to the company. A short time later, the company picked up the laptop, diagnosed a software problem, repaired it, and returned it with a new battery, all without charge. "I'd call that outstanding service," said Mr. Jones.

Adapted from a newspaper

a If you have a problem with something you bought, or with the service in a store, do you usually complain? Who to? If not, why not?

b Read the article about complaining and number the paragraphs in order 1–7.

c Read the article again in the right order and complete the chart.

	Mr. Jones	Mr. Olsen
1 What did he complain about?		
2 What was the problem?		
3 How did he try to solve it?		
4 Why wasn't he successful?		
5 Who did he write to?		
6 What happened as a result?		

d Match the highlighted words or phrases with their meanings.

1 _____ a store or office that is part of a larger organization
2 _____ employees
3 _____ things that are for sale
4 _____ available in the store
5 _____ things that other people do for you, e.g., repair your TV
6 _____ money or things you give somebody because you have treated them badly
7 _____ a written promise from a company that it will repair something if it breaks in a certain period of time

e Now read the last part of the article. Complete the tips with a phrase from below. Which two tips do you think are the most important?

Be reasonable   Keep a record   Don't lose your temper
Act quickly   Always go to the top

Top tips for complaining

1 _____ when there's a problem and give the company a chance to solve the problem.

2 _____, and ask to speak to the manager. He / She is the one who can compensate you.

3 _____. Note the date, time, and name of the person you've spoken to, and what was agreed.

4 _____. Getting angry won't help at all.

5 _____. If a company apologizes and makes a genuine effort to satisfy you, be prepared to meet it halfway.

6 GRAMMAR reported speech: commands

a Look at the sentences below from the article. What do you think were the exact words the salespeople used?

1 They told him to buy a new one.
2 They told him to come back in a week.

b Look at pictures 1–4. Complete the sentences with an affirmative or negative infinitive (e.g., *to be* or *not to be*).

1 She asked the salesperson _____ her a refund.

2 He told the people at the next table _____ so much noise.

3 She asked the clerk _____ her a bigger room.

4 He told the taxi driver _____ so fast.

c ⊙ **p.140 Grammar Bank 6A.** Read the rules for reported speech: commands and do exercise **b**.

7 LISTENING & SPEAKING

a ◖ **6.4** ◗ Listen to part of a radio program where people are talking about bad service. Then answer the questions.

The taxi

1 Why did the man get annoyed?
2 What did he ask the taxi driver to do?
3 What happened in the end?

The hotel

4 What problems were there with the woman's room?
5 What happened when she told the front desk clerk?
6 What did she tell him to do? Did he do it?

The restaurant

7 Why did the man ask the waitress to change his soup?
8 Why wasn't he happy with the check?
9 What happened in the end?

b Talk to a partner.

1 Who's best at complaining in your family? Why?
2 Can you remember a time when you (or someone in your family) complained…?

to a taxi driver
to a front desk clerk
to a waiter
to someone else

Why did you complain? What did you ask the person to do? What happened?

c ⊙ **Communication** *I want to speak to the manager A p.118 B p.121.* Role-play complaining in a store and a restaurant.

6 B

G passive: *be* + past participle
V movies
P sentence stress

See the movie... get on a plane

1 READING

a Have you ever seen a movie that made you want to go to the place where the movie was made?

b Read the article and try to complete each text with the name of the movie and the country where it was made. Use the photos to help you.

Out of Africa	*The Lord of the Rings*	*The Beach*
New Zealand	Thailand	Kenya

Famous movies that moved us (literally!)

Sometimes when you see a movie, the sense of place is so strong that it makes you think "I have to go there one day." Here are three movies, from three different decades, that have made thousands of people pack their suitcases and catch a plane. There's travel information too, in case you want to go there yourself…

1 *The Beach*

The movie is set in the 1990s on a small tropical island. It is based on a best-selling book by Alex Garland and it was directed by Danny Boyle. It's about a young traveler (played by Leonardo DiCaprio) who finds a group of young people living on a beautiful, uninhabited island. But paradise soon turns into a nightmare…

Where was it filmed?

The movie was shot on the beautiful island of Phi Phi Leh in *Thailand*, which is now visited by more than a million tourists every year. Most of the hotels were destroyed in 2004 by the tsunami, but they have now been rebuilt.

How do I get there?

Fly to Phuket International Airport and travel to the island by boat or small plane.

2 *Out of Africa*

This movie was nominated for 11 Oscars and it won seven. It's about a Danish writer (played by Meryl Streep) who goes to Africa to help her husband run a coffee plantation. To her surprise, she finds herself falling in love with the country, the people, and a mysterious hunter (Robert Redford). The movie was based on an autobiographical novel by Isak Dinesen, and was directed by the American director Sydney Pollack.

Where was it filmed?

The story is set in *Kenya* in 1914 and was shot on location in the Masai Mara National Park. Aside from the actors, the "stars" of the movie are the breathtaking scenery and the exotic wildlife, which look so wonderful on the big screen. The movie also had an unforgettable soundtrack guaranteed to move even the most unromantic.

The movie won the Oscar for Best Picture, and the following year tourism replaced agriculture as the country's top industry.

How do I get there?

Fly to Nairobi and then drive to the Masai Mara National Reserve, where the cast and movie crew lived during filming. Then take a three-day safari to see giraffes, elephants, lions, and much more.

3 *the lord of the rings*

This trilogy of movies won a total of 17 Oscars, including Best Picture and Best Director.

They are based on the books written by J.R.R. Tolkien. They tell the story of a hobbit, Frodo Baggins, who has to try to destroy a magic ring in order to defeat the evil forces of the Dark Lord Sauron. He is helped on his journey by a group of friends.

Where was it filmed?
The story is set in an imaginary land called Middle Earth. All three movies were filmed in *New Zealand*, which was chosen because of its magnificent and dramatic scenery. The director of the movie, Peter Jackson, was born there. The success of the movies has attracted thousands of tourists to the country.

How do I get there?
You can either fly to Auckland or Wellington, the capital city (where you will be greeted by a huge sign saying "Welcome to Middle Earth"). From there you can travel to visit all the fantastic movie locations, including the battlefields. There are guided tours by road or helicopter.

c Read the article again and answer the questions.
Which movie(s)…?
1 had three parts *the lord the rings*
2 were based on a book *all the B...*
3 was set at the beginning of the 20th century
4 was set in a place where later there was a natural disaster *Phi Phi (off thailand)*
5 was filmed in a wildlife park *out of Africa*
6 didn't win an Oscar
7 was a romantic movie *The beach*
8 was directed by a man born in the country where the movie was made
Peter Jackson

d Answer the questions.
Have you seen any of these movies? Did you like it / them? *yes the*
Which of the three places would you most like to visit?
Thailand, new zealand

2 GRAMMAR passive: *be* + past participle

a Read about *The Beach* again. Underline an example of the present passive, the past passive, and the present perfect passive. How do you form the passive?

b Look at the active sentences in the chart below and underline the verbs. What tense are they? In pairs, complete the chart with passive verbs.

Active	Passive
Movies inspire people to travel.	People *are inspired* to travel by movies.
Sydney Pollack directed *Out of Africa*.	*Out of Africa* *was directed* by Sydney Pollack.
They're making the movie on location.	The movie *was made* on location.
They will release the movie next year.	The movie _____ next year.
Thousands of fans have visited the country.	The country *had visited* by thousands of fans.

c ⟳ **p.140 Grammar Bank 6B.** Read the rules and do the exercises.

3 PRONUNCIATION sentence stress

a 6.5 **Dictation.** Listen and write six passive sentences.

b Listen again. Underline the stressed words.

c Listen and repeat the sentences. Copy the rhythm.

4 VOCABULARY movies

a Try to remember words or phrases from **READING** on pages 88 and 89 which mean…

1 the music from a movie.   the s _oundtrack_
2 the person who directs a movie.   the d _irector_
3 all the actors in a movie.   the c _ountry_
4 all the people who make a movie.   the c _reator_
5 (filmed) in the real place, not in a studio.   o _____ l _____
6 the part of a theater or TV where the image appears.   the s _cens_

b Look at **READING** (text 2) again and check your answers.

c ◉ **p.154 Vocabulary Bank** *Movies.*

5 SPEAKING

a Read the questionnaire and think about your answers.

b In pairs, interview each other. Do you have similar tastes?

The movie questionnaire

1 Can you think of a movie which…?
made you laugh a lot
made you cry
put you to sleep
made you feel good
you've seen several times
made you buy the soundtrack

2 Do you prefer…?
seeing movies on TV or DVD, or in the theater
seeing foreign movies dubbed or with subtitles
movies from your country or foreign movies

3 Think of a really good movie you've seen this year:
Where was it set? When?
Who was in it? Who was it directed by?
Did it have a good plot?
What was the soundtrack like?

4 Have you ever…?
met an actor or a director
used a video camera
appeared in any kind of movie
seen a movie being made

To Dagmara, You have been the most valuable help to me and this film and I am eternally grateful.

Your friend, Steven Spielberg

a Look at the photograph. In pairs, answer the questions.

1 Who do you think the man and woman are?
2 Where do you think they are?
3 What movie do you think was being made?
4 What do you think is happening?

b 🔊 6.6 Listen to the first part of an interview with Dagmara and check your answers to **a**.

c Listen again and answer these questions.

1 Where does Dagmara live?
2 What was she doing before the shooting of the movie started?
3 Was that her real job?
4 Where did she meet Spielberg?
5 What did she have to do there? Why?
6 How well did she do it?
7 What happened afterwards?

d 🔊 6.7 Now listen to the second part of the interview and then make notes under the headings below.

> What she had to do during the movie
> *go to the set every day, translate*
> The most difficult thing about the job   *Repeat again*
> The worst moment
> What it was like to work with Spielberg
> Her opinion of the movie
> How she feels when she watches the movie
> *remember*

e Compare with a partner. Then listen again and complete your notes.

6C

G relative clauses: defining and non-defining
V what people do
P word stress

I need a hero

1 GRAMMAR relative clauses: defining and non-defining

a **6.8** In pairs, do the quiz. Choose a, b, or c. Compare with another pair and then listen and check.

What do you know about...

1 He was born in...
a Cuba   b Colombia   (c) Argentina

2 His first name was...
a Alejandro   (b) Ernesto   c Eduardo

3 In college he studied...
a law   b politics   (c) medicine

4 He helped...in the Cuban Revolution.
(a) Fidel Castro   b Eva Perón   c Emiliano Zapata

5 He was captured and shot in...
a Chile   (b) Bolivia   c Venezuela

6 When he died he was in his late...
a twenties   (b) thirties   c forties

7 He died in...
a 1960   (b) 1967   c 1973

b Look at the photos and cover the texts. Guess what the connection is between each of the things, people, or places and Che Guevara.

c Now read texts A–E and check.

d Cover the texts. Complete the sentences with **who**, **whose**, **which**, **that**, or **where**. In some cases, two answers are possible.

1 The movie, _whose_ theme song won an Oscar, is based on the motorcycle journey _that_ Che made with Alberto across South America.
2 It was the poverty _that_ he saw on this trip _which_ made him decide that revolution was the only answer to South America's problems.
3 Gael García Bernal is the actor _whose_ played Che.
4 Rosario is the town in Argentina _where_ Ernesto "Che" Guevara was born.
5 The photo, _which_ was taken in 1960, is probably one of the best-known photos in the world.
6 The people _who_ wear Che T-shirts tend to be people _who_ don't conform.

e Compare your sentences 1 and 2 with text **A**. Find two differences.

f ⇨ **p.140 Grammar Bank 6C.** Read the rules and do the exercises.

g Cover the text and look at the photos. Can you remember the connections with Che?

Che Guevara?

a Norton 500cc motorcycle

Alberto Korda

Aleidita

Gael García Bernal

Rosario

A This is the motorcycle that was used in the movie *The Motorcycle Diaries*. It is a 1939 Norton 500cc, which is the same model as the motorcycle that belonged to Che's friend Alberto. The movie, whose theme song won an Oscar, is based on the motorcycle journey Che made with Alberto across South America. Che was from a rich family in Argentina, and it was the poverty he saw on this trip that made him decide that revolution was the only answer to South America's problems.

B **Gael García Bernal** is the actor who played Che in the movie *The Motorcycle Diaries*. He is from Guadalajara in Mexico, and has also starred in *And Your Mother Too* and Pedro Almodovar's *Bad Education*.

C **Rosario** is the town in Argentina where Ernesto "Che" Guevara was born on June 14, 1928. He was the first of five children, and his parents, Ernesto and Celia, were political radicals. From the age of two the young Che suffered from asthma, but his father told him that learning to live with his illness would make him a stronger person.

D **Alberto Korda** was the photographer whose photo now appears on T-shirts and posters all over the world. The photo, which was taken in 1960, is probably one of the best-known photos in the world – but Korda never received a penny in royalties. However, in 2000 he took some people who had made money from the photo to court, and won $50,000, which he gave to the Cuban health service.

E **Aleidita**, daughter of Che and his second wife Aleida, was his favorite child. She says that she doesn't think that Che would mind that his photo has been so commercialized. "Look at the people who wear Che T-shirts," she says. "They tend to be people who don't conform, who are wondering if they can be better human beings. My father would have liked that."

2 LISTENING & SPEAKING

a 🔊 **6.9** Listen to a contest on a radio program. With a partner, try to write down the eight heroes and icons. Check your answers on page 120.

b ⊃ **Communication** *Relatives quiz A p.118 B p.121.* Make questions to ask a partner.

3 READING

a In pairs, look at the photos 1–5 and match them with the names below. Do you know what they are famous for?

Wangari Maathai ☐ 3 Bernard Kouchner ☐
Bono ☐ 1 Queen Rania of Jordan ☐ 5
Thierry Henry ☐

b Now read the article and complete it with the five names.

c Read the article again and answer the questions.

1 Who was asked for some help that he / she couldn't give?
2 Who is trying to fight disease? How?
3 Who encouraged women to play a stronger role in protecting the environment? How?
4 Who used to be a politician? Why was he / she unusual?
5 Who used their celebrity status to raise money? What are they trying to change?

d Read the article again. Find the nouns from these verbs and adjectives.

1 found (vb) _____*foundation*_____
2 modern (adj) _____
3 hungry (adj) _____
4 poor (adj) _____
5 deforest (vb) _____
6 operate (vb) _____
7 sell (vb) _____

e In pairs, look at the photos and say why these people are heroes.

Heroes and icons of our time

Time magazine has chosen a list of people called the *Time 100*. These are people who, the magazine believes, have an enormous impact on today's world and who inspire millions of people. The category *Heroes and Icons* includes a whole variety of people from a queen to a soccer player, from politicians to a multimillionaire rock star.

A _____, one of the world's greatest soccer players, has used his hero status on the field to fight racism in soccer. After he saw black players from the England team being insulted by spectators in an international game, he started the campaign "Stand up, Speak out." He has raised nearly $16 million for anti-racism groups through the sales of black and white bracelets.

"You probably can't change the racists," he says, "but you can make the silent majority stand up and speak out against them. That way we will make them feel less comfortable. In a few years, I want to be able to watch a soccer game and not hear a single racist insult."

B _____ is helping her husband to "try to reconcile tradition with modernity" in their country. But outside her country, along with the Bill & Melinda Gates Foundation and others, she is working to try to make sure that all children everywhere get vaccinated. As she reminds us, there are more than 30 million children a year who get no vaccinations during their first year of life, so up to 10% of them will die.

C _____, one of the world's biggest rock stars, is also Africa's biggest defender. When he and his wife Ali first went to Africa, they worked in a refugee camp for a month. On the day they were leaving, a man approached him carrying a baby. "This is my son," the man said. "Please take him with you when you leave. If you do, he will live. Otherwise he will die." He couldn't take the child, but since then he has been working tirelessly to raise money to free Africa from hunger and poverty.

1

2

3

4

D ___S___, who won
the Nobel Peace Prize in 2004, is an
environmental leader known in her
native Kenya as the "Tree Woman." In
1977, she founded the Green Belt
Movement, an organization, consisting
mostly of women, that has fought
deforestation by planting more than
20 million trees in Kenya. She wanted
to prove that "women could improve
the environment without much
technology or financial resources." The
movement has spread to other African
nations, but her work has also met
with opposition, and at one time she
was jailed for her fight against
deforestation. Today she continues to
work for environmental causes,
women's rights, and democracy.

E ___2___ first came
to the public eye when he helped to
save many of the boat people who
escaped Vietnam. He carried sacks of
rice himself, even though he was a
French government minister, in
"Operation Restore Hope" in Somalia.
Nelson Mandela once said to him,
"Thank you for helping in matters
which aren't your problem." He co-
founded Médecins sans Frontières
(Doctors without Borders), which was
awarded the 1999 Nobel Peace Prize,
and later Médecins du Monde.

4 VOCABULARY & PRONUNCIATION   what people do, word stress

> ⚠ Most words which tell us what people do end in *-er*, *-or*, *-ian*, or *-ist*, e.g.,
> Wangari Maathai is an environmental **leader**.

a Add an ending and put the words in the correct column.

act	compose	conduct	cycle	design	direct	guitar
invent	lead	music	paint	photograph	physics	play	politics
present	science	sculpt	violin			

-er	-or	-ian	-ist
composer	actor	musician	cyclist
conducter	director	physicus	guitarist
Painter	sculptor	politician	violinist
Photographer		sciences	
Plyer	lead		

b 🔊 **6.10** Listen and <u>under</u>line the stressed syllable. Practice saying the words.

5 SPEAKING

a Think of a person (living or dead) you admire for three of the categories below.

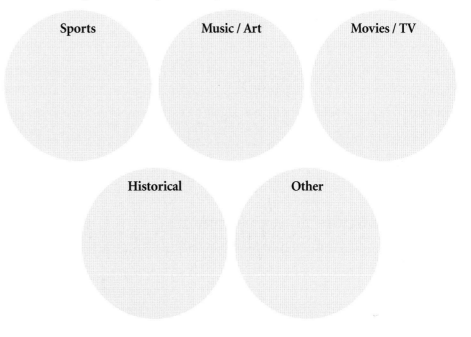

Sports   **Music / Art**   **Movies / TV**

Historical   **Other**

b In groups, talk about the people you chose. Explain who they are, what they
have done, and why you admire them.

6 🔊 **6.11** SONG ♫ *Holding out for a hero*

GIVING AND REACTING TO NEWS

a 〔 6.12 〕 Cover the conversation and listen. What news does Ben have? Who is more surprised, Jacques or Nicole?

b Read the conversation. In pairs, what do you think the missing words are? **Don't write them in yet.**

Ben	Hi.
Nicole / Jacques	Hi. / Hello.
Nicole	Did you have a nice weekend?
Ben	Oh yeah. You'll never guess who I saw on Saturday.
Nicole	Who?
Ben	Allie… and Mark. In the Louvre… together.
Nicole	Really?
Jacques	You're joking.
Ben	It was definitely them. And they looked really close. I think they were holding hands.
Jacques	No! I don't believe it.
Ben	It's true, I'm telling you! And I think they saw me because they turned and left really quickly.
Jacques	Are you serious?
Nicole	You know, I'm not surprised. I think they've been seeing each other ever since Mark arrived. Or maybe even before.
Jacques	That's weird. What makes you say that?
Nicole	When I went to look at Mark's new apartment, I'm sure Allie called him on his mobile. And I've seen her looking at him in a certain way…
Ben	Hey, quiet everyone. It's Mark.

c Listen again and complete the conversation.

d 〔 6.13 〕 Listen and repeat the highlighted phrases. Copy the rhythm.

e Cover the conversation. Try to remember five ways of reacting to news with surprise or interest.

f In pairs, invent some news about a famous person to tell other students. Take turns telling your news. React with surprise / interest.

> You'll never guess what happened! — What?

SOCIAL ENGLISH For your eyes only

a 〔 6.14 〕 How does Allie reply to Mark's e-mail?

b Listen again and mark the sentences T (true) or F (false).

1 Jacques had a busy weekend. F
2 Mark invites Ben and Jacques to his place for a meal on Saturday. F
3 Mark says he went to the Louvre with a friend. F
4 Ben says he saw Mark at the Louvre. F
5 Everybody gets the same e-mail from Allie. T

USEFUL PHRASES

That would be very nice.
So didn't you go out at all?
I felt like (getting a bit of culture).
That's funny. I went to the Louvre on Saturday, too.
I didn't see you either.

c 〔 6.15 〕 Complete the USEFUL PHRASES. Listen and check.

d Listen again and repeat the phrases. How do you say them in your language?

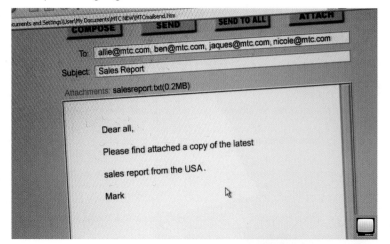

"Must-have" DVDs: *Cinema Paradiso: 1989*

Tim Hudson reviews a DVD that every movie lover should own.

1 *Cinema Paradiso* was directed [1] _by___ Giuseppe Tornatore.
It stars Philippe Noiret as Alfredo, and Salvatore Cascio, who plays
the part of the boy. The movie won an Oscar in 1989 [2] _____
Best Foreign Language film.

2 The movie is set in an Italian village in the 1940s and 50s. It was
filmed on location in Sicily.

3 It is [3] _____ a little boy called Salvatore who ends up becoming
a famous movie director. [4] _____ the beginning of the story, he
goes [5] _____ to his village for the first time in thirty years, for
the funeral of an old friend, Alfredo. The rest of the movie is a
"flashback" about his childhood. [6] _____ his village there is only
one movie theater, called Cinema Paradiso. Salvatore is crazy
[7] _____ movies, so he spends all his time there. He becomes
friends with Alfredo, the man who shows the movies, and later he
works [8] _____ his assistant. But when he is a teenager he leaves
the village and goes [9] _____ work in Rome, and [10] _____ the
end he becomes a famous director. He never sees Alfredo again.

4 I strongly recommend *Cinema Paradiso*. It makes you laugh and
cry, it has a memorable soundtrack, and it is a moving tribute
to the magic of the early days of movies.

a Look at the title and the photos. Have you seen
the movie? Would you like to see it?

b Read the movie review. Number the paragraph
summaries below in order, 1–4.

> **Paragraph** ☐
> The plot
>
> **Paragraph** ☐
> The name of the movie, the director, the
> stars, and any prizes it won
>
> **Paragraph** ☐
> Why you recommend this movie
>
> **Paragraph** ☐
> Where and when it was set

c Read the review again and complete it with the
missing words.

| about (x2) at as back ~~by~~ in (x2) for to |

d Look at the third paragraph again. What tense do we
usually use to tell the story of a movie or book?

Useful language: describing a movie

It was directed / written by…
It is set in…
It is based on the book…
It's about…
It stars…
My favorite scene is…

> **WRITE** a movie review about a movie that you would
> recommend people buy on DVD.
>
> **PLAN** what you're going to write in the four paragraphs.
> Use the **Useful language** box and **Vocabulary Bank**
> **p.154** *Movies* to help you.
>
> **CHECK** the review for mistakes (grammar ,
> punctuation , and spelling).

GRAMMAR

Complete the second sentence with **two words** so that it means the same as the first.

1 "Do you want to have dinner?" he asked.
  James asked me if _____ _____ to have dinner.
2 "I'll pay," she said.
  Jacqueline said that _____ _____ pay.
3 "Where am I?" the man asked.
  The man asked me where _____ _____.

4 "Can you open the window, please?"
  My mother asked me _____ _____ the window.
5 "Don't talk!"
  The teacher told the students _____ _____ talk.
6 They made the movie in a studio.
  The movie _____ _____ in a studio.
7 They're building a new school.
  A new school is _____ _____.
8 An Asian company has bought our company.
  Our company has _____ _____ by an Asian company.
9 That man's son goes to my school.
  That's the man _____ _____ goes to my school.
10 This is a machine. It cuts paper.
  This is a machine _____ _____ paper.

| 10 |

VOCABULARY

a Underline the word that is different. Say why.

1	bakery	shoe store	store window	newsstand
2	buy	sale	sell	pay
3	cast	extras	special effects	actors
4	horror movie	thriller	sequel	comedy
5	dubbed	filmed	directed	plot

b Write words for the definitions.

1 A store where you can buy bread. **b**_____
2 The piece of paper you are given when you buy something. **r**_____
3 What salespeople use to make a sale. **c**_____ **r**_____
4 A basket on wheels that people use at supermarkets. **c**_____
5 The words of a movie translated on the screen. **s**_____
6 The music from a movie. **s**_____
7 The people who watch a movie in a theater. **a**_____
8 Something you buy more cheaply than usual. **b**_____

c Complete with one word.

1 Can I try _____ these pants, please?
2 You can pay _____ credit card.
3 People always complain _____ high prices.
4 If it's broken, take it _____ to the store.
5 The movie is based _____ a book.
6 *Schindler's List* was directed _____ Spielberg.
7 *Les Misérables* was set _____ 18th century Paris.

| 20 |

PRONUNCIATION

a Underline the word with a different sound.

1		sell	special	sale	center
2		cart	market	compare	star
3		bakery	scene	discount	sequel
4		director	manager	drugstore	supermarket
5		schedule	chain store	each	watch

b Underline the stressed syllable.

| subtitles | complain | receipt | soundtrack | customer |

| 10 |

CAN YOU UNDERSTAND THIS TEXT?

Designer brands aren't for me!

Although I follow fashion, I hate the phrase "must-have." If I read that Ugg boots or Prada sunglasses are the latest "must-haves," my immediate reaction is to think, "Why must I have them?" Why should I fall for the designer's manipulative tactics, which are only intended to increase his bank balance at the expense of mine?

Designer brands, in general, are for people who are too insecure to trust their own taste. These people decide that everything at Prada must be "cool," so if you shop there, you can't go wrong. I find it much more satisfying to stop by one of the cheap chain stores and buy a copy of the designer's clothes for a tenth of the price. OK, you have to have a good eye to find the one garment in three

that looks great. But it's worth it! It's like finding a piece of gold in a river. The find gives you immense satisfaction.

Which is why, according to a survey done by one bank, young people with money are abandoning the designer stores and buying their clothes in chain stores, second-hand stores, and in street markets. This is the best news I've heard all week. It means that young people have the confidence to trust their judgement. They are prepared to take risks to look individual and not mass-produced.

That has always been my shopping philosophy. The exorbitant prices in designer stores are outrageous. Even if I had the money, I would think of all the other things I could spend it on!

LOUIS VUITTON
Salvatore Ferragamo

GIANFRANCO
FERRÉ
LIU·JO

BOSS
HUGO BOSS

C E L I N E
PRADA

V E C U A

a Read the text and choose a, b, or c.

1 The writer thinks…
  a fashion is ridiculous.
  b Prada sunglasses are "must-haves."
  c designers just want to make a lot of money.

2 She thinks people who buy designer brands…
  a are "cool."
  b don't have good taste.
  c are afraid of making a mistake.

3 She thinks…
  a it's easy to find great, cheap clothes.
  b you feel good if you find good, cheap clothes.
  c the clothes in chain stores are better than designer clothes.

4 According to the bank survey, rich young people…
  a now want to look different from each other.
  b don't have as much money to spend as they used to.
  c are now buying more designer clothes.

5 The writer…
  a thinks the price of designer clothes is fair.
  b thinks there are better things to spend her money on.
  c would like to have the money to buy designer clothes.

b Look at the highlighted phrases. Try to guess their meaning. Check with your teacher or your dictionary.

CAN YOU UNDERSTAND THESE PEOPLE?

a 🔊 **6.16** Listen and circle the correct answer, a, b, or c.

1 What was the problem with the woman's steak?
  a It wasn't cooked enough.   b It was cold.   c It was overcooked.

2 What didn't the man like about the movie?
  a The acting.   b The music.   c The plot.

3 How much did the sweater cost?
  a $25   b $67   c $77

4 How did the man feel after he saw the movie?
  a Disappointed.   b Nervous.   c Excited.

5 What did Brunel do?
  a He was an architect.   b He was an engineer.   c He was a boxer.

b 🔊 **6.17** Listen to the guide showing tourists around Mark Twain's house in Hartford, Connecticut. Complete the sentences with one word.

Mark Twain, or Samuel Clemens, was born on November 30, _____.
When Sam was 11 years old, his father _____.
After that, Sam worked for a local _____.
Clemens and his wife, Olivia, were _____ married.
His novel *Tom Sawyer* is based on his life as a _____ near the Mississippi River.
Twain died at the age of _____.

CAN YOU SAY THIS IN ENGLISH?

Can you…? Yes (✓)

☐ talk about a time you complained in a store or restaurant
☐ describe a movie
☐ talk about a person who you admire

7 A

G third conditional
V making adjectives and adverbs
P sentence stress

Can we make our own luck?

1 READING & LISTENING

a Read the article **Bad luck?** In pairs, decide what you think happened next.

b 🔊 **7.1** Now listen to what happened. Were you right?

c Listen again and check. Then in pairs, write two sentences to explain how the story ended.

d 🔊 **7.2** Now do the same for **Good luck?**

Bad luck?
I missed you!

an Johnson, a 27-year-old builder, went to work in Australia for a year, leaving behind his girlfriend, Amy. Ian and Amy missed each other a lot and after being apart for six months, Ian planned a surprise. Without telling Amy, he caught a plane back to England to see her. After a 24-hour flight via Singapore and a 17,600-kilometer journey, he finally arrived at her house in Yorkshire in the north of England, carrying flowers and an engagement ring. He rang the doorbell, but nobody answered. He had a key to her house, so he opened the door and went in. The house was empty. Ian thought Amy had gone out for the evening and sat down to wait for her to come back. Tired after his long journey, he fell asleep. When he woke up, his phone was ringing...

Good luck?
Is there a doctor on the plane?

rs. Dorothy Fletcher was traveling with her daughter and her daughter's fiancé on a flight from London to Florida. Her daughter was going to be married there the following week. When they changed planes in Philadelphia, they had to rush between terminals to catch the connecting flight and Mrs. Fletcher, age 67, began to feel sick.

"I didn't say anything to my daughter because I didn't want to worry her or miss the wedding," said Mrs. Fletcher. But when the plane took off from Philadelphia, she suddenly got a terrible pain in her chest, back, and arm – she was having a heart attack. The cabin crew put out a desperate call to the passengers: "If there is a doctor on the plane, could you please press your call button..."

Adapted from a newspaper

2 GRAMMAR third conditional

a Complete the two sentences from the listening in **1c**.

> **1 Ian**
> If one of us had ~~Stay~~ at home, we _____ have met.
>
> **2 Mrs. Fletcher**
> If those doctors _____ been on the plane, I would ~~don't~~ died.

b 🔊 **7.3** Listen and check.

c Look at sentences 1 and 2 above and answer the questions.

1 Did Ian or Amy stay at home? Did they meet?
2 Were the doctors on the plane? Did Mrs. Fletcher die?
3 Do sentences 1 and 2 refer to something that happened or something that didn't happen?

d ⬅ **p.142 Grammar Bank 7A.** Read the rules and do the exercises.

3 PRONUNCIATION sentence stress

a 🔊 **7.4** Listen and repeat the sentences. Copy the rhythm.

1 If you'd told me earlier, I would have gone, too.
2 If the weather had been better, we would have stayed longer.
3 If I hadn't stopped for gas, I would have arrived before he left.
4 We would have been late if we hadn't taken a taxi.
5 She wouldn't have come if she'd known he was here.
6 It would have been cheaper if we'd gone last month.

b ➡ **Communication** *Guess the conditional A p.118 B p.121.*

4 SPEAKING

a Read the questionnaire and mark your answers.

b Compare your answers with a partner. Give more information if you can.

c Now look at what your scores mean. Do you agree with the results?

How lucky are you?

Read the following statements and write a number 1–3 in the box

3 = This is usually true about me.
2 = This is sometimes true about me.
1 = This is hardly ever true about me.

1 I enjoy talking to people I haven't met before. ☐
2 I don't worry or feel anxious about life. ☐
3 I enjoy trying new food and drink. ☐
4 I listen to my instincts. ☐
5 When I need to calm down, I just go to a quiet place. ☐
6 I try to learn from my mistakes. ☐
7 I try to get what I want from life. ☐
8 I expect people I meet to be pleasant, friendly, and helpful. ☐
9 I'm an optimist. I look on the bright side of life. ☐
10 When things are bad, I think things will get better soon. ☐
11 I don't think about bad luck I have had in the past. ☐
12 I expect good things to happen to me in the future. ☐

Your score

12–18 You are naturally unlucky and you don't attract good luck. You need a more positive and more adventurous attitude to life.

19–27 You are quite lucky, but you could be luckier. Look back at situations where you were lucky or unlucky and analyze why. Try to learn from the past.

28–36 You are probably someone who is lucky, but you could become even luckier. Don't be afraid of taking risks, as they will probably end up being positive for you.

5 READING

a Look at the title of the article. What do *you* think?

b Read the article. Match exercises A–D to paragraphs 1–4.

Can we make our own luck?

Some people seem to be born lucky – they meet their perfect partners, achieve their ambitions, and live happy lives.

Psychologist Dr. Richard Wiseman has done a lot of research to discover why some people are luckier than others. After interviewing hundreds of people with the questionnaire on page 101, he has concluded that people who *think* they are lucky achieve more success and happiness than those who don't. Without realizing it, they are creating good fortune in their lives.

Using Dr. Wiseman's techniques, you too can understand, control, and increase your own good fortune.

1 Lucky people make the most of their opportunities.
Be open to new experiences and vary your routine. For example, get off the bus a stop earlier than usual. You may see something interesting or new, or bump into an old friend.
Exercise ☐

2 Lucky people trust their instincts.
When you are trying to decide what to do, first make an effort to relax. Then when your mind is clear, listen to what it is telling you and act on it.
Exercise ☐

3 Lucky people expect to be lucky.
Convince yourself that your future will be bright and lucky. Set realistic but high goals. If you fail, don't give up. Be open to the idea of trying a different way to achieve your goals.
Exercise ☐

4 Lucky people use bad luck to their advantage.
If something bad happens, imagine how things could have been worse. You will then realize that things aren't so bad after all. Compare your situation with that of other people who are in an even worse situation. Take a long view of things. Even if things seem bad now, expect them to get better. Learn from your past mistakes and think of new ways to solve your problems.
Exercise ☐

EXERCISES

A Make a list of your goals. They must be specific, not vague, e.g., "I want to spend more time with my family," not "I want to be happy." Now make a second list of all the advantages you would get if you achieved your goals, and the disadvantages. Compare the advantages with the disadvantages and you will see which goals are worth trying to achieve.

B Make a list of six new experiences you'd like to try. These could be simple, like eating at a new restaurant, or long term, for example, learning a new language. Number the experiences 1–6. Then throw a dice and whatever experience is chosen, go out and do it.

C When you experience bad luck, first cry or scream for 30 minutes. Then put your bad luck behind you. Do something to make the situation better, e.g., ask friends for advice and focus on a solution to the problem.

D If you are trying to decide between two options, write one of them down in the form of a letter. For example, if you are unhappy about a relationship, write to your boyfriend or girlfriend explaining that it's all over. Read the letter. Would you really like to send it, or is something telling you that it doesn't *feel* right? If so, don't do it.

c Read just the article again (not the EXERCISES). Cover the text and from memory complete the expressions below with a verb or phrase. Then look at the text again and check your answers.

1 **s**_____ to be = give the impression of being
2 **a**_____ their ambitions = make their ambitions come true
3 **v**_____ your routine = change your routine, make it different
4 **b**_____ **i**_____ an old friend = meet an old friend by chance
5 **m**_____ an **e**_____ to relax = try hard to relax
6 **c**_____ yourself that your future will be bright = make yourself believe that your future will be bright
7 **r**_____ that things aren't so bad = understand that things aren't so bad

d Read EXERCISES **A–D** on page 102 again. Which one do you think is the best for making you luckier?

HOW WORDS WORK...

When you are trying to decide `what` to do, first make an effort to relax. Then when your mind is clear, listen to `what` it is telling you.

We often use *what* as a relative pronoun. It means "the thing (or things) that."

Complete the sentences with *what* or *that*.

1 Can you speak a bit louder? I can't hear _____ you're saying.
2 **A** What's this?
   B It's a machine _____ makes ice cream.
3 This is the song _____ won the MTV award.
4 Everybody was very surprised by _____ she said.
5 We went to the restaurant _____ Ann recommended.
6 I didn't get _____ I wanted for my birthday!

6 VOCABULARY making adjectives and adverbs

> **Lucky** people use bad **luck** to their advantage.

a Look at the adjectives and adverbs that can be made from the noun *luck* in the chart below. Then in pairs complete the chart.

noun	+ adjective	− adjective	+ adverb	− adverb
luck	lucky	unlucky	luckily	unluckily
care	careful	careless	_____	_____
comfort	_____	_____	_____	_____
patience	_____	_____	_____	_____
fortune	_____	_____	_____	_____

b Underline the stressed syllable in the three two-syllable nouns. How does that help you stress the adjectives and adverbs correctly? Practice saying them.

c Complete the sentences with the right form of the **bold** noun.

1 The beach was beautiful but _____ it rained every day. **FORTUNE**
2 If the beds had been more _____, we would have slept better. **COMFORT**
3 You would have gotten better grades if you hadn't been so _____ on the exam. **CARE**
4 We were really _____. We missed the flight by just five minutes. **LUCK**
5 Don't be so _____. The program will start in a minute. **PATIENCE**
6 I fell off my bicycle last week, but _____ I wasn't badly hurt. **LUCK**
7 There was a very long line to pay, but we waited _____. **PATIENCE**
8 If you had been more _____, you wouldn't have had an accident. **CARE**
9 It was freezing cold, but _____ we'd all brought jackets. **FORTUNE**
10 Are you sitting _____? Then I'll begin the story. **COMFORT**

7 🔊 7.5 SONG ♫ *Ironic*

7

B

G tag questions, indirect questions
V compound nouns
P intonation in tag questions

Murder mysteries

1 READING & LISTENING

a Read *Jack the Ripper – case closed?* and answer these questions.

1 Where and when did the murders take place?
2 How did "Jack the Ripper" get his name?
3 How many murders were there?
4 How long did the murders continue?
5 Who do the suspects include?
6 What does Patricia Cornwell usually do?
7 How did she try to solve the mystery?

Jack the Ripper – case closed?

One of the great unsolved murder mysteries of all time is that of Jack the Ripper.

In the fall of 1888, a brutal murderer walked the dark, foggy streets of London, terrorizing the inhabitants of the city. The victims were all women, and the police seemed powerless to stop the murders. Panic and fear among Londoners was increased by a letter sent by the murderer to Scotland Yard. In the letter he made fun of the police attempts to catch him and promised to kill again. It finished, "Yours truly, Jack the Ripper." This was the first of many letters sent to the police. The murders continued – seven in total. But in November, they suddenly stopped, three months after they had first begun.

Jack the Ripper was never caught, and for more than a century historians, writers, policemen, and detectives have tried to discover and prove his identity. Hundreds of articles and books have been written and many movies made about the murders. But the question "Who was Jack the Ripper?" has remained unanswered. There have been plenty of suspects, including a doctor, a businessman, a painter, and even a member of the royal family.

Three years ago the American crime writer Patricia Cornwell left aside her fictional detective, Kay Scarpetta, and tried to solve the real-life murder mystery of Jack the Ripper. After spending a considerable amount of time and money on her investigation, and analyzing DNA samples, Cornwell thinks she has proved who Jack the Ripper really was…

Johnny Depp hunts Jack the Ripper in the movie *From Hell*

b **7.6** Now listen to the first part of an interview with Ken Morton, an expert on Jack the Ripper. Complete the information about the suspects. Check (✔) the person who Patricia Cornwell says is Jack the Ripper.

Prince Albert,
Queen Victoria's *grandson*

James Maybrick,
a cotton merchant

Walter Sickert,
an *artist/painter*

c **7.7** Listen to the second part of the interview and mark the sentences T (true) or F (false). Correct the false sentences.

1 Cornwell's evidence is mainly scientific. *T*
2 She took DNA samples from a letter written by Sickert. *T*
3 Art lovers were angry with Cornwell. *T*
4 Sickert was probably abroad at the time of the murders. *F*
5 Maybrick confessed to the murders in a letter. *T*
6 Ken Morton thinks that Prince Albert was a serial killer. *F*
7 He doesn't want to say who he thinks the murderer is. *T*
8 He thinks the mystery will never be solved. *F*

police officers just for jolly wouldnt you. Keep this letter back till I do a bit more work. then give it out straight. My knife's so nice and sharp I want to get to work right away if I get a chance. Good luck.
yours truly
Jack the Ripper
Dont mind me giving the trade name

Extract from one of Jack the Ripper's letters

2 GRAMMAR tag questions

a **7.8** Listen to four questions the interviewer asked Ken Morton and complete them with the missing words.

1 You were a detective with Scotland Yard, _____ _____?
2 It's incredible, *isn't it*?
3 But you don't think she's right, *do you*?
4 There's been another recent theory, *hasn't there*?

b Now look at questions 1–4. Does the interviewer think she knows how the inspector is going to answer?

c ○ **p.142 Grammar Bank 7B** and read the rules for tag questions. Do exercise **a** only.

3 PRONUNCIATION & SPEAKING intonation in tag questions

a **7.9** Listen and complete the conversation between a police officer and a suspect.

P Your last name is Jones, _____? *isn't it*
S Yes, it is.
P And you're 27, *aren't you*?
S Yes, that's right.
P You weren't at home last night at 8:00, _____?
S No, I wasn't. I went for a walk.
P But you don't have any witnesses, *do you*?
S Yes, I do. My brother was with me.
P Your brother wasn't with you, *was he*?
S How do you know?
P Because he was at the police station. We arrested him last night.

b **7.10** Listen and repeat. Copy the rhythm and intonation.

c ○ **Communication** *Just checking A p.118 B p.121.* Role-play a police interview.

4 GRAMMAR indirect questions

a Do you like reading detective stories or watching detective movies / TV shows? Who are your favorite detectives?

b **7.11** Listen to and read an extract from a Donna Leon detective novel. Which questions does Inspector Brunetti ask? <u>Underline</u> them.

c How do Inspector Brunetti and Signora Trevisan behave during the interview? Do you think Signora Trevisan killed her husband?

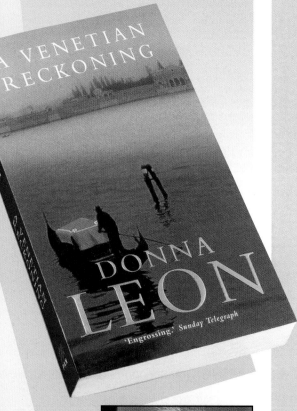

Carlo Trevisan, an important international lawyer, is found dead on a train in Italy. Inspector Brunetti goes to interview Signora Trevisan, the wife of the victim.

Donna Leon is an American crime writer whose detective novels are all set in Venice. Her detective is Inspector Brunetti.

"I'd like to ask you some questions about your personal life, signora."

"Our personal life?" she repeated, as though she had never heard of such a thing.

When he didn't answer this, she nodded, signaling him to begin.

"Could you tell me how long you and your husband were married?"

"Nineteen years."

"How many children do you have, signora?"

"Two. Claudio is seventeen and Francesca is fifteen."

"Are they in school in Venice, signora?"

She looked up at him sharply when he asked this.

"Why do you want to know that?"

"My own daughter, Chiara, is fourteen, so perhaps they know each other," he answered, and smiled to show what an innocent question it had been.

"Claudio is in school in Switzerland, but Francesca is here. With us. I mean," she corrected, rubbing a hand across her forehead, "with me."

"Would you say yours was a happy marriage, signora?"

"Yes," she answered immediately, far faster than Brunetti would have answered the same question, though he would have given the same response. She did not, however, elaborate.

"Could you tell me if your husband had any particularly close friends or business associates?"

She looked up at this question, then as quickly down again at her hands. "Our closest friends are the Nogares, Mirto and Graziella. He's an architect who lives in Campo Sant'Angelo. They're Francesca's godparents. I don't know about business associates: you'll have to ask Ubaldo."

"Other friends, signora?"

"Why do you need to know all this?" she said, voice rising sharply.

"I'd like to learn more about your husband, signora."

"Why?" The question leaped from her, almost as if beyond her volition.

"Until I understand what sort of man he was, I can't understand why this has happened."

"A robbery?" she asked, voice just short of sarcasm.

"It wasn't robbery. Whoever killed him intended to do it."

102

From *A Venetian Reckoning* by Donna Leon

d Look at the four questions. How are 1 and 3 different from 2 and 4?

1 Could you tell me how long you and your husband were married?

2 How many children do you have, signora?

3 Could you tell me if your husband had any particularly close friends or business associates?

4 Why do you need to know all this?

e ⬤ **p.142 Grammar Bank 7B.** Read the rules for indirect questions, and do exercise **b**.

f 〔7.12〕 Listen to six direct questions and turn them into indirect ones.

1 Could you tell me _____?

2 Do you know if _____?

3 Could you tell me _____?

4 Can you tell me if _____?

5 Can you tell me _____?

6 Do you know if _____?

g Imagine you are interviewing somebody on the street. Ask your partner these questions. Begin *Can / Could you tell me…* Then change roles.

What's your name?
Where do you live?
What do you do?
Do you have a TV?
How much TV do you watch a week?

5 VOCABULARY   compound nouns

a Make compound nouns using a word from each box.

~~detective~~		mystery	
	murder		movie
horror		~~novel~~	
	crime		writer
police		station	
	police		inspector

b 〔7.13〕 Compare in pairs. Then listen and check. Which word is stressed in compound nouns?

c In pairs, try to answer all the questions in two minutes with a compound noun from Files 1–6.

Compound noun race

1 **What do you use to pay for things you buy on the Internet?**

2 **Where do you catch a train?**

3 **What does Steven Spielberg do?**

4 **What do you call the time of day when trains and buses are full?**

5 **What should you put on when you get into a car?**

6 **What do you call a big store that sells many different things?**

7 **Where do you play tennis?**

8 **What do you need before you can get on a plane?**

9 **What's the opposite of a private school?**

10 **Where do you buy gas?**

11 **What do you call the noise a phone makes?**

12 **What do you call a long line of cars that can't move?**

7 C

G phrasal verbs
V television, phrasal verbs
P review of sounds, linking

Turn it off

1 VOCABULARY & SPEAKING television

a Look at the **bold** words in the TV survey below. What do they mean? How do you pronounce them?

b In pairs, ask and answer the questions.

Your TV habits

How many TVs are there in your house? Where are they?

Do you know anybody who doesn't have a TV?

How many **channels** do you have?

Do you have **satellite** or **cable TV**?

Which channels do you watch the most?

Do you watch any foreign channels? Which one(s)?

How much TV do you watch during the week / on weekends?

Who watches most / least TV in your family?

What kind of TV programs do you like? What kind do you hate? Write L (like), H (hate), or DM (don't mind) in the boxes.

☐ **quiz shows**
☐ **reality shows**
☐ **comedy shows**
☐ **talk shows**
☐ **soap operas**
☐ **the news**

☐ **cartoons**
☐ **documentaries**
☐ **drama series**
☐ **movies**
☐ **sports programs**

Do you think there are too many **ads** on TV in your country?

Do you think TV programs in your country are getting better or worse? Why?

2 GRAMMAR phrasal verbs

a How many phrasal verbs can you think of connected with television?

b Read the three stories on p. 109 and complete them with phrasal verbs A–G.

> A look out
> B sold out
> C picked up
> D turn off
> E looking forward to
> F find out
> G passed away

c Read the texts again. Then cover them and look at the pictures. In pairs, tell the stories from memory.

d Now look at how *look forward to* and *turn off* appear in a dictionary. How does the dictionary show you if the verb and the particle (e.g., *off*, *on*, etc.) can be separated or not?

> **look forward to sth** to wait with pleasure for something to happen
>
> **turn sth off** to stop the flow of electricity, water, etc., by moving a switch, tap, etc.

e ⊙ **p.142 Grammar Bank 7C.** Read the rules and do the exercises.

TV-B-Gone

An American, Mitch Altman, went to a restaurant with some friends. He was ¹_____ some lively conversation. But instead of talking, his friends spent the whole time watching a TV in the corner. This suddenly gave Mitch an idea for a new gadget. He invented TV-B-Gone, a remote control that allows you to ²_____ any TV within 17 meters of where you are. When the gadgets were first marketed on the Internet, they ³_____ after the first two days.

Dead or alive?

The BBC was planning to make a program about the Bob Marley hit song *No Woman No Cry*. A researcher contacted the Bob Marley Foundation to ⁴_____ if they could interview him during the summer. The researcher added that filming was scheduled for June, July, and August but "our schedule is flexible." Unfortunately, Marley's schedule was not: he had died in 1981. A friend of the Marley family told the *Daily Mirror*: "We didn't think there was anyone on the planet who didn't realize Bob ⁵_____ years ago." A BBC spokesman admitted: "We're very embarrassed."

Can I speak to Bob Marley, please?

BOB MARLEY FOUNDATION

Furious soccer fan forgiven

Two people were nearly killed when a Romanian soccer fan threw his TV out of the window. Ghita Axinte said he was so angry with the national side when they lost their World Cup qualifier against the Czech Republic 1-0 that he ⁶_____ the TV _____ and threw it out of the window.

Radu Demergiu, his neighbor, was discussing the game on the balcony below with his brother. Suddenly his brother shouted, "⁷_____!" and the TV set crashed onto the balcony, almost hitting the two of them. But Radu is not going to take any action against his neighbor. "At first I was angry with him, he could have killed us. But when he told me he had been watching soccer, I completely understood. We had also been watching it and I was furious with the Romanian team, too."

3 PRONUNCIATION   review of sounds, linking

a Look at the pink letters in each sentence. What's the sound? Write the sound word and symbol.

	Sound word	Symbol
1 We can't go. It's sold out.	_phone_	oʊ
2 I'd like to find out about train times.	_____	___
3 I'm looking forward to Saturday morning.	_____	___
4 I was talking to my mother but we were cut off.	_____	___
5 In the future, remember to turn off the kitchen lights.	_____	___
6 Philip's not old enough to take care of a five-year-old.	_____	___
7 We put on our seat belts before the flight took off.	_____	___
8 They don't get along with each other.	_____	___

b ⟳ **p.157 Sound Bank**. Check your answers.

c ⟨7.14⟩ Listen and repeat sentences 1–8.

d ⟨7.15⟩ You're going to hear some phrases where three words are linked together. Listen and write down the missing words.

1 There's a towel on the floor. _____ _____ _____.
2 I hate this music. _____ _____ _____.
3 Your jacket's on the chair. _____ _____ _____.
4 You don't need a coat. _____ _____ _____.
5 I can't hear the TV. _____ _____ _____.
6 Coffee is bad for you. _____ _____ _____.

4 VOCABULARY & SPEAKING

a ⟳ **p.155 Vocabulary Bank** *Phrasal verbs.*

b Choose and check (✓) six questions to ask your partner.

1 Is there anything you're trying to **give up** right now?

2 How do you feel when a plane **takes off**?

3 Are you going to **keep on** studying English next year?

4 What are you most **looking forward to** right now?

5 Have you ever tried to go to a concert but it was **sold out**?

6 Where and when do you **turn off** your cell phone?

7 Have you ever **thrown away** something really important by mistake?

8 How often do you **go away** for the weekend?

9 Would you like to **set up** your own business?

10 Are people in your country trying to **slow down** and work less?

c Ask and answer the questions. Ask for more information and try to keep each "mini-conversation" going for as long as possible.

Couple turns on after 37 years without power

An **elderly couple** is going to trade candles for light bulbs after 37 years without electricity at their home in Suffolk, England. Pat Payne, 74, and his wife Margaret, 72, brought up their large family in their farmhouse, without any modern appliances.

Their children left home years ago but now one of them has moved back and is paying £19,000 (almost $40,000) to have electricity put in the 200-year-old house next month. Mrs. Payne said that she was looking forward to "being modernized" but does not feel that she has missed much by not having electricity.

"It would have been nice to have been able to do the ironing or to have a vacuum cleaner instead of having to sweep the floor, but we got by," she said. "I think our children are more excited about us getting electricity than we are."

The couple has mostly lived off the land. Mr. Payne, a former farm laborer, grows vegetables in the garden. Without a refrigerator or freezer in the three-bedroom house, milk is delivered every other day and fresh meat is bought as needed. Water comes from a well.

Mrs. Payne used to wash clothes by hand, and with nine children that was a lot of clothes, but she believes that not having electricity may have been a good thing for her children while they were growing up. "Instead of watching television, they played together and used to make up games or read books," she said.

The life also suited her and her husband. "Neither of us has ever been seriously ill and we rarely get a cough or cold," Mrs. Payne said. "With our fresh vegetables and not having central heating, it's been a very healthy way to live." The couple has 24 grandchildren and eight great-grandchildren.

5 READING

a You're going to read an article about a couple who lived without electricity for 37 years. Which **two** of these things do you think they missed most?

central heating	an iron
electric light	a TV
a freezer	a vacuum cleaner
a refrigerator	a washing machine

b Read the article once. Were you right? Do they regret living without electricity for so long?

c Read the article again. Then cover the text and say what the following numbers refer to.

37   74 and 72   19,000   200   3   9   24   8

d Answer the questions in pairs.

1 Do any of their children still live with them?
2 How does Mrs. Payne feel about the house being modernized?
3 Was it a big problem for her not to have an iron or a vacuum cleaner?
4 Where did they get most of their food from?
5 Why does Mrs. Payne think that not having electricity was good for the children?
6 How was it good for her and her husband?

e Match the highlighted phrasal verbs with their definitions. Write the base forms in the chart.

Phrasal verbs	Meaning
1 _____ _____	to develop into an adult
2 _____ _____	to manage to live or do something with difficulty
3 _____ sth _____	to install something in your house, e.g., central heating
4 _____ _____	to return to live in a place where you lived before
5 _____ sth _____	to invent
6 _____ _____ sb/sth	to depend on sb / sth in order to live
7 _____ sb _____	take care of a child until he / she is an adult

6 LISTENING

a **7.16** Listen to four people answering the question "If you had to live without electricity for a week, what two things would you miss most?" Write the two answers for each person.

Cindy   1 _____   2 _____
Why? _____

Andy   1 _____   2 _____
Why? _____

Julia   1 _____   2 _____
Why? _____

Tyler   1 _____   2 _____
Why? _____

b Listen again and write their reasons.

c In pairs, say what **two** things *you* would miss and why.

APOLOGIZING, GIVING EXCUSES

a **7.17** Cover the conversation. Who does Allie apologize to? Why?

b Read the conversation. In pairs, what do you think the missing words are? **Don't write them in yet.**

Mark	Mark Ryder.
Allie	Mark, can you come in?
Mark	Sure.
Allie	Thanks for the sales report.
Mark	I think there's something more important to talk about right now.
Allie	What do you mean?
Mark	That message you sent me. You hit "reply to all." You sent it to everyone in the office.
Allie	Oh no. You're joking. Oh, Mark. I'm _so_ sorry. I did it without _thinking_.
Mark	It's _alright_, Allie. It's an easy mistake to make.
Allie	How could I be so _stupid_? I just wasn't _concentrating_
Mark	Allie...
Allie	I'm _really_ sorry.
Mark	Don't _worry_ about it. It doesn't _matter_. But I think we should talk to the others.
Allie	Yes, you're right. I'll do it. It was my _fault_.
Allie	Listen, everybody. I just want to say that I'm _terribly_ sorry. I haven't been honest with you. Uh, we... Mark and I...
Nicole	That's OK, Allie. We had already guessed. It wasn't really a surprise.

c Listen again and complete the conversation.

d **7.18** Listen and repeat the highlighted phrases from the dialogue. Copy the rhythm.

e Look at the highlighted phrases in the conversation. Put them in the right place in the chart.

Apologizing	Admitting responsibility/ Explaining	Responding to an apology
I'm so sorry _Concentrated_	_I did it without thinking._ _concentrated_	_It's all right_ _I'm really sorry_

f ⟳ **Communication** *I'm so sorry! A p.118 B p.121.*

SOCIAL ENGLISH   A walk by the Seine

a **7.19** Listen. How does the story end?

b Listen again and answer the questions.

1 According to Allie, how did the people in the office discover their secret? _No Blanchu_
2 Does Mark agree with her?
3 Is Mark sorry everybody knows? Why (not)? _His not Blame Blame_
4 Why doesn't Allie hear what Mark's saying? _Blame him_
5 What's the last thing Mark asks Allie to do? _Married Him_

c **7.20** Complete the USEFUL PHRASES. Listen and check.

d Listen again and repeat the phrases. How do you say them in your language?

USEFUL PHRASES

So if it w_asn't_ me, it must have been you.
You're h_opeless_ (at keeping secrets)!
Don't b_laim_ me.
But it's now or n_ever_.
I didn't hear a w_ord_ you said.
Can you c_onfirm_ that (in an e-mail)?

a Read an article for a student magazine about the advantages and disadvantages of living without a TV. The computer has found <u>ten mistakes</u> (grammar, punctuation, or spelling). Can you correct them?

Living without a TV

ALMOST every family today ¹<u>have</u> a TV, in fact probably more than one, and people everywhere spend hours watching it. But a few families choose to live without a TV because they think there are advantages.

The first advantage is that families spend more time ²<u>talk</u> to each other. Second, they spend more time doing more creative things like reading or painting. Third, they spend more time outdoors, and are usually in ³<u>gooder shape</u>.

On the other hand, there are also disadvantages. For example, children who don't have a TV may feel ⁴<u>differents</u> from ⁵<u>there</u> school friends, and often won't know what they are talking about. Also it is not true that all TV ⁶<u>programes</u> are bad. There are also good ones, like ⁷<u>documentarys</u>. People who live without a TV may know less about ⁸<u>whats</u> happening in the world.

In conclusion, ⁹<u>althought</u> living without a TV has some advantages, I think today it's unrealistic and that we should just try to turn the TV ¹⁰<u>out</u> when there's nothing good on.

b Read the article again. Then cover it and in pairs answer the questions from memory.

   1 What are the three advantages of life without a TV?

   2 What are the two disadvantages?

   3 Is the writer for or against having a TV?

c You are going to write a similar article about cell phones. First, with a partner, make a list of the advantages and disadvantages.

d Now decide which are the three biggest advantages and number them 1–3 (1 = the biggest). Do the same with the disadvantages.

Useful language: writing about advantages and disadvantages

Listing advantages

First,… Second,… Third,…

Listing disadvantages

On the other hand, there are also (some) disadvantages.

For instance,… / For example,…

Also,…

Conclusion

In conclusion / To sum up, I think…

WRITE an article called *Cell phones – a great invention?*

Begin the article with this introduction:
Almost everybody has a cell phone. But is it a great invention? I think there are both advantages and disadvantages.

Write three more paragraphs.

PLAN what you're going to write. Use the paragraph summaries below and the **Useful language** box to help you.

Paragraph 2   Write two or three advantages.
Paragraph 3   Write two or three disadvantages.
Paragraph 4   Conclusion – decide if you think cell phones are a great invention or not.

CHECK the article for mistakes (grammar , punctuation , and spelling).

GRAMMAR

a Choose a, b, or c.

1 If we hadn't gone to that meeting, we _____ each other.
   a wouldn't meet
   b hadn't met
   c wouldn't have met

2 Could you tell me what _____?
   a is your name
   b your name is
   c your name

3 Do you know _____ after lunch?
   a if the store does open
   b if opens the store
   c if the store opens

4 You aren't coming tonight, _____?
   a are you
   b aren't you
   c you aren't

5 If you've finished watching TV, _____.
   a turn off it
   b turn it off
   c turn off

b Complete the second sentence with **two words** so that it means the same as the first.

1 We were late because we got lost.
   If we _____ _____ lost, we wouldn't have been late.

2 What time did you arrive home last night?
   Could you tell me what time _____ _____ home last night?

3 Does this train stop in Buffalo?
   Do you know _____ this train _____ in Buffalo?

4 I think the movie finishes at 8:00.
   The movie finishes at 8:00, _____ _____?

5 I'm excited about our vacation.
   I'm looking _____ _____ our vacation.

`10`

VOCABULARY

a Complete with an adjective or adverb formed from the **bold** noun.

1 He's very intelligent, but _____ he's not very good-looking. **fortune**
2 He hates waiting. He's very _____. **patience**
3 Let's buy this sofa. It's definitely the most _____. **comfort**
4 I was very _____ on the exam. The questions were all on things I'd studied the night before. **luck**
5 He writes very _____ and makes a lot of spelling mistakes. **care**

b Complete the compound nouns.

1 Excuse me? Where's the nearest **police** _____?
2 **A** Do you like _____ **movies**?
   B No. I don't enjoy feeling frightened!
3 They lived in a large _____ **building**.
4 Yesterday I had to pay a $50 **parking** _____.
5 I don't like _____ **operas**. I prefer comedy shows.

c Complete the phrasal verbs.

1 _____ **out!** There's a car coming.
2 Could you **turn** the music _____? I can't hear it.
3 Could you **give** me _____ my book, please!
4 My uncle has **set** _____ a small company.
5 I always feel nervous when planes _____ **off**.
6 _____ **down!** You're walking much too fast.
7 Do you _____ **along well with** your boss?
8 If you **keep** _____ watching TV, you'll get square eyes.
9 My grandmother **brought** _____ eight children without any help.
10 They _____ **up** last month, and now she has a new boyfriend.

`20`

PRONUNCIATION

a Underline the word with a different sound.

1	(↑)	lucky	comfortable	plug in	put on
2	(cat)	patient	traffic jam	ad	reality
3	(phone)	down	show	soaps	slow
4	(bird)	murder	birthday	careful	turn
5	(owl)	channel	machine	chat	watch

b Underline the stressed syllable.

impatient   comfortable   documentary   cartoons   detective

`10`

CAN YOU UNDERSTAND THIS TEXT?

The man who missed the lottery bus

YESTERDAY bus driver Dennis Hassall was behind the wheel as usual, reflecting on his fate as one of the unluckiest men in the world. Just six months earlier, he decided to **give up** playing the lottery with his 11 coworkers after four years of playing every week but winning almost nothing.

But last Saturday night, his coworkers, who had **kept on** playing, each received a check for £744,126. While they celebrated their success, Mr. Hassall worked his morning shift, driving a number 7 bus between Plymouth and Plymstock in Devon, England. He refused to talk to journalists.

The winners said they felt very sorry for Dennis, but they were not going to share the money with him. "He hasn't paid his contribution since last summer," winner Chris Robinson said. "He must be feeling pretty bad. But as far as I know, he has wished us all the best of luck." All the winners are now planning to retire. For Les Read, 53, the win couldn't have come at a better time. Two weeks ago he failed an eye test and is no longer able to drive. "If I hadn't won the lottery, I'd have been unemployed." Fellow winner Ian Crampton, 46, the man who **picked out** the six winning numbers, has been out of work for several weeks and is having chemotherapy and radiotherapy for a cancer-related illness. "Now I don't have to worry about **going back** to work," he said.

The leader of the lottery group, Dave Mallet, said, "We all feel very sorry for Dennis, but he knew the rules. It's OK if you don't pay for two weeks, but any more than that and you're out. It wouldn't be fair to the others. I haven't spoken to Dennis yet, but we will be inviting him to the party we're going to have at the social club. But I don't know if he'll **turn up**."

a Read the article and mark the sentences T (true), F (false), or DS (doesn't say).

1 Dennis stopped playing the lottery four years ago.
2 Dennis didn't celebrate with the lottery winners.
3 He gave an interview to journalists.
4 He stopped playing the lottery because he was short of money.
5 Dennis is the only person who will continue working.
6 Two of the winners had health problems.
7 Dave Mallet feels bad about what has happened to Dennis.
8 Dennis doesn't want to go to the party.

b Look at the highlighted phrasal verbs. What do they mean?

CAN YOU UNDERSTAND THESE PEOPLE?

a 🔊 **7.21** Listen and circle the correct answer, a, b, or c.

1 Had the man saved his article (on his computer)?
  a Yes. b No. c Some of it.
2 Why didn't the man wear his lucky T-shirt?
  a Because he didn't need it.
  b Because he had lost it.
  c Because he couldn't.
3 What kind of books does the woman read?
  a Several kinds. b Only science fiction. c Only detective novels.
4 Where does Jonathan say he was last night?
  a At home and at a cafe. b At home and at a store.
  c At home and at a basketball game.
5 What time do the children usually go to bed?
  a 10:00 b 9:15 c 9:30

b 🔊 **7.22** Listen and complete the missing information.

Time	Channel	Program
8:00	PBS	*Eight-legged Wonders.* A documentary film about [1] _____
8:00	ABC	*The Silent* [2] _____, a new crime series
[3] _____	ABC	*Who wants to be a millionaire?* Quiz show
10:05	[4] _____	Great Films: *Fanny and Alexander*
10:30	ABC	[5] _____ _____ _____ A tribute to Sydney Pollack

CAN YOU SAY THIS IN ENGLISH?

Can you...? Yes (✓)
☐ complete these three sentences in a logical way
  If I hadn't gone to bed so late,...
  If I had known it was your birthday,...
  I would have arrived on time if...
☐ ask your partner three polite questions and check three things you think you know about him / her
☐ talk about how much TV you watch and what kind of programs

2B Are you hungry? Yes, I'm starving! Student A

a Say your sentences to **B**. He / she must respond with the phrase in parentheses.

1 Is the water cold? *(Yes, it's freezing.)*
2 Was the movie good? *(Yes, it was great.)*
3 Were you tired after the exam? *(Yes, I was exhausted.)*
4 Is the kitchen dirty? *(Yes, it's filthy.)*
5 Is it a big house? *(Yes, it's enormous.)*
6 Was the weather bad? *(Yes, it was awful.)*

b Respond to **B**'s questions. Say *Yes, it's / I'm*, etc., + the **strong** form of the adjective which **B** used in the question. Remember to stress the **strong** adjective.

c Repeat the exercise. Try to respond as quickly as possible.

3B Who do you think they are? Students A + B

a In pairs, look at the people. You will have to match them with one of the jobs in the list below.

boxer	racecar driver	violinist	university professor	comedian

b Discuss person A with your partner.
- Eliminate the jobs you think are impossible for that person. Use *He / She can't be a…* Say why.
- Now say which jobs you think are possible. Use *He / She might be…*
- Now make a final choice for person A. Use *He / She must be…* Say why.

c Now do the same for B–E.

d Finally, check your answers on page 119.

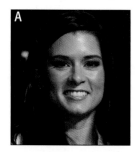
A

B

C

D

E

3C Guess the sentence Student A

a Look at sentences 1–5 and complete them with the correct form of *be able to* + a verb.

1 I've never _____ the guitar well.
2 I'm sorry I won't _____ to your party next weekend.
3 I used to _____ a little Japanese, but I can't now.
4 I love _____ in bed late on weekends.
5 Will you _____ all the work before Saturday?

b Read your sentence 1 to **B**. If it's not the same, try again until **B** tells you "That's right." Continue with 2–5.

c Now listen to **B** say sentence 6. If it's the same as your sentence 6 below, say "That's right." If not, say "Try again" until **B** gets it right. Continue with 7–10.

6 I won't **be able to see** you tonight. I'm too busy.
7 It was the rush hour, but luckily I **was able to park** near the theater.
8 They haven't **been able to find** a house yet. They're still looking.
9 It must be fantastic **to be able to speak** a lot of languages.
10 You must **be able to do** this exercise! It's very easy.

Practical English 3   How do I get there?   **Student A**

a   You are a tourist in Boston. You are at South Station. Ask **B** how to get to the places below. **B** will explain how to get to the nearest subway station or "T-stop." Draw the route on the map. Write the name of the place next to the T-stop. Then change roles.

The Science Museum
Harvard University
Boston Museum of Fine Art

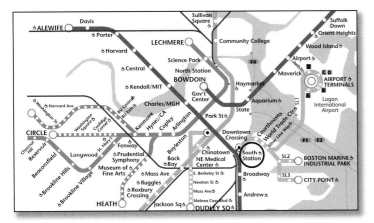

b   You live in Boston. **B** is a tourist. You are both at South Station. **B** will ask you how to get to the three places below. Look at the map to find the subway station, or "T-stop" nearest to **B**'s destination and give **B** directions.

> Excuse me. How can I get to the Science Museum?

> Take the Red Line toward Alewife. Change at Park Street and …

Paul Revere's House (nearest T-stop Haymarket – Green Line)
Boston Public Garden (nearest T-stop Arlington – Green Line)
New England Aquarium (nearest T-stop Aquarium – Blue Line)

4B   What would you do if…?   **Student A**

a   Ask **B** your questions. Put the verbs in parentheses in the simple past.

What would you do if you…?
(meet) your English teacher at a party
(find) a lot of extra money in your bank account
(get) a present from your boyfriend / girlfriend that you really didn't like
(hit) somebody's car in a parking lot
(have) to sing at a karaoke evening
(be) invited to a really good concert by somebody you didn't like
(see) your best friend's personal diary open on a table

b   Answer **B**'s questions. Ask *What about you?*

5C   Test your memory   **Student A**

a   Ask **B** these questions. See if he / she can remember the answers.

1   What's the program called? (*The Pretenders.*)
2   How many judges are there? (Three.)
3   What do the judges have to decide? (Who is pretending to be a professional.)
4   Where does Jessica work? (In her local library.)
5   How did Jessica react when the TV company called her? (She thought it was a joke and she said no.)
6   What job did she have to learn to do? (A TV reporter.)
7   What did she have to do in her final test? (A live TV interview with the secretary of education.)
8   What did she have to learn to do? (How to interview people / look more confident / speak clearly.)
9   How was she feeling before she started? (Nervous and terrified of being on TV.)

b   Answer **B**'s questions. Who has the best memory?

Practical English 5 What do you think?
Student A

a   Ask **B** question number 1. Then say if you agree or disagree. If you disagree, say why. Use *I don't agree,…, Personally, I think…,* etc.

b   Now answer **B**'s first question. Use *Personally, I think* or *In my opinion.* Say why.

c   Continue taking turns asking questions and giving your opinions.

1   Which do you think is easier, speaking English or writing it?
2   Do you think that school vacations are too long?
3   What do you think is the best sport for a young person to take up?
4   Do you think that life in your country is faster or slower than it used to be?
5   Who do you think are safer drivers, women or men?

Communication

6A I want to speak to the manager
Student A

a Look at the situations and role-play the conversations. Spend a few minutes preparing what you are going to say.

> **1** You're a **customer**. You bought something on sale at a clothing store yesterday (decide what) and there's a problem (decide what). Go back to the store. **B** is the salesperson. You'd like to exchange it for another identical one. If you can't, you'd like a refund. If you aren't satisfied, ask the salesperson to call the manager.
>
> **You** start. *Excuse me. I bought...*

> **2** You're the **manager** of a restaurant. Your normal chef is off this week, and you have a temporary chef who is not very good. One of the waiters has had a problem with a customer, who would like to speak to you. When customers complain you usually offer them a free drink or coffee. If it's absolutely necessary, you might give a 10% discount on their check, but you would prefer not to. **B** is the customer.
>
> **B** will start.

6C Relatives quiz Student A

a Complete the questions to describe the **bold** word. Begin with *who, which, that, whose, where* (or no relative pronoun when there is a new subject).

1 **selfish**
   What do you call a person...?
2 **neighbors**
   What do you call the people...?
3 **a private school**
   What do you call a school...?
4 **a helmet**
   What do you call the thing...?
5 **a boss**
   What do you call the person...?
6 **traffic light**
   What do you call the thing...?
7 **the bakery**
   What do you call the place...?
8 **a salesperson**
   What do you call a person...?

b Ask **B** the questions.

c Answer **B**'s questions.

7A Guess the conditional Student A

a Look at sentences 1–5 and think of the missing verb. Remember ➕ = affirmative verb, ➖ = negative verb.

1 If it had been cheaper, I _____ it. ➕
2 If I _____ that it was your birthday, I would have made a cake. ➕
3 I _____ so angry if you had told me the truth. ➖
4 I would have written to you if I _____ your e-mail address. ➖
5 If you _____ to me, you wouldn't have married him. ➕

b Read your sentence 1 to **B**. If it's not the same, try again until **B** tells you "That's right." Then write it in. Continue with 2–5.

c Listen to **B** say sentence 6. If it's the same as 6 below, say "That's right." If not, say "Try again" until **B** gets it right. Continue with 7–10.

6 If I had listened to that CD first, I **wouldn't have bought** it.
7 I would have paid for the meal today if I **hadn't paid** last time!
8 If you **had put** the milk in the fridge, it wouldn't have gone bad.
9 I would have gone with you last night if I **hadn't seen** the movie before.
10 If I'd recognized him, I **would have said** hello.

7B Just checking Student A

a You are a police officer. **B** is a suspect. Ask **B** the questions below but **don't write anything down**. Try to remember **B**'s answers.

What's your name?	What do you do?
Where do you live?	What car do you drive?
How old are you?	How long have you lived in this town?
Where were you born?	What did you do last night?
Are you married?	Where were you this morning at 7:00?

b Now check the information with **B** using a tag question.

> Your name's Angela, isn't it?

> You live in Seattle, don't you?

c Change roles. Now you are the suspect and **B** is the detective. Answer his / her questions. You can invent the information if you want to.

d **A** will now check the information he / she has. Just say, "Yes, that's right" or "No, that's wrong." Correct the wrong information.

Practical English 7 I'm so sorry! Student A

a **B** has done some very irritating things! You are going to tell **B** what he / she has done. **B** will apologize and make an excuse.

You forgot my birthday!	You took my dictionary home last night!
You've broken my glasses!	You didn't answer your cell phone
You've just eaten the last cookie!	when I called you last night!

b Now **B** is going to tell you about some things you've done. Apologize and make an excuse.

2B Are you hungry? Yes, I'm starving! **Student B**

a Respond to **A**'s questions. Say *Yes, it's / I'm* etc. + the **strong** form of the adjective which **A** used in the question. Remember to <u>stress</u> the **strong** adjective.

b Say your sentences to **A**. He / she must respond with the phrase in parentheses.

1 Are you afraid of flying? *(Yes, I'm terrified.)*
2 Is the soup hot? *(Yes, it's boiling.)*
3 Was the teacher angry? *(Yes, he / she was furious.)*
4 Is the bedroom small? *(Yes, it's tiny.)*
5 Are the children hungry? *(Yes, they're starving.)*
6 Is the chocolate cake good? *(Yes, it's delicious.)*

c Repeat the exercise. Try to respond as quickly as possible.

Practical English 2 Requests **Students A + B**

a Look at the verbs below. Choose **one** thing you would like someone to do for you.

take care of (my children, my dog, my cat, etc.)
lend me (some money, a car, a book, etc.)
give me a ride (home, downtown, etc.)
help me (with my homework, to paint my apartment, etc.)

b Ask as many other students as possible. Be polite, and explain why you want the favor. How many people agree to help you?

3C Guess the sentence **Student B**

a Look at sentences 6–10 and complete them with the correct form of *be able to* + a verb.

6 I won't _____ you tonight. I'm too busy.
7 It was the rush hour, but luckily I _____ near the theater.
8 They haven't _____ a house yet. They're still looking.
9 It must be fantastic _____ a lot of languages.
10 You must _____ this exercise! It's very easy.

b Listen to **A** say sentence 1. If it's the same as your sentence 1 below, say "That's right." If not, say "Try again" until **A** gets it right. Continue with 2–5.

1 I've never **been able to play** the guitar well.
2 I'm sorry I won't **be able to go** to your party next weekend.
3 I used to **be able to understand** a little Japanese, but I can't now.
4 I love **being able to stay** in bed late on weekends.
5 Will you **be able to finish** all the work before Saturday?

c Now read your sentence 6 to **A**. If it's not the same, try again until **A** tells you "That's right." Continue with 7–10.

Answers to communication 3B on page 116.
A Danica Patrick (racecar driver)
B Jon Stewart (comedian)
C Gunter Weller (university professor)
D Leila Ali (boxer, Mohammad Ali's daughter)
E Nigel Kennedy (violinist)

119

Communication

Practical English 3 How do I get there? **Student B**

a You live in Boston. **A** is a tourist. You are both at South Station. **A** will ask you how to get to the three places below. Look at the map to find the subway station, or "T-stop" nearest to **A**'s destination and give **A** directions.

The Science Museum (nearest T-stop Science Park – Green Line)

Harvard University (nearest T-stop Harvard – Red Line)

Boston Museum of Fine Art (nearest T-stop Museum of Fine Arts – Green Line)

> Excuse me. How can I get to the Science Museum?

> Take the Red Line toward Alewife. Change at Park Street …

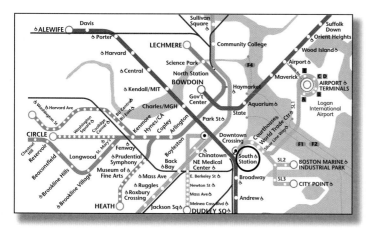

b You are a tourist. You are at South Station. Ask **A** how to get to the places below. **A** will explain how to get to the nearest subway station or "T-stop." Draw the route on the map. Write the name of the place next to the T-stop. Then change roles.

Paul Revere's House

Boston Public Garden

New England Aquarium

4B What would you do if...? **Student B**

a Answer **A**'s questions. Ask *What about you?*

b Ask **A** your questions. Put the verbs in parentheses in the simple past.

What would you do if you...?

(have) an exam the next day and somebody offered to sell you the answers

(be) offered a job in Australia

(wake up) and (see) a snake in your bedroom

(meet) your girlfriend / boyfriend in the street with an ex-boyfriend / girlfriend

(get) too much change from a salesperson

(see) somebody stealing something in a store

(borrow) a friend's car and broke one of the headlights

5C Test your memory **Student B**

a Answer **A**'s questions.

b Now ask **A** these questions. See if he / she can remember the answers. Who has the best memory?

1 How long do the contestants have to learn to do the new job? (One month.)

2 What does the contestant have to do at the end of the month? (Take a test – they do the new job with three real professionals.)

3 How old is Jessica? (26.)

4 What did Jessica study at the university? (English Literature.)

5 Why did she agree to be on the program? (Her friends and family persuaded her.)

7 What was Jessica like before the program? (Quiet and shy.)

8 Who were her teachers? (A political journalist and a politician.)

9 What did she have to learn about? (The world of politics.)

Practical English 5 What do you think?
Student B

a Answer **A**'s first question. Use *Personally, I think* or *In my opinion*. Say why.

b Ask **A** your question number 1. Then say if you agree or disagree with **A**. If you disagree, Use *I don't agree,…, Personally, I think…*, etc.

c Continue taking turns asking questions and giving your opinions.

1 Do you think it is easier to learn to drive or to learn to swim?

2 Do you think it's better to be an only child or have brothers or sisters?

3 Do you think that men are better cooks than women?

4 Which do you think is more dangerous, traveling by plane or traveling by car?

5 Do you think that it is a waste of money to buy designer clothes?

Answers to 2a on page 94.	
1 Bill Gates	5 Jackie Onassis
2 Nelson Mandela	6 Martina Navratilova
3 Madonna	7 George Clooney
4 Giorgio Armani	8 Maria Callas

6A I want to speak to the manager Student B

a Look at the situations and role-play the conversations. Spend a few minutes preparing what you are going to say.

1 You're a **salesperson** in a clothing store. **A** is going to come to you with a problem with something he / she bought on sale yesterday. You can't exchange it for an identical one because there are no more in his / her size.
Try to persuade **A** to exchange it for something else because you don't usually give refunds on sale items.

A will start.

2 You're a **customer** in a restaurant. The waiter has just brought your meal and something is wrong with it (what is wrong with it?). You complained to the waiter but he/she didn't solve the problem. You have asked to speak to the manager.
Try to get at least a 50% discount on your meal.
A is the manager.

You start. Good evening. Are you the manager?

6C Relatives quiz Student B

a Complete the questions to describe the **bold** word. Begin with *who, which, that, whose, where* (or no relative pronoun when there is a new subject).

1 **shy**
What do you call a person…?
2 **a referee**
What do you call the person…?
3 **a classroom**
What's the name of the place…?
4 **a (shopping) cart**
What do you call the thing…?
5 **a dentist**
What do you call a person…?
6 **a receipt**
What do you call the piece of paper…?
7 **a taxi stand**
What do you call the place…?
8 **a close friend**
What do you call a person…?

b Answer **A**'s questions.

c Ask **A** your questions.

7A Guess the conditional Student B

a Look at sentences 6–10 and think of the missing verb. Remember ⊞ = affirmative verb, ⊟ = negative verb.

6 If I had listened to that CD first, I _____ it. ⊟
7 I would have paid for the meal today if I _____ last time! ⊟
8 If you _____ the milk in the fridge, it wouldn't have gone bad. ⊞
9 I would have gone with you last night if I _____ the movie before. ⊟
10 If I'd recognized him, I _____ hello. ⊞

b Listen to **A** say sentence 1. If it's the same as 1 below, say "That's right." If not, say "Try again" until **A** gets it right. Continue with 2–5.

1 If it had been cheaper, I **would have bought** it.
2 If I **had known** that it was your birthday, I would have made a cake.
3 I **wouldn't have been** so angry if you had told me the truth.
4 I would have written to you if I **hadn't lost** your e-mail address.
5 If you **had listened** to me, you wouldn't have married him.

c Read your sentence 6 to **A**. If it's not the same, try again until **A** tells you "That's right." Then write it in. Continue with 7–10.

7B Just checking Student B

a You are a suspect. **A** is a police officer. Answer **A**'s questions. You can invent the information if you want to.

b **A** will now check the information he / she has. Just say, "Yes, that's right" or "No, that's wrong." Correct the wrong information.

c Change roles. Now you are a police officer and **A** is a suspect. Ask **A** the questions below but **don't write anything down**. Try to remember **A**'s answers.

What's your name?	What do you do?
Where do you live?	What car do you drive?
How old are you?	How long have you lived in this town?
Where were you born?	What did you do last night?
Are you married?	Where were you this morning at 7:00?

d Now check the information with **A** using a tag question.
Your name's Angela, isn't it?   You live in Seattle, don't you?

Practical English 7 I'm so sorry! Student B

a **A** is going to tell you about some things you've done. Apologize and make an excuse.

b **A** has done some very irritating things! Tell **A** what he / she has done. **A** will apologize and make an excuse.

You didn't pay me back the money I lent you!
You haven't introduced me to your friend!
You're sitting in my seat!
You finished all the milk in the refrigerator!
You didn't reply to my e-mail yesterday!

Audioscripts

🔊 1.1

Interviewer Rumiko, what do you eat on a typical day?

Rumiko I don't usually have breakfast because I can't get up early enough to eat! I normally just buy coffee and drink it in the office. I usually have lunch in a restaurant near the office with people from work. When I was younger, I used to go to fast-food restaurants and have pizza, or fried chicken and French fries. Now I prefer eating something healthier, so I go to sushi restaurants or restaurants that serve organic food. And for dinner I eat out a lot, too.

Interviewer Do you ever cook?

Rumiko Well, I like to cook, but I work very late every day and also my kitchen's too small. My boyfriend's a better cook anyway.

Interviewer Do you ever eat unhealthy food?

Rumiko Well, I don't eat a lot of sweet things but I drink a lot of coffee every day. I think I'm addicted to caffeine.

Interviewer Are you trying to cut down on anything right now?

Rumiko No. I eat healthily and I exercise regularly, so I don't think I need to cut down on food.

Interviewer Are people's diets in your country getting better or worse?

Rumiko Oh, probably worse. I think the diet in Japan today is much more westernized than before and that's why some people are getting fatter. But personally, I like the fact that there are more different kinds of food and restaurants now. I enjoy the variety, it makes eating out much more fun.

🔊 1.5

Interviewer Kevin, why did you decide to open a restaurant in Chile?

Kevin I'd always wanted to have my own restaurant. I'd visited Chile as a tourist and loved it, and I thought it would be a good place because Chileans are pretty open to new things, new ideas. So I opened Frederick's.

Interviewer Why did you call the restaurant Frederick's?

Kevin Because Frederick's my father's name. It's my middle name, too.

Interviewer What kind of food do you serve?

Kevin Mainly international dishes like pasta, steak and French fries, risotto – but we also serve several English dishes as well.

Interviewer Were Chilean people surprised when they heard that an English chef was going to open a restaurant here?

Kevin Yes, they were – very! I think… people don't usually expect the English to be good cooks.

Interviewer Is your chef English?

Kevin No, he's Chilean – but I've taught him to make some English dishes.

Interviewer What kind of English dishes do you have on your menu?

Kevin Well, we're open in the morning, so we serve traditional English breakfasts, eggs, sausage, toast and so on, and then we have a lot of English desserts at lunchtime, for example, trifle – that's a popular English dessert made with fruit and cake and cream.

Interviewer Are the English dishes popular?

Kevin Yes, especially the desserts and cakes. I think people here in Chile have a very sweet tooth.

Interviewer I hear that you've met a lot of famous people in your career as a chef.

Kevin Yes, I used to cater for the tennis tournament at Wimbledon, and I've also worked for the royal family. I've met a lot of famous people who are very interesting, from every point of view.

Interviewer You said earlier that your chef was a man. Do you have any women working in your kitchen?

Kevin Yes, one, but the rest are all men. In fact, I think that's typical all over the world – there are far more men than women in restaurant kitchens.

Interviewer Why do you think that is?

Kevin I think there are a lot of reasons. The most important reason is probably the unsocial hours. Most women don't want a job where you have to work until late at night. Then there's the atmosphere. Women don't like being shouted at, and there's a lot of shouting in restaurant kitchens. It's also usually extremely hot, and I think women don't like that either.

Interviewer Do you think you'll stay in Chile?

Kevin Yes! I love Chile and its people, and the climate is perfect. The language is the most difficult thing for me, but the Chileans are very understanding.

🔊 1.6

Interviewer What was the most exciting game you refereed?

Juan Antonio It's difficult to choose one game as the most exciting. I remember some of the Real Madrid–Barcelona games, for example, the first one I ever refereed. The atmosphere in the stadium was great. But really it's impossible to pick just one – there have been so many.

Interviewer Who was the best player you ever saw?

Juan Antonio During my career, I've met many great players. It's very difficult to say who was the best, but there's one player who stands out for me, not just for being a great soccer player but also for being a great human being, and that was the Brazilian international player Mauro Silva, who used to play here in Spain.

Interviewer What was the worst experience you ever had as a referee?

Juan Antonio The worst? Well, that was something that happened very early in my career. I was only 16 and I was refereeing a game and the home team lost. After the game, I was attacked and injured by the players of the home team and by the spectators. After all these years I can still remember a mother who had a little baby in her arms and was trying to hit me. She was so angry with me that she nearly dropped her baby. That was my worst moment, and it nearly made me stop being a referee.

Interviewer Do you think that there's more cheating in soccer than in the past?

Juan Antonio Yes, I think so.

Interviewer Why?

Juan Antonio I think it's because there's so much money in soccer today that it has become much more important to win. Also, the game is much faster than it used to be so it's more difficult for referees to detect cheating.

Interviewer How do soccer players cheat?

Juan Antonio Oh, there are many ways, but for me the worst is what we call "simulation." Players pretend there has been a foul when there has been no foul at all! For example, sometimes a player falls down and says someone pushed him or hit him when, in fact, nobody has touched him. In my opinion, when a player does this, he's cheating not only the referee and the players of the other team, but also the spectators. The spectators pay money to see a fair contest, not to watch people cheat!

Interviewer What's the most difficult thing about being a referee?

Juan Antonio Ah, the most difficult thing is to make the right decisions during a game. It's difficult because you have to make decisions when everything's happening so quickly – soccer today is *very* fast. Also, important decisions often depend on the referee's *interpretation* of the rules. Things aren't black and white. And of course making decisions would be much easier if players didn't cheat.

Interviewer So, in your opinion fair play doesn't exist any more.

Juan Antonio No, I didn't mean that. I think fair play does exist – the players who cheat are still the exceptions.

🔊 1.9

1 **A** So what are you going to do next year, dear? Are you going to go to college?
  B No, Gran. I've already told you three times. I'm not going to college. I'm going to look for a job. I want to earn some money.
  A All right, dear, you don't need to shout. I'm not deaf. What time is it now?
  B Ten after five. I'll make you a cup of tea.
  A Oh yes, dear, that'd be very nice.
2 **A** See you tomorrow, then.
  B Hold on a minute. Where are you going?
  A Out. It's Friday night, remember?
  B What time are you coming back?
  A I'm not coming back. I'm staying at Mom's tonight.
  B I think you need a hat. It's going to be cold tonight.
  A Dad! Nobody wears hats any more! Bye!
3 **A** Can I use your car tonight?
  B No.
  A Why not?
  B You'll crash it again.
  A I won't. I'll be really careful. I'll drive slowly. I promise.
  B OK. Here you are. But be careful.
  A Thanks. See you later.

🔊 1.11

Announcer It's eight o'clock and time for *Breakfast Time*.

Presenter Good morning, everyone. Our guest this morning is the writer Norah Levy. Norah's here this week promoting her new book *We are family*, which is all about how our position in the family affects our personality. Welcome, Norah.

Norah Thank you.

Presenter Now is this really true, Norah? That our position in the family affects our personality?

Norah Sure. OK, other factors can influence your personality too, but your position in the family is definitely one of the strongest.

Presenter So tell us a little about the oldest child in the family – the firstborn.

Norah Well, the oldest children get maximum attention from their parents and the result is that they're usually pretty self-confident people. They make good leaders. Did you know that fifty-two percent of the US presidents were firstborn children? Firstborn children are often ambitious and they're more likely to go to college than their brothers or sisters. They often get the top jobs, too. Oldest children are often responsible people because they often have to take care of their younger brothers or sisters. The downside of this is that sometimes this means that when they're older they worry a lot about things. They can also be a little bossy, or even aggressive, especially when they don't get what they want.

Presenter Well, what about the middle child?

Norah Well, middle children are usually independent and competitive.

Presenter Competitive?

Norah Yes, because they have to fight with their brothers and sisters for their parents' attention. And they're usually sociable. They like being with people, probably because they've always had other children to play with. However, on the negative side, middle children are often jealous of their brothers and sisters, and they can be moody.

Presenter And the youngest children?

Norah If you're the youngest in a family, you'll probably be very charming, very affectionate, and a pretty relaxed person. This is because parents are usually more relaxed when they have their last child. On the other hand, youngest children are often a little lazy. This is because they always have their older brothers and sisters to help them. And they can be pretty manipulative. They use their charm to get what they want.

Presenter OK, that's all very interesting. Now, I'm an only child. People often have the idea that only children like me are spoiled. Is that true?

Norah Well, it's true in many cases! Only children are the only ones. They don't have to share with anyone, so they're often spoiled by their parents and their grandparents. As a result, they can be somewhat selfish. They think of themselves more than of other people.

Presenter OK. Well, that sounds like a good description of me! Is there any good news?

Norah Yes, there is. On the positive side, only children are usually very organized and responsible, and they can be very imaginative, too.

Presenter Well, thank you, Norah, and good luck with the book. And now it's time for the news headlines…

1.13

My name's Allie Gray and I'm from Cambridge in England. I met Mark about a year ago. He's from San Francisco. We both work for MTC, a music company. I was working in the London office and he came there on business. We got on really well and we really liked each other.

Anyway, at the end of his trip, he invited me to go to a conference in San Francisco. We had a great time again. And then something amazing happened. When I was in San Francisco, I was offered a job in our new office in Paris.

When I told Mark, he told me that he was going to work in the Paris office, too!

There's just one little thing. His job is marketing director, but mine is managing director, so I'm going to be his boss. I've been in Paris for three weeks now, and I love it. Mark arrived from San Francisco yesterday. He's coming into the office this morning.

1.16

Allie What a lovely view! The river's beautiful, isn't it?

Mark Paris is so romantic. I can't believe we're here together at last.

Allie Yes, it's weird.

Mark Weird? It's wonderful. I really missed you.

Allie Me too.

Mark Why don't we sit down?

Allie So did you like the office?

Mark Yes, it's great. How do you get on with everyone?

Allie OK. But we'll see. I've only been here three weeks. What did you think of them?

Mark I thought Jacques was very nice, and Nicole …

Allie What about Nicole?

Mark She was very friendly.

Allie You know we have to keep things a secret.

Mark What things?

Allie You know, us. Our relationship. I don't want the people in the office to know we're together.

Mark No, of course not. But it isn't going to be easy.

Allie No, it isn't. How's the hotel?

Mark It's OK, I guess, but it's not like having my own place. I have to find an apartment.

Allie Don't worry. It won't take you long. What are you thinking?

Mark Do you really want to know? I was wondering what kind of a boss you'll be.

Allie Well, you'll find out tomorrow.

2.5

Good evening. I'm Rafael Perez with the six o'clock news.

At least 17 people have been injured in an accident on the freeway near San Francisco. The police said that the truck that caused the accident was traveling at about 85 miles an hour, well over the 65-mile-an-hour speed limit.

Meanwhile, hundreds of transit workers have walked off the job in protest against the transit authority's pay offer. The unions have asked for a raise of 8.5 percent over two years. There will be a meeting between their leaders and city officials later today.

Just released, the latest unemployment figures show that the total number of unemployed people, 6.9 million, is essentially unchanged this month. Over the year unemployment has gone up slightly from 4.6 to 4.8 percent, which means 138,000 more unemployed for the year. The secretary of labor says some of this increase has been caused by the shutdown of auto plants in the Midwest.

In real estate, agents are predicting that housing prices will continue to go up this year, making it extremely difficult for first time buyers to get into the housing market. It's estimated that house prices have increased by one third over the last five years. The average price of a single family home in the US is now about $226,000.

And now the weekend weather report …

2.6

Interviewer So, how long have you been living here?

Angela For about six months now.

Interviewer Why did you choose Ecuador?

Angela Because I have always been interested in the culture and language of Latin America.

Interviewer Why did you want to take a year off?

Angela Basically I wanted a break from teaching. I love teaching children but I needed a change. Also, I've been drawing and painting since I was a child and I took art classes in college. I've always wanted an opportunity to study the art of the Andean countries, such as Peru and Ecuador.

Interviewer What have you been doing here since you arrived?

Angela Well, I've been taking some art classes at the university and getting to know some of the local artists. Luckily, many of them speak a little English, as I don't know much Spanish yet. But I am learning the language as quickly as I can.

Interviewer Is Spanish a difficult language to learn?

Angela Not really. A lot of words are similar in English and Spanish. Listening is probably the most difficult thing for me. I often have to ask people to repeat things more slowly.

Interviewer Are the other students in your classes helpful when you don't understand something?

Angela Yes, very. I think they're happy to find that a foreigner loves the Ecuadorian culture and wants to learn about it.

Interviewer You also teach English?

Angela I've been teaching for about three months now. It's a great way to meet people and of course earn a little money to pay for my classes!

Interviewer What's the best thing about living in Ecuador so far?

Angela The people! The hospitality of the people here is absolutely amazing.

2.11

1

Sharon Hello?

Kylie Hi, Sharon. It's me… Kylie.

Sharon Oh. Hi, Kylie.

Kylie Hey, you sound awful – what's been happening?

Sharon Oh, nothing. Well, OK… Kenny and I have been arguing.

Kylie What about? What's he been doing this time?

Sharon He's been sending text messages to his ex-girlfriend again.

Kylie No!

Sharon I knew this vacation was a mistake. I shouldn't have come.

2

Wife You are so red! How long have you been sunbathing? All morning?

Husband I haven't been sunbathing. I've been reading.

Wife Yes, but in the sun! Didn't you put any sunscreen on?

Husband No.

Wife You'd better go and put some lotion on now. You're going to feel terrible tonight…

3

Woman 1 You two look exhausted. What have you been doing?

Man We've been sightseeing in the town. We've been walking all afternoon.

Woman 2 Yes, my feet are killing me.

Woman 1 Well, come and sit down and have a nice cup of coffee.

2.12

I left at six. It was still dark when I put my suitcase in the car and drove off. It was fast and easy to go through London because it was Saturday, so there was no rush hour traffic. Soon I was on the highway heading toward Folkestone on the south coast. I stopped at a gas station for a cup of coffee and a sandwich. I didn't buy any gas because it's much cheaper in France.

I arrived in Folkestone at 8:10. The problem with traveling by car from England to France is that Britain is an island. There are 35 kilometers of water between England and France. You can get across it by ferry, but there's a much better and quicker way – the Channel Tunnel.

The Channel Tunnel is only a train tunnel, not a road tunnel, and so you have to put your car on a train. The trip takes an hour and a half, and drivers have to sit in their cars because there are no seats on the train for passengers. I arrived at the terminal and joined the line of cars waiting for the next train.

At 10:30 the train arrived in Calais and I drove my car off the train and onto the road – a French road. It was nice to drive on the right again, although that was not so easy with an English car.

The traffic in Calais was really bad. Finally, I got out of Calais and onto the highway to the South of France. The speed limit on French highways is 130 kilometers an hour and the road was clear, so now I could travel quickly. But first I stopped at a gas station to fill up.

Gas is cheaper in France than in Britain but, on the other hand, you have to pay to travel on French highways. In Britain they are free.

It's 960 kilometers from Calais to Avignon, and the trip on the highway was boring. I listened to my favorite music to pass the time and I stopped again for lunch. At eight o'clock I finally arrived in Avignon. I found my hotel and I was looking forward to a delicious French meal.

2.15

TV host And this evening on *Behind the Wheel* we talk to Brian Russo, who is an expert on road safety. Brian, you did some tests to find out how dangerous it is to do other things when we're driving. According to your tests, what's the most dangerous thing to do?

Expert Well, the first thing I have to say is that doing anything else when you're driving is dangerous and can cause an accident. Because when you're driving you should concentrate 100 percent on controlling the car and anything else you do is a distraction.
The tests we did in a simulator showed that the most difficult and most dangerous thing is to try and open a bag of chips or a can of soda. The reason is that most people actually need two hands to open a bag of chips or a can of soda, so they take both hands off the wheel for a second or two. And, of course, that's the most dangerous thing you can possibly do. In fact, one of the drivers in the simulator actually crashed when he did this.

TV host And which is the next most dangerous?

Expert The next most dangerous thing is to select a specific CD from the passenger seat. This is extremely dangerous too because to do this you have to take your eyes off the road for one or two seconds.

TV host And number three?

Expert Number three was making a phone call on a cell phone. What we found in the tests was that drivers drove more slowly when they did this, but that their control of the car got worse.

TV host Yes, I can believe that. And Number four?

Expert Number four was listening to your favorite music. In the tests most drivers drove more quickly and less safely when they were listening to music they already knew. If the music was fast and heavy, some drivers even drove more aggressively.

TV host So no heavy metal when you're driving?

Expert Absolutely not.

TV host And in fifth place?

Expert In fifth place was talking to other passengers. The problem when we talk to other people in the car is that we pay too much attention to what we're saying or what we're hearing and not enough attention to what's happening on the road.

TV host So the least dangerous is listening to music you *don't* know?

Expert That's right. The least dangerous of all these activities is listening to unfamiliar music on the radio or on a CD player. It seems that if we *don't know* the music then we're less distracted by it. In this part of the tests, all drivers drove safely and well.

2.18

Nicole Have you started looking for an apartment?

Mark No, I haven't had time yet.

Ben Anyway, it's best to get to know Paris first.

Mark Yeah – it's a big city.

Nicole Merci.

Ben Merci.

Mark Merci beaucoup.

Nicole Very good, Mark!

Mark Thanks. That's nearly all the French I know!

Ben Hi, Beatrice. … Yeah … just a minute. Sorry.

Nicole How do you like the office?

Mark Oh, it's great.

Nicole And the people?

Mark Really friendly! I like Ben a lot. He's amazing with computers. And Jacques's a really nice guy!

Nicole Oh, Jacques, he's very charming. Everybody likes him. And he has a lovely wife. She used to be a pop star when she was young. Have you heard of Isabelle?

Mark No, I'm sorry, I haven't.

Nicole She's very pretty. Allie is very attractive, too.

Mark Allie? Yeah, I guess.

Nicole Although her clothes are very English. And she's very formal. You know, today, I asked if I could have a day off, and she wanted me to send her an e-mail!

Mark Well, the English have their funny ways.

Nicole Oh yeah. Oh, hello, Allie.

Allie Hi.

Mark Allie! Hi, let me get you a drink.

Allie Thanks. I'll have a Diet Coke™.

3.2

1
I'm a salesperson and I work in a clothing store. What really makes me angry is when I'm waiting on somebody and suddenly their cell phone rings, and they answer the phone and start having a conversation. It's really annoying. I think that if you're in a store and talking to a salesperson, then you shouldn't answer the phone.

2
What most annoys me is people who use their phones on a plane. I mean, everybody knows that you have to turn off your cell phone on a plane and that you must not use it until you get off the plane. But some people turn on their phones the moment the plane lands and they start making calls. Why can't they wait another 15 minutes?

3
I hate it when people talk very loudly on their cell phones in a public place. The other day I was in the waiting room at the doctor's, and there was a man there whose cell phone rang about every two minutes and we all had to listen to him talking loudly to his wife, then to his boss, then to a garage mechanic… I think that if you're in a public place and someone calls you, you should talk really quietly or go somewhere else. And you don't have to shout – the other person can hear you perfectly well.

4
What really annoys me are people who use their phones a lot when they're with other people – like when you're out for dinner with someone and they spend the whole time talking on their cell phones or texting other people to arrange what they're doing the next day. I think it's really rude.

5
I hate people who use their cell phones in the car, even if they're hands-free. Whenever you see someone driving badly, nine times out of ten they're on the phone.

3.4

Clare
In a store in the US, when you go to the checkout counter to pay, the salesperson always thanks you and says, "Have a nice day." For Americans this is standard polite behavior. However, some visitors to the US find this expression "Have a nice day!" very annoying. They say it's a sign that Americans are not sincere. You know, the salesperson doesn't really care if you have a nice day or not. I understand what they mean, but personally I really like it. I prefer the people who serve me in stores and restaurants to be polite and friendly, even if they are not 100% sincere. And the Americans are very good at that.

Paul
Well, some Chinese refer to Americans as "the thank-you people," because of our constant use of the phrase. You don't usually hear the Chinese say *please* or *thank you*. It's just not part of their culture. In fact, the standard Chinese answer to "Thank you" means something like "You don't have to be that polite!" So I would say yes, we are polite and we do use *please* and *thank you* a lot. A Chinese friend suggested that this might be because Americans generally don't know any other words in Chinese, but I don't think this is really fair. I think it's more a cultural thing.

Andrea
I saw a survey the other day that said that Americans themselves feel they are not as polite as they used to be. Sixty-nine percent said that Americans are ruder now than they were 20 or 30 years ago. Many people blamed this on the faster pace of life in the US today. About 70 percent said that parents were to blame for not teaching their children good manners. They also said that kids saw too many examples of rude behavior on TV. I agree. I think we used to be polite, but we aren't anymore, especially young people.

Marcos
In my job, I've met a lot of Americans and I think they're polite in the way they talk and also in the way they respect other people's opinions. And their manners in general are good. OK, this isn't true of all Americans. Some of the tourists that come here can be pretty loud and pushy, especially if they don't get the service they want, and they don't always know or respect some of our customs. I mean, you see Americans dressed in shorts, T-shirts, and sandals trying to go into a really nice restaurant. Then they don't understand why they can't do that, even when they see that all the local people are very nicely dressed – but, in general, I think the majority are OK.

3.5

Policeman OK now, can you describe the man you saw in the bank?

Woman 1 Well, he was, uh, sort of medium height, you know, not short – but not tall either. And quite skinny, you know, thin.

Woman 2 Yes. And he had a beard and a little mustache.

Woman 1 No, he didn't. He had a mustache but not a beard. It's just that I think he hadn't shaved.

Woman 2 No, it was a beard, I'm sure.

Woman 1 And anyway, Doris, you weren't wearing your glasses, so you probably didn't see him very well.

Woman 2 Yes, I did. I saw him very well.

Policeman OK, OK. So, no mustache then.

Woman 1 No, he had a mustache but he didn't have a beard.

Policeman And what about his hair?

Woman 2 Dark.

Woman 1 Yes, short, dark hair.

Policeman Straight?

Woman 1 No, I think it was curly. What about you, Doris?

Woman 2 Yes, very curly.

Policeman So, dark, curly hair?

Woman 1 Yes. That's what we said.

Policeman And what time was it when…?

3.8

Interviewer Rafael Lloyd. A Spanish first name and an English last name?

Rafael Yes. My mother was Spanish and my father, English.

Interviewer Is Rafael your real name then or your stage name?

Rafael It's my real name: my mother was from Cordoba in Spain and Rafael's the patron saint of Cordoba. But it's also my stage name.

Interviewer What nationality are you?

Rafael I'm Spanish and British. I was born in Spain and I was brought up there. I've spent a lot of time in Britain, too. I've been living in England for the last ten years.

Interviewer Oh, good. Are you bilingual?

Rafael Yes, I am.

Interviewer And, it's a strange question, do you feel more Spanish than British or vice versa?

Rafael Well, I think I feel more Spanish in most respects, especially as a big part of my life revolves around Spanish culture. But I do like individuality, eccentricity, and tea. I must feel a little British too, I suppose!

Interviewer Do you think you look more Spanish than English?

Rafael Well, I think I look Spanish, but when I travel, people always think I'm from their country and people have stopped me in the street, for example, in Cairo and in Rome, to ask me for help, so I must have an international face… Maybe I should be a spy!

Interviewer When did you start learning to play the guitar?

Rafael I started when I was nine, when my family lived in Madrid. A teacher used to come to our apartment and give me lessons.

Interviewer I see, so how long have you been working professionally as a flamenco guitarist?

Rafael I started when I was 17, I mean, that's when I started to get paid for my first concerts. I'm now 39, and that's, uh, 22 years?

3.9

Interviewer As a flamenco guitarist living in Britain, is it easy to make a living?

Rafael I think life as a musician is never easy. But I think it's easier in Britain than in Spain, because there are fewer flamenco guitarists there.

Interviewer And where's flamenco popular, apart from in Spain?

Rafael Well, the biggest markets for flamenco outside Spain are really the US, Germany, and Japan, but I've found that it's popular all over the world. It has a strong identity that people relate to in every corner of the planet.

Interviewer Now, you don't look like the stereotype of a flamenco guitarist. People imagine flamenco guitarists as having long, dark hair...

Rafael That's true. I used to have really long hair, but I decided to cut my hair short.

Interviewer Are people in Britain surprised when they find out that you're a flamenco guitarist?

Rafael No, not really. That's one of the things I like about Britain: no one judges on appearance.

Interviewer And what about in Spain?

Rafael Well, actually, in Spain people find it much harder to believe that I'm a flamenco guitarist. I think Spanish people believe in stereotypes more than in Britain. And they judge you more on your appearance. But as soon as people hear me play the guitar, they know that I'm the real thing.

Interviewer Could you play something for us?

Rafael Of course.

3.13

Interviewer Hello and welcome to this week's edition of *All about you*. Today's program's about taking up new activities, and how to succeed at them. With us is psychologist Dr. Maggie Prior. Good afternoon.

Psychologist Good afternoon.

Interviewer Dr. Prior, what tips can you give our listeners who are thinking of learning to do something new?

Psychologist Well, first of all, I would say choose wisely. On the one hand, don't choose something completely unrealistic. For example, don't decide to take up sailing if you can't swim, or parachute jumping if you're afraid of heights. But, on the other hand, don't generalize and think that just because you aren't very good at one sport, you won't be able to do any sports at all. I mean, just because you were bad at gymnastics at school, doesn't mean that you might not love playing tennis.

Interviewer So think positive?

Psychologist Definitely. And never think you'll be bad at something before you've even tried it.

Interviewer OK, so, let's imagine I've started to learn to play tennis and I'm finding it very hard work.

Psychologist Well, first don't give up too quickly, keep on trying for at least a few months. It often takes time to begin to enjoy learning something new. Another thing that can help, if you're having problems learning something, is to give it a break and then try again, perhaps a month or two later.

Interviewer But what if I find I really don't have a talent for tennis.

Psychologist I think the important thing is not to be too ambitious. I mean, if you've never been active in sports and you decide to learn to play tennis, don't expect to become the next Wimbledon champion. Just aim to enjoy what you're doing, not to be the best in the world at it.

Interviewer But what if, even after all this, I still feel I'm not getting anywhere?

Psychologist Well, sometimes you do have to accept it and say, "OK, this really isn't my thing," and you need to give it up. But why not try something else? There are lots of other things you can learn to do. But remember that if you take up an activity that you're really interested in, even if you aren't very good at it, you'll make new friends because you'll be meeting other people who have similar interests.

Interviewer So it might be good for my love life?

Psychologist Exactly.

Interviewer Dr. Maggie Prior, thank you very much.

3.17

Landlady This is the apartment. *Je vous laisse visiter. Je serai en bas.*

Mark Merci, madame. Sorry, Nicole. What did she say?

Nicole She said that we can have a look at the flat. She's going to wait downstairs.

Mark Thanks. So, what do you think?

Nicole Well, it's a long way from the station. And it's on the fourth floor. It's a pity there isn't a lift.

Mark Who needs one? The stairs are good exercise. Look, there's a great view from here.

Nicole It's also very noisy.

Mark Sure, but it has character. It's just how I imagined an apartment in Paris.

Nicole Everything's old, including the heating. It will be very cold in the winter.

Mark Oh, hi.

Allie Well, what's it like?

Mark Nice – really Parisian.

Allie Are you going to take it?

Mark I think so, yeah …

Allie I can't wait to see it!

Mark Yeah …

Allie Are you OK? Are you on your own?

Mark No, I'm with the woman who owns the apartment. I'll call you back.

Allie OK, speak later. Love you.

Mark Love you too, bye. Sorry about that. That was…that was my… my daughter.

Nicole Calling from America?

Mark You know. She's just taking an interest.

Nicole Taking an interest. That's nice.

4.3

Reporter So, you just took the Scholastic Aptitude Test, the SAT. What parts did you take?

Carla Well, I took the main parts of the test. Those include critical reading, math, and writing.

Reporter Was it difficult?

Carla Well, yeah, some parts were and I need to get a pretty high score.

Reporter Why?

Carla Because I want to be a doctor, and I want to get into a pre-med program at one of the big universities, like maybe the University of California. They probably won't admit me unless I get 650 or higher.

Reporter Do you think you'll get it?

Carla I don't know. I think I did OK, but I'm a little worried about the math.

Reporter When will you get the results?

Carla They'll go online next week. Believe me, as soon as they're online, I'll look up my scores.

Reporter And how will you celebrate if you get high scores?

Carla I don't want to plan any celebrations until I get the results.

Reporter And what will you do if you don't get the scores you need?

Carla I don't want to think about it. If I don't get into college, my parents will kill me. No, I'm joking. I suppose I could apply to some schools that don't require such high scores.

Reporter Well, good luck!

Carla Thanks.

4.4

Reporter What test did you take?

Ruben The TOEFL. That's the Test of English as a Foreign Language.

Reporter Was it difficult?

Ruben Well, not really, but I need at least 550 to get into a college. One of the schools I've applied to requires 640! But I'm optimistic. I think I did pretty well.

Reporter When will you get the results?

Ruben When they score the tests, they'll mail the results. It takes about six or seven weeks!

Reporter And how will you celebrate if you get a high score?

Ruben I'll go out for pizza with the other people in my class – well, with the people who did well on the test.

Reporter Will you keep on studying English?

Ruben Probably not – at least formally. I mean, if I'm taking college classes, I'll be learning a lot every day anyway.

Reporter And if you don't get a high enough score?

Ruben I'll take the test again in June.

4.6

Reporter Carla – I can see from your face that the results, uh, weren't exactly what you wanted. Am I right?

Carla Yeah. I got a 700 on critical reading but only 620 on math.

Reporter So what are you going to do now?

Carla Well, my reading score was pretty good, so I'm going to wait and see if one of the universities I want will still accept me. If not, I'll try to find other schools that will take me.

Reporter Were your parents angry?

Carla No, they've been really nice about it. They know how disappointed I am. Besides, it's not that my scores were really bad.

Audioscripts

Reporter Well, Ruben, did you get a good score on the TOEFL?

Ruben Yes, I got a 650! I'm very happy. I didn't think I'd get such a high score.

Reporter And your friends?

Ruben They all did well, too, except one. But he didn't expect to do very well. He didn't do any work.

Reporter So are you going out to celebrate?

Ruben Oh yes. We're going out for pizza tonight and then we're going dancing.

4.7

Presenter Hello and welcome to our review of international TV programs. With me today is the television critic Michael Stein... So, Michael, what interesting foreign TV shows have you seen recently?

Michael I saw a British series called *That'll Teach 'Em*. I must say I found the whole series absolutely fascinating. They took a group of 30 16-year-old students and sent them – as an experiment – to a boarding school for one month. But it wasn't a modern boarding school; it was a 1950s boarding school. They recreated exactly the same conditions as in the 1950s – the same food, the same discipline, the same exams. The idea was to compare education today with education in the 1950s.

Presenter Well, I bet it was a shock for today's teenagers.

Michael Well, it was, of course. It wasn't just the classes – it was the whole atmosphere – I mean, they had to wear the uniform from the 50s – horrible uncomfortable clothes – they hated them and they weren't allowed to leave the school once for the whole month, or watch TV, or use cell phones. And they had to take cold showers every morning, and go for cross-country runs!

Presenter Well, what was the worst thing for them?

Michael The food, definitely! Most of them hated it. They said it was cold and tasteless. And the girls didn't like the cold showers much either...

Presenter What about the classes?

Michael Well, of course the biggest difference for the kids was the discipline. It was silence all the time during the classes – only the teacher spoke. And anyone who misbehaved had to go to the principal and was either hit on the hand or made to stay after school and do extra work. And of course they couldn't use computers or calculators, but strangely enough the kids didn't really mind that, and in fact most of them found the classes interesting. Some of them said they were more interesting than their normal classes. They had to work very hard, though.

Presenter So what happened in the end? Did they pass the 1950s exams?

Michael No. Most of them failed – although they were all really bright kids. There was only one student who actually passed all the subjects.

Presenter So, do you think that school subjects really used to be harder in the 1950s?

Michael No, I think that the kids failed because the exams in the 1950s were very different. The students in the program will probably do very well in their own exams. On the other hand, 1950s students would probably find today's subjects very difficult.

Presenter How did the kids themselves feel about the experiment?

Michael They were really positive. In general, they had a good time and they all felt they learned a lot. I think it made them appreciate their own lifestyle more. Some of them actually said it was the best month of their lives. It was an interesting experiment and the program was really well made. I really enjoyed watching it.

4.9

1

When I retire, if I can afford it, I'd love to have a cottage down at the lake, where we could go for the summer. I'd like to have a garden there. I've never been able to have one, as we live in an apartment in the city. Not too big, though. I'd like to grow vegetables and flowers and some fruit trees. I'd spend all my time either in the garden or sitting by the lake.

2

My dream house would be in the mountains, high up on the hillside with a beautiful view. It'd be modern and quite simple, with wooden floors and big windows, and from every window you'd be able to see the mountains and the forest. It'd be quite isolated, with no neighbors for miles and miles. Can you imagine? Just the sound of the wind in the trees.

3

I'd love to have a big old townhouse, maybe one of those beautiful houses with big rooms, high ceilings, and a lovely staircase going down to the hall. But the bathrooms and kitchen would have to be modern, because old ones are cold and impractical. I'd need some help looking after it, though...

4

If I won the lottery, which of course I won't, I'd buy a big penthouse apartment near the river with a great view, a really hi-tech place, you know, with one of those intelligent refrigerators that orders food from the supermarket all by itself when you're running out and a huge TV and music system – but all very stylish and minimalist.

4.11

Carol

When Robert answered my e-mail, I got really excited. He didn't say very much about himself. He just told me that he was now a teacher, which surprised me because he always used to say that he would hate to teach. He also told me that he'd been married but was now divorced.

Anyway, I answered his e-mail, and we agreed to meet for lunch at a restaurant I like – a place where I often go on weekends.

When I got there, I looked around to see if I could see him, but I couldn't, and I thought, "Typical! Same old Robert," because, he always used to be late. So I sat down and ordered a drink. I was just sipping my drink when a man came over to my table and said, "Carol, how are you?" I could hardly believe it – I mean, I know neither of us is young anymore, but I think I look pretty good for my age. People usually say I look five years younger than I am. But Robert looked like an old man. His lovely long hair was all gone – in fact, he was bald, with a few strands of hair sort of combed over his head – and he was wearing the most hideous jacket. Well, I know you shouldn't judge by appearances, so I smiled at him and we started talking – and well, I enjoyed the lunch and we talked a lot about the past – but I knew as soon as I saw him that we didn't have anything in common anymore. And I was right. Instead of the rebel he used to be, he was now, well, much more conventional than me. In fact, he seemed just like the sort of teachers we used to hate when we were young.

4.12

Alex

I got to the restaurant late because I couldn't find it, but when I walked in I saw a whole group of young people at a table. I thought that must be them, though I didn't really recognize anybody. So

I went up and they all said hello. They all recognized me, which was great, though it felt a little strange. I must admit I was feeling really nervous. Anyway, I sat down and we started talking. They told me lots of things that I used to do when I was at school, like play on the school basketball team – they said I used to be really good – and they told me about all sorts of other things: places we used to go to, things like that. Some of my friends had even brought photos, and we looked at them. I'd completely forgotten that I used to wear these really awful big glasses – and I sort of relaxed and I felt that I was getting to know them again, and getting to know more about myself and my past. Anyway, since we met that evening, we've all been e-mailing each other and I've started going out with Anna – one of the girls who was at the restaurant that night. She says she used to like me a lot at school, but that I didn't use to take any notice of her then! I can't remember any of that, but I know I like her a lot now!

4.14

1

I don't agree at all. I think it's much easier. Today you can text, you can e-mail, you can chat online and things like that. I'm still in touch with some friends I met on vacation last year, even though they live miles away.

2

Actually, I think it's probably true. Because I know a lot of men who are still friends with people they went to elementary school with, but I don't know many women who are. For example, my brother has a friend named Tim who he's known since they were three years old. But I think the reason is that men's friendships are less intense, sort of less intimate than women's friendships. As men only ever talk about sports or superficial things, it doesn't matter if they've completely changed and don't have much in common anymore – they can still talk about baseball.

3

You definitely shouldn't. I mean, that's the quickest way to lose a friendship. If you don't like a friend's boyfriend or girlfriend, you should just keep quiet. You have to wait until they break up, and of course then you can say how awful you thought the person was and your friend will agree and think you're being supportive. But if you say anything bad while they're still madly in love, it's a disaster. I know because it happened to me once with a friend of mine. I said something negative about his girlfriend. And now we're not friends any more.

4.17

Mark So ... Scarlett. What would you like?

Scarlett Nothing.

Mark Aren't you hungry?

Scarlett Sure. But this food's really horrible.

Allie This is one of the finest restaurants in Paris.

Scarlett Well, I can't eat this stuff. I never touch meat...

Allie The seafood looks good...

Scarlett Hey, fish have feelings, too.

Mark What about the mushroom risotto?

Scarlett Mushrooms? No way! Didn't they tell you guys about my allergies? I'm allergic to mushrooms, strawberries, nuts...

Mark Shall we go some place else?

Scarlett Whatever. I'm going to the restroom.

Allie Well, that was a disastrous morning. The boat trip made her feel sick and she wouldn't go up the Eiffel Tower. "I can't stand heights."

Mark It's a pity we didn't just take her shopping.

Allie She's so spoiled.

Mark Oh, come on, she's just a kid really.

Allie So, what are we going to do about lunch? Shall we leave now?

Mark No, hang on. I have an idea. Let me talk to the waiter.

Waiter Monsieur?

Mark Do you think you could possibly do me a favor?

Waiter Yes, of course, sir. What would you like?

Mark Well, I think this place is great. More wine, Allie?

Allie No, thanks.

Waiter Mademoiselle…

Scarlett What's this?

Mark It's your lunch, Scarlett.

Scarlett But I didn't order anything.

Waiter Voilà!

Scarlett Hey, pizza margherita! Cool!

5.3

Tip Number 1. Eat breakfast sitting down. Most people stay in bed until the last minute and then have a cup of coffee and a piece of toast standing up. This is really bad for you because it means that you start the day in a hurry. Your body and mind are already moving too fast. So do yourself a favor. Get up ten minutes earlier every day and have breakfast – nice and slowly.

Tip number 2. Forget the gym, and do yoga instead. Many people go to the gym after work to exercise because they think that this relaxes them, but it doesn't, believe me. I really think that a gym is a very stressful place. Exercising hard, for example doing aerobics, makes your heart beat more quickly, so it doesn't relax your body at all. In fact, it does the opposite. So, forget the gym and try doing yoga. Yoga will not only help you get fit, but it will also slow your body down and help you think more clearly.

Tip number 3. Go for a long walk. Walking is the most traditional form of exercise, but many people have just forgotten how to do it. These days we all just get into our cars. The great thing about walking is that you can't walk very fast, so walking actually slows you down. And when we walk, we look around us at the birds, the trees, the stores, other people. It reminds us of the world we live in and it helps us stop, and think, and relax.

Tip number 4. Spend 10 minutes each day in silence. Meditation isn't new. People have been doing it for thousands of years and now it is becoming really popular again. In the United States you can find meditation rooms in companies, schools, airports, and even hospitals. Meditation is a fantastic way to teach your mind to slow down and to think more clearly. And spending time in silence every day will also benefit your general health.

And finally, tip number 5. Take a bath not a shower. Taking a shower is very quick and convenient, but it is another part of our fast-living culture. When you come home from work, instead of taking a shower, take a bath and spend half an hour there. A bath is one of the most relaxing things you can do. It will really help to slow you down at the end of a hard day.

5.8

Voice-over 1 The body polish

Joanna So? What did you think?

Stephen It was just horrible! Horrible. Fruit's for eating, not putting on your body. It was hot and sticky and extremely uncomfortable. And I felt so stupid. I'd never do that again. I give it zero out of ten.

Joanna Sticky? It was fruit, for goodness sake! I thought it was wonderful. It smelled so good and it was incredibly relaxing. I mean, how could anybody not like it? And the head massage was fantastic! That was one of my favorite spa treatments ever. Ten out of ten. OK, so now, the facial.

Stephen Hmm. How long is this one?

Joanna One hour 40 minutes.

Stephen Oh, you're joking? That's too long

Joanna Too long? It'll be heaven. See you later.

5.9

Voice-over 2 The facial

Stephen Oh, that was so boring. It went on forever.

Joanna I loved it.

Stephen Well, I must admit my face feels different – much smoother. But I'm not sure I really want a smooth face. And it was nearly two hours and she used about 12 different creams and things. It normally only takes me a minute to wash my face – and I just use soap and water – the therapist said I ought to buy *five* different products!

Joanna Well, I enjoyed every second. My skin feels great – really healthy. I give it nine out of ten.

Stephen Hmm… I give it four.

Joanna Your problem was that you were hungry, so you couldn't relax. We could have a glass of fruit juice before the last treatment…

Stephen Fruit juice? Oh, OK then, if you really want one.

5.10

Voice-over 3 The foot treatment

Stephen Wow!

Joanna Don't tell me, you liked it!

Stephen It was wonderful!

Joanna I must say, your feet look …well, better. Clean anyway.

Stephen Well, I've never liked my feet much to be honest, but now they look and feel great. That was definitely worth the time and money. Nine out of ten. What do you think?

Joanna Yes, it was great. A real luxury. And I love the color they painted my nails. I agree – nine out of ten. You see, I knew…

5.14

Voice-over Week one.

Jessica When I got to the studio on the first day, I was really nervous. I met my teachers, Adam and Sally. They were very nice to me, but I could see that they thought it was going to be impossible to teach me to be a reporter in just a month.

Adam The problem with Jessica at the beginning was that she was too shy and too nice. Political reporters need to be hard – almost aggressive sometimes – and I've never met anyone less aggressive than Jessica. And also she knew nothing about politics. She knew who the president was but not much else!

Jessica I spent the first week watching lots of political interviews on TV, and Adam and Sally taught me how to speak more clearly and more confidently. In the evenings they made me read the political sections of all the newspapers. It was very boring. At the end of the week, I was exhausted.

5.15

Voice-over Week two

Jessica Adam and Sally said I had to change my image for TV, so I had my hair cut and colored, and I got new, more stylish clothes. I must say I liked my new look. I spent the week learning how to interview someone in front of a camera.

Adam Then came Jessica's first big challenge. The president was arriving home after a visit to Asia. They'd arranged an informal news conference at the airport, and she had to wait with the other reporters and try to ask him a question.

Jessica It was a disaster. I was so nervous I was shaking. There were a lot of other reporters pushing and shouting. They didn't let me get near the president. I tried to ask my question, but he didn't hear me. I felt really stupid.

5.16

Voice-over Week three.

Adam Jessica was finally making some progress. She was more relaxed. This week she had to interview a politician from the Republican party in the studio.

Jessica In the beginning it was fine. But then I made a stupid mistake.

Jessica *So could you tell us what the Democratic party is going to do about…sorry, I mean the Republican party, what they're going to do about the…*
I said the "Democratic party" instead of the "Republican party." And after that I was really nervous again.

Adam We all make mistakes sometimes. Jessica just has to learn to keep going and not to lose her confidence.

5.17

Voice-over Week four.

Jessica I spent the last week preparing for the test. It was going to be a live interview with the secretary of education. There would be three professional reporters and me, all asking him questions. I'd done lots of research, so although I was nervous, I felt well prepared.

Jessica *Secretary, many people think that the real reason there aren't enough teachers is that their salaries are so low. Are you proposing an increase in teachers' salaries?*

Secretary *Well, let's not forget that salaries are much higher today than they were under the previous government.*

Jessica *Yes, but you haven't answered my question. Are you going to increase them?*

Secretary *Well, we're planning to spend a lot more money on education in the next two years.*

Jessica *Is that a yes or a no?*

Secretary *There are no immediate plans to increase teachers' salaries…*

Jessica *So it's a no then. Thank you, Secretary.*

Jessica When it was all over, came the worst part. I had to wait while the judges decided which of us they thought *wasn't* a professional reporter.

Adam The judges gave their verdict – and incredibly *none* of the three realized that Jessica wasn't a professional! She did very well. Who knows, maybe one day soon you'll be seeing her on TV… and this time she'll be a real reporter, not pretending!

Jessica It was a great experience and I was pleased how I did, but actually I *wouldn't* like to change jobs. I'm much happier working in the library.

5.20

Allie It's great to be on our own again.

Mark Yeah.

Allie Is this the first time you've been to the Louvre?

Mark Uh huh.

Allie What's the matter? Is this about the meeting? Because I agreed with Jacques and not with you?

Mark Yeah, well, we knew it wouldn't be easy. Working together, I mean.

Allie It's difficult for me as well. But if I don't agree with you…

Mark I know, I know, you're the boss.

Audioscripts

Allie And I have to do my job. I really thought that Jacques's idea was better. And so did Scarlett.

Mark It's not a big deal, Allie. I'm fine, really. So who exactly was the Mona Lisa?

Allie I'm not sure. I think she was the wife of a banker…

Mark Is that why she's smiling? Because her husband has a good salary?

Allie I also read somewhere that she was a self-portrait of Leonardo.

Mark A self-portrait? You're kidding. Now, I don't know much about art, but Leonardo da Vinci was a man, right?

Allie Well, it's just a theory. Why do you think she's smiling?

Mark Well, in my opinion, she's the managing director of a music company.

Allie What?

Mark She lives in Paris, she's in love with her marketing director, and she has a lot of fun telling him what to do.

Allie That's really unfair!

Mark Hey, we're not in the office now – you can't tell me I'm wrong! Let's get a coffee.

Allie Good idea.

Mark Don't turn around!

Allie What is it?

Mark I've just seen Ben from the office.

Allie Where?

Mark I said don't look! I don't think he's seen us. Let's get out of here. Come on.

6.4

1
I was in a taxi in Greece, in Athens, and I was going downtown to do some shopping, and the taxi driver started talking to me. He asked me where I was from. When I said I was American, he started getting really aggressive. He said that he didn't like Americans and that all Americans were loud and pushy. He went on and on – he just wouldn't stop. I got really annoyed. I mean, I thought, "Why do I have to listen to all of this?" So I asked him to stop the taxi and let me get out. Luckily, he stopped and I got out – and of course I didn't pay him anything.

2
This happened to me recently when I was traveling around on business. I was really tired because I'd been working and traveling all day. Anyway, when I got to the hotel in Philadelphia – it was the evening – I checked in and the front desk clerk gave me the key to my room. So I went up to my room and opened the door, but it was a complete mess! The bed wasn't made, there were dirty towels on the floor, and the bathroom was *filthy*. I went downstairs and told the clerk, and he said that I would have to wait for half an hour while they prepared the room. But I was exhausted and needed to rest, so I told him to give me another room right away. Luckily, he did.

3
This happened to me last week. I went to a restaurant in San Francisco with my family to celebrate my dad's birthday. Anyway, my dad ordered soup and when the soup arrived, he saw that it had a long, black hair in it. So he asked the waitress to take it back and bring him another bowl. She brought him another bowl of soup and it was fine, and we finished our meal. But when my dad asked for the check, he saw that they had charged us for the soup. He didn't think that was right. He thought the soup should be free because he had found a hair in it. So he asked the waitress to take it off the check. She went away and spoke to the manager, and he came out and apologized and he took the soup off the check.

6.6

Interviewer So how did you get involved in the film, Dagmara?

Dagmara Well, as you probably know, a lot of the film *Schindler's List* was shot in Krakow, in Poland, which is where I live. And before the actual shooting of the film started, the film company had an office in Krakow and I got a job there translating documents and parts of the script – things like that – I was a university student at the time.

Interviewer But how did you get the job as Spielberg's interpreter in the film?

Dagmara It's a funny story. I didn't think I would ever get to meet Spielberg or any of the actors. But then, just before the shooting started, there was a big party in one of the hotels in Krakow and I was invited.
At first, I wasn't going to go – I was tired after working all day, and I didn't think I had anything suitable to wear. But in the end, I borrowed a jacket from a friend and I went. But when I arrived at the party, the producer – who was Polish – came up to me and said, "Dagmara, you're going to interpret for Steven Spielberg. You have to translate his opening speech, because the girl who was going to do it couldn't come."

Interviewer How did you feel about that?

Dagmara I couldn't believe it! I was just a student – I had no experience of interpreting – and now I was going to have to speak in front of hundreds of people. But when I started speaking, I was so nervous that I confused the dates of the Second World War – but luckily I managed to get to the end without making any more mistakes.
And afterward, during the party, Spielberg came up to speak to me to say thank you – he was really nice to me and said he was impressed by the way I had interpreted. And then he said, "I'd like you to be my interpreter for the whole film." I couldn't believe it. I had to pinch myself to believe that this was happening to me.

6.7

Interviewer So what exactly did you have to do?

Dagmara I had to go to the film set every day. A car came every day to pick me up from my house – I felt really important! And then what I had to do was to translate Spielberg's instructions to the Polish actors, as well as the extras. I had to make them understand what he wanted. It was really exciting – sometimes I felt as if I was a director myself.

Interviewer Was it a difficult job?

Dagmara Sometimes it was really difficult. The worst thing was when we kept having to shoot a scene again and again because Spielberg thought it wasn't exactly right. Some scenes were repeated as many as 16 times – and then sometimes I would think that maybe it was my fault – that I hadn't translated properly what he wanted, so I'd get really nervous. I remember one scene where we just couldn't get it right and Spielberg started shouting at me because he was stressed. But in the end we got it right and then he apologized, and I cried a little, because I was also very stressed – and after that it was all right again.

Interviewer So, was Spielberg difficult to work with?

Dagmara Not at all. – I mean he was very demanding – I had to do my best every day – but he was really nice to me. I felt he treated me like a daughter. For instance, he was always making sure that I wasn't cold –it was freezing on the set most of the time – and he would make sure I had a warm coat and gloves and

things. It was hard work but it was fascinating – an amazing experience.

Interviewer What did you think of the finished film?

Dagmara I believe that *Schindler's List* is truly a great movie, a masterpiece. I think the actors were brilliant, especially Liam Neeson and Ben Kingsley – and I love the way it was shot in black and white, with color in just one scene.
But, as you can imagine, I can't be very objective about it – I mean, I lived through nearly every scene. And when I watch it – and I've seen it a lot of times – I always remember exactly where I was at that moment. I can't help thinking, "Oh there I am, hiding under the bed, or standing behind that door."

6.8

Che Guevara was born in the city of Rosario, Argentina, on June 14, 1928. His first name was really Ernesto. He was the oldest of five children in his family. At the university, he studied medicine and had plans to be a doctor. He spent many vacations traveling around Latin America by motorcycle. The poverty he saw convinced him that revolution was the answer to Latin America's problems. In 1956, he met Fidel Castro in Mexico and joined him in the Cuban Revolution. In 1966, Guevara went to Bolivia to lead a revolution in that country. On October 8, 1967, he was captured by the Bolivian army and shot.

6.9

It's 12:00 noon and so it's time for today's contest. Today the topic is "Heroes and Icons." As usual, the rules are very simple. I'm going to give you eight clues and you have to identify the people. If you know all the answers, e-mail them to me right away. The first person who sends me the correct answers wins a prize. Today's prize is two plane tickets to … the Big Apple, New York City!

OK, so let's get started with those clues. I'll say each one twice only. And remember, I always give you the first letter or letters of the word I'm looking for. Today they are all people's names.

Let's start with an easy one. Two letters, B and G. It's a man who's probably the richest man in the world, the founder of Microsoft. That's BG, the man who started Microsoft.

Number 2. Two letters again, N and M. He's a man whose courage and humanity made him an icon for millions of people all over the world. He spent many years in prison in South Africa because of his fight against apartheid, but he eventually became president of that country.

Number 3 begins with M, just one word. It's the name of a woman who's had a lot of different jobs. She's been an actress, she's even written children's books, but she's most famous as a singer. One word beginning with M.

And number 4.This time it's a man, and the letters are G and A, though many people just know him by his last name. He's an Italian designer whose clothes are considered among the most elegant in the world, and whose name is also on perfume bottles everywhere. G and A, for an Italian fashion designer.

On to number 5. Two letters, J and O. It's the name of a famous American woman, whose first husband was president of the United States and whose second husband was a Greek millionaire. Although she died in 1994, she is still admired for her style all over the world. Two letters, J and O.

And number 6. It's a woman again and the letters are M and N. She's the woman who changed the shape of women's tennis, and is possibly the greatest female player of all time. She was born in

Prague but later became a US citizen. M and N for the greatest ever woman tennis player.

Number 7 is an American actor. He was born in Kentucky in 1961, and he is often called the most attractive male actor in Hollywood today. He first became famous in a TV hospital drama in which he played the part of a doctor. His first name begins with G and his last name with C. So that's a Hollywood actor, G and C.

Finally, number 8. Two letters. M and C. She was born in Greece and died in Paris, and she is the woman whose voice is familiar to lovers of opera all over the world. Nicknamed "La Divina" her life was tragic, but her voice will never be forgotten. MC, "La Divina."

So if you think you have the eight correct answers, e-mail them to me now at this address, Guessthenames@hitmail.com. That's Guessthenames@hitmail.com. And the first person with the correct answers will win those two tickets to New York.

Time for some music.

6.14

Mark Dear all, Please find attached a copy of the latest sales report from the USA. Mark.

Mark So, did you guys have a good weekend?

Ben Yes, fine.

Jacques Not bad. Very quiet.

Ben What about you, Mark?

Mark Oh, I spent most of the time at home … just being domestic, you know. The apartment's looking pretty nice, now. You must come round for a meal one evening.

Jacques That would be very nice.

Ben So didn't you go out at all?

Mark Oh sure. I went to the Louvre on Saturday. I felt like getting a bit of culture.

Jacques On your own?

Mark Yeah. I kind of prefer going to museums and galleries on my own. You can look at everything at your own pace.

Ben That's funny. I went to the Louvre on Saturday, too.

Mark Really? I didn't see you.

Ben Well, it's a big place. I didn't see you either.

Nicole I've just had an e-mail from Allie.

Jacques So have I.

Mark Me, too...

Nicole Dear Mark, Thank you for the information. And thank you, darling, for a wonderful weekend. Allie.

7.1

Narrator Ian thought Amy had gone out for the evening and sat down to wait for her to come back. Tired after his long journey, he fell asleep. When he woke up, the phone was ringing. Ian answered the phone. It was Amy.

Ian I said, "Where are you?" She said, "Ian, I'm sitting in your flat in Australia." At first, I didn't believe her, but then she gave the phone to Eddie, who lives in my flat in Sydney, and he told me it was true. I was so shocked I couldn't speak.

Narrator Amy had had the same idea as Ian. She had flown from London to Sydney via Singapore at exactly the same time Ian was flying in the opposite direction. Incredibly, both their planes stopped in Singapore at the same time. Ian and Amy were sitting in the same airport lounge, but they didn't see each other.

Amy I had saved all my money to buy a ticket to Sydney. I wanted it to be a fantastic surprise for Ian. I couldn't wait to see his face when I arrived. You can't imagine how I felt when I arrived at his flat and his friend Eddie told me he had gone to England! I just couldn't believe it! When I spoke to Ian on the phone, he told me that he had

flown back to England for a special reason and then he asked me to marry him. I didn't know whether to laugh or cry but I said "Yes."

Ian It was just bad luck. If one of us had stayed at home, we would have met. It's as simple as that.

7.2

Narrator The cabin crew put out a desperate call to the passengers: "If there's a doctor on the plane, could you please press your call button..." The cabin crew were hoping to hear this: [bell on airplane]. But they didn't. They heard this: [lots of bells]. Incredibly, there were fifteen doctors on the plane, and all of them were cardiologists. They were from different countries and they were traveling to Florida for a medical conference. Four of the doctors rushed to give emergency treatment to Mrs. Fletcher. At one point, they thought she had died, but finally they managed to save her life. The plane made an emergency landing in North Carolina and Mrs. Fletcher was taken to a hospital. After being in the hospital for four days, she was able to go to her daughter's wedding.

Mrs. Fletcher I was very lucky. If those doctors hadn't been on the plane, I would have died. I can't thank them enough.

Narrator But now that she's back in England, Mrs. Fletcher has been less lucky with the British hospitals.

Mrs. Fletcher I had fifteen heart specialists on that plane, but I'll have to wait three months until I can see one in this country!

7.6

Interviewer Good morning and thank you for coming, Mr. Morton – or should it be Inspector Morton – you were a detective with Scotland Yard, weren't you?

Ken Yes, that's right. For 25 years. I retired last year.

Interviewer People today are still fascinated by the identity of Jack the Ripper, more than a hundred years after the crimes were committed. It's incredible, isn't it?

Ken Well, it's not really that surprising. People are always interested in unsolved murders – and Jack the Ripper has become a sort of cult horror figure.

Interviewer Who are the main suspects?

Ken Well, there are a lot of them. But probably the best known are Prince Albert, Queen Victoria's grandson, the artist Walter Sickert, and a Liverpool cotton merchant named James Maybrick.

Interviewer Patricia Cornwell in her book Jack the Ripper – case closed says that she has identified the murderer. Who does she think he was?

Ken Well, she's convinced that Jack the Ripper was Walter Sickert, the painter.

7.7

Interviewer What evidence did she discover?

Ken Well, she mainly used DNA analysis. She actually bought a painting by Sickert at great expense and she cut it up to get the DNA from it. People in the art world were furious.

Interviewer I can imagine.

Ken And then she compared the DNA from the painting with DNA taken from the letters that Jack the Ripper sent to the police. Patricia Cornwell says that she's 99 percent certain that Walter Sickert was Jack the Ripper.

Interviewer But you don't think she's right, do you?

Ken No, I don't. I don't think her scientific evidence is completely reliable and there's a lot of evidence which says that Sickert was in France not London when some of the women were killed.

Interviewer There's been another recent theory, hasn't there? About James Maybrick? Do you think he was the murderer?

Ken Well, somebody found a diary, which is supposed to be his, where he admits to being Jack the Ripper. But nobody has been able to prove that the diary is genuine and, personally, I don't think he was the murderer.

Interviewer And Prince Albert, the queen's grandson?

Ken This for me is the most ridiculous theory. I can't seriously believe that a member of the royal family could be a serial murderer. In any case, Prince Albert was in Scotland when at least two of the murders were committed.

Interviewer So, who do you think the murderer was?

Ken I can't tell you because I don't know.

Interviewer So you don't think we'll ever solve the mystery?

Ken No, I wouldn't say that. I think that some day the mystery will be solved. Some new evidence will appear and we'll be able to say that the case of Jack the Ripper is finally closed. But at the moment it's still a mystery, and people like a good mystery.

7.16

Cindy Well, it wouldn't be electric light because I love candles. And I could live without a washing machine for a week – I often do when I'm on vacation. I think I would miss the refrigerator, though. I'd hate not having cold drinks, and it would mean having to go shopping every day for food or it would go bad. So a refrigerator would be one thing, and then probably my laptop. It has a battery, but I could only use it for three hours or so without charging it. So I wouldn't be able to do much work.

Andy Uh, well, it depends. I'd really miss the TV, but I suppose I could live without it for a week if I had to. And, uh, what else – oh no, my cell phone. I wouldn't be able to charge it. I couldn't live without my cell. I mean, that's how I keep in touch with all my friends. And my MP3 player. I need my music. Yes, definitely those two.

Julia I think for me it would have to be first and foremost the dishwasher. Because with a family and so many dishes to do, I would just be at the sink forever. It would be a nightmare for me to have no dishwasher because I've gotten so used to it. So that would be the first thing. And the second thing, probably again because of having a family, a young family, would be an iron, because there's so much ironing. If I had to go without that, everyone would look terrible. Nobody would look very neat. So those would be my two things.

Tyler Well, I suppose the first thing I'd miss most would be my cell phone, because I couldn't charge it, so I couldn't use it, and I'd get very upset about that. There are some people's numbers that are only stored in the phone. I don't have them written down, and I wouldn't be able to get in touch with those people. So cell phone. And the other thing I'd miss would be the lights. At this time of year especially, when the days are short, the mornings are dark, late afternoon's dark too, I'd miss lights. So cell phone and lights.

1

1A present tenses: simple and continuous, action and non-action verbs

simple present: *I live, he works*, etc.

> They **work** in a bank.
> Where **do** you **live**?
> He **doesn't wear** glasses.
> She **usually has** cereal for breakfast.
> I'**m never** late for work.

- Use the simple present for things that are always true or happen regularly.
- Remember the spelling rules, e.g. *lives, studies, watches*.
- Remember the word order for questions: (question word), auxiliary, subject, base form of verb.
- Put adverbs of frequency, e.g., *usually*, before the main verb and after *be*.

present continuous: *be* + verb + *-ing*

> A Who **are** you **waiting for**?
> B I'**m waiting** for a friend.
> A What **are** you **doing** after class?
> B I'**m going** to the cafe.

- Use the present continuous (not simple present) for actions in progress at the time of speaking or for future arrangements.
- Remember the spelling rules, e.g., *living, studying, getting*.

action and non-action verbs

> A What **are** you **cooking** tonight?
> B I'**m making** pasta.
> A Great! I really **like** pasta.

- Verbs that describe actions, e.g., *make, cook*, can be used in the simple present or continuous.
- Verbs that describe states or feelings (not actions), e.g., *like, want, be*, are <u>not</u> normally used in the present continuous.
- Common non-action verbs are **agree, be, believe, belong, depend, forget, hate, hear, know, like, love, matter, mean, need, prefer, realize, recognize, seem, suppose**.

> ⚠ A few verbs have an action and a non-action meaning. The most common is *have*.
> *I have a big car.* = possession (non-action)
> *I can't talk now. I'm having lunch.* = an activity (action)

1B past tenses: simple, continuous, perfect

simple past: *worked, stopped, went, had*, etc.

> They **got** married last year.
> What time **did** you **wake up** this morning?
> I **didn't have** time to do my homework.

- Use the simple past for finished past actions.

past continuous: *was / were* + verb + *-ing*

> A What **were** you **doing** at six o'clock last night?
> B I **was watching** TV. It was a cold night and it **was raining**.

- Use the past continuous to describe an action in progress at a specific time in the past.

past perfect: *had* + past participle

> When they turned on the TV, the game **had finished**.
> I **felt** nervous because I **hadn't flown** before.

- Use the past perfect when you are talking about the past and you want to talk about an earlier past action.

using narrative tenses together

> When John **arrived**, they **had** dinner. (First John arrived. <u>Then</u> they had dinner.)
> When John **arrived**, they **were having** dinner. (When John arrived, they were <u>in the middle of</u> dinner.)
> When John **arrived**, they **had had** dinner. (They had dinner <u>before</u> John arrived.)

- Remember **Irregular verbs** p.156.

1C future forms

be going to + base form

> future plans and intentions
> My sister'**s going to adopt** a child.
> **Are** you **going to buy** a new car?
> I'**m not going to go** to New York next week.

> predictions
> I think they'**re going to win**. (They're playing very well.)
> It'**s going to rain**. (The sky is very dark.)

- Use *going to* NOT *will / won't* when you have already decided to do something.
- With the verb *go* you can leave out the infinitive.
  I'm not going (to go) to New York.

present continuous: *be* + verb + *-ing*

> future arrangements
> We'**re getting** married in October.
> They'**re meeting** at 10:00.
> She'**s leaving** on Friday.

- You can usually use present continuous or *going to* for future plans / arrangements.
- *going to* shows that you have made a decision.
  We're going to get married in the summer.
- Present continuous emphasizes that you have made the arrangements.
  We're getting married on July 12th (e.g., we've booked the church).

will + base form

> I'**ll have** the steak. (instant decision)
> I **won't tell** anybody where you are. (promise)
> I'**ll carry** that bag for you. (offer)
> You'**ll love** the movie! (prediction)

- Use *will / won't* (NOT the simple present) for instant decisions, promises, offers, and predictions.
- In sentences with *I* and *we*, *shall* (and not *will*) is sometimes used to offer to do something or to make a suggestion, but this is very formal.
  Shall we go for a walk?

1A

a Correct the mistakes in the highlighted phrases.

Ouch! You stand on my foot!   *You're standing*

1 They have always breakfast in bed on Sunday morning.
2 She can't come to the phone now. She takes a shower .
3 We are needing an answer from you before Wednesday.
4 I'm studing a lot now because I have exams next week.
5 She don't eat meat at all. *doesn't*
6 They always are late. *they are always*
7 Do you go out tonight? *are you going out*
8 He never replys to my e-mails! *Replised*
9 A Are you going to the park this afternoon?
   B I don't know. It's depending on the weather. *depends*

b Write questions in the present continuous or simple present.

A What *are you eating*? (you / eat)   B A cheese sandwich.

1 A Where *are you Have* lunch today? (you / have)
  B At home. My mother's making pasta.
2 A What *he do* ? (he / do)
  B He's an accountant.
3 A *Are you goa* this weekend? (you / go away)
  B No, we're staying here.
4 A _____ to eat out tonight? (you / want)
  B Yes, that would be nice.
5 A What *are she* ? (she / cook) *cooking*
  B I don't know, but it smells good.

1B

a Combine the two sentences. Use the verb in **bold** in the past continuous or past perfect.

Sarah **took** a nap from 3:00 to 5:00. Peter picked up the tickets at 4:00.
Peter picked up the tickets when Sarah *was taking* a nap.

1 They **watched** TV from 7:00 until 9:00. I arrived at 7:30.
  When I arrived, they *watching* TV.
2 He **left** the office at 7:00. She called him at 8:00.
  When she called him, he *lefted* the office.
3 I **studied** for the test the night before. The test didn't go well.
  The test didn't go well although I *had* the night before.
4 He **drove** to work this morning. In the middle of his trip, he had an accident.
  When he *driving* to work this morning, he had an accident.
5 He only **had** five lessons. He passed his driving test.
  When he passed his driving test, he *has* (only) five lessons.

b Complete with the simple past, past continuous, or past perfect.

We *didn't realize* that we *had been* there before. (not realize, be)

1 A How _____ ? (the accident / happen)
  B He *was* back from Chicago when he *hit* a tree. (drive, hit)
2 I *had all* to cook dinner when they _____ me to say they couldn't come. (already / start, call)
3 When I got home, I was very tired, so I _____ a shower and *when* to bed. (take, go)
4 I arrived too late. The concert *arrive* and my friends *go* home. (finish, go)
5 The driver *Lost* control of his car because he *was* on his cell phone. (lose, talk)

1C

a Circle the correct form. Put a check (✔) next to the sentence if both are possible.

(*I'm not going*)/ I won't go to work tomorrow because it's Saturday.

1 *I'm going to study* / I'll study English here next year.
2 *We'll go* / *We're going* to Brazil next week. I can't wait.
3 What *are you going to wear* / *are you wearing* to the party?
4 Do you think *it will rain* / *it's going to rain* tomorrow?
5 A This is heavy.   B *I'll help* / *I help* you.
6 *I'm meeting* / *I meet* a friend this evening.
7 I'm really sorry. I promise *I won't do* / *I'm not going to do* it again.
8 *They're getting* / *They're going to get* married in May.

b Complete B's replies with a correct future form.

A Sorry, Ann's not in.
B OK. *I'll call back* later. (call back)

1 A There's no milk.
  B Don't worry. I *got* some. (get)
2 A Can we meet on Tuesday?
  B Sorry, I can't. I *can't going* to Boston on Tuesday. (go)
3 A Can we have pizza for lunch?
  B No, we *Have a* chicken. I've already put it in the oven. (have)
4 A Is that the phone?
  B Yes, but don't get up. I *Have* it. (answer)
5 A Jane's put on a lot of weight!
  B She's pregnant. She *having* a baby in August. (have)

2

2A present perfect and simple past

present perfect simple: *have* / *has* + past participle (*worked*, *seen*, etc.)

past actions at an indefinite time in the past	unfinished states or actions that started in the past and are true now	with *already* and *yet*
I've **been** to Miami, but I **haven't been** to Tampa. She's never **used** an ATM. **Have** you ever **lost** your credit card?	I've **known** her for ten years. How long **have** they **worked** here? They've **worked** here since 2004.	I've already **seen** the movie. **He hasn't found** a job yet? **Have** they **left** yet?

- We often use *ever* and *never* with the present perfect. They go before the main verb.
- Use *for* + a period of time. e.g., *for two weeks*; use *since* with a point of time, e.g., *since Wednesday*.
- Use *How long … ?* + present perfect to ask about a period of time from the past until now.
- For irregular past participles see page 156.

- *already* goes before the main verb in ⊕ sentences; *yet* goes at the end in ⊖ and ? sentences.
- The words *already* and *yet* are also used with the simple past with the same meaning. *We've already eaten. = We already ate.* *He hasn't done it yet. = He didn't do it yet.*

present perfect or simple past?

I've **been** to Miami twice. (= in my life up to now)	I **went** there in 1998 and 2002. (= on two specific occasions)
How long **have** you **been** married? (= you are married now)	How long **were** you married? (= you are not married now)
I've **bought** a new computer. (= I don't say exactly when)	I **bought** it on Saturday.(= I say when)

- Use the present perfect when there is a connection between the past and the present.
- Use the simple past to ask or talk about **finished** actions in the past, when the time is mentioned or understood. We often use a past time expression, e.g., *January*, *last week*, etc.

2B present perfect continuous

present perfect continuous for unfinished actions

How long **have** you **been studying** English?
He's **been working** here since April.
They've **been going out** together for three years.

- *have* / *has been* + verb + *-ing*
- Use the present perfect continuous with *for* or *since* with **action verbs** (e.g., *learn*, *go*, etc.).

⚠ With **non-action verbs** (e.g., *know*, *be*, etc.) use the present perfect simple NOT the present perfect continuous with *for* or *since*. *I've known her for ages.* NOT ~~I've been knowing her for ages.~~ With *live* and *work* you can use the present perfect simple or continuous with *for* or *since*. *I've been living here for six months.* *I've lived here for six months.*

present perfect continuous for recent continuous actions

A Your eyes are red. **Have** you **been crying**?
B No, I've **been cutting** onions.

- Use the present perfect continuous for actions that have been going on very recently. They have usually just stopped.

2C comparatives and superlatives

comparing two things (or actions)

My sister is a little **taller than** my brother. San Francisco is **more expensive than** Chicago. This test is **less difficult than** the last one.
Olive oil is **better** for you **than** butter. You drive **more slowly than** I do. Atlanta played **worse** today **than** last week.
Flying isn't **as comfortable as** going by train. He doesn't smoke **as much as** she does. Her new car looks **the same as** the old one.

superlatives

He's **the tallest** player on the team. What is **the most expensive** capital city in Asia? This book is **the least difficult** to understand. She's the **best student** in the class.
Who drives **the most carefully** in your family? That's **the worst** they've ever played.

- Form superlatives like comparatives but use *-est* instead or *-er* and *most* / *least* instead of *more* / *less*.
- You normally use *the* before superlatives, but you can also use possessive adjectives, e.g., *my best friend*, *their most famous song*.

- Regular comparative adjectives / adverbs:
  hard>harder, big>bigger, easy>easier, modern>more modern, difficult>more difficult, carefully>more carefully
- Irregular comparative adjectives / adverbs: *good* / *well>better, bad* / *badly>worse, far>farther* / *further*
- After *than* or *as* we can use an object pronoun *me, him, her*, etc., or a subject pronoun (*I, he, she*) + auxiliary verb, e.g., *She's taller than me* OR *She's taller than I am* but NOT ~~She's taller than I.~~

2A

a Correct the mistakes in the highlighted phrases.

I've never saw *Star Wars*.   *I've never seen*

1 He left pretty early, but he yet hasn't arrived .
2 We don't see each other since we graduated.
3 Have you ever wrote a poem?
4 She have never been to Seoul.
5 I've lent him $50 last week, but he hasn't paid me back yet.
6 I don't see them often but I've known them since ten years .
7 What year have you graduated ?
8 We're lost. We already have been down this road twice.
9 I sent her an e-mail last week, but she doesn't reply yet .
10 They live in that house since 1980.

b Complete the dialogues with the simple past or present perfect.

I've *already seen* that movie twice. (already / see)

1 **A** How long _____ at the university? (you / be)
  B I _____ two years ago. I'm in my third year now. (start)
  A Do you live with your parents?
  B I _____ with them for the first two years but then I _____ into a student residence last September and I _____ there since then. (live, move, live)
2 **A** _____ a job yet? (your brother / find)
  B Yes, he _____ work in a hotel. (already / start)
3 **A** _____ to Nobu – that new Japanese restaurant? (you / ever / be)
  B Yes, we _____ there for my birthday. (go)
  A What was it like?
  B The food _____ fantastic but it _____ a fortune! (be, cost)

2B

a Make sentences with the present perfect continuous (and *for* / *since* if necessary).

she / work there / 2003 [+]
She's been working there since 2003.

1 how long / they / go out together [?]
2 I / study English / two years [+]
3 he / feel very well recently [−]
4 you / read that book / months! [!]
5 you / wait / a long time [?]
6 we / spend much time together [−]
7 how long / she / live there [?]
8 I / rent this house / three years. [+]
9 the elevator / work / 10 o'clock [−]
10 she / work here / a long time [?]

b Complete with a verb from the list in the present perfect continuous.

bark	cry	do	eat	play	shop	not sleep	watch

  A Your sister's lost a lot of weight!
  B Yes. She *'s been eating* a lot less recently.
1 **A** Your eyes are red. __DO__ you __crying__?
  B Yes. I __watching__ a sad movie.
2 **A** It's very late. Why aren't you in bed?
  B I can't sleep. That dog __barking__ for the last two hours.
3 **A** You look tired.
  B I know. I __don sleeping__ well recently.
4 **A** Wow! You bought a lot of things!
  B Yes, we __shopping__ all day.
5 **A** You look hot! What __are__ you __doing__?
  B I __playing__ at the park with the children.

2C

a Complete with one word.

She's much *more* intelligent than her brother.

1 He's not as smart __then__ he thinks he is.
2 It's _____ best book I've read in a long time.
3 The trip took longer _____ we expected.
4 I think it was the saddest movie I've _____ seen.
5 Is Texas the biggest state _____ the US?
6 He's the _____ selfish person I've ever met.
7 Your watch is the same _____ mine.
8 My father speaks _____ quickly than I do.
9 We don't go swimming _____ often as we did before.
10 Her brother's about 10 and she's a year younger than _____ .

b Complete with the comparative or superlative of the **bold** word.

Mexican food is much *spicier* than Italian food.   **spicy**

1 It's _____ than it was this time last year.   **hot**
2 Jan's _____ of all my sisters.   **competitive**
3 He's _____ person in the office.   **lazy**
4 He looks much _____ with shorter hair.   **good**
5 I sat next to _____ person at the party!   **boring**
6 Could we meet a little _____ tomorrow?   **early**
7 It was _____ movie I've seen this year.   **bad**
8 Sue is _____ member of my family.   **ambitious**
9 The _____ way to travel is by train.   **safe**
10 The beach was _____ from the hotel than we expected.   **far**

3A   *must, have to, should* (obligation)

obligation / necessity: *have to* / *must* (+ base form)

> You **have to** wear a seat belt in a car.
> **Do** you **have to** work on Saturdays?
> I **had to** wear a uniform at my elementary school.
> I'**ll have to** get up early tomorrow. My interview is at 9:00.

> I **must** remember to call Emily tonight – it's her birthday.
> You **must** be on time for class tomorrow – there's a test.

- *Must* and *have to* have a very similar meaning.
  Have to is more common in speaking and for **general**, **external** obligations, for example rules and laws.
  Must is more common in official forms, notices, and signs and for **specific** (i.e. on one occasion) or **personal** obligations.
  Compare:
- *Have to* is a normal verb and it exists in all tenses.
- *Must* is a modal verb. The only forms are *must* and *must not*.
- You can also use *have to* or *must* for strong recommendations,
  e.g., *You have to / must see that movie – it's fantastic.*

no obligation / necessity: *don't have to*

> You **don't have to** pay for the tickets. They're free.
> You **don't have to** go to the party if you don't want to.

prohibition: *must not* (+ base form)

> Passengers **must not** leave bags unattended.

- *Don't have to* and *must not* are completely different.
  Compare:
  You must not drive down this street. = It's prohibited, against the law.
  You don't have to drive. We can get a train. = You can drive if you want to but it's not necessary / obligatory.
- You can often use *can't* or *not allowed to* instead of *must not*.
  You must not park here. You can't park here. You're not allowed to park here.

> ⚠ *Have got to* is sometimes used instead of *have to* in spoken English, e.g., *I've got to go to now.*

advice or opinion: *should* / *shouldn't* (+ base form)

> You **should** take warm clothes with you to Quito. It might be cold at night.
> I think the government **should** do something about unemployment.

- *Should* is not as strong as *must* / *have to*. We use it to say if we think something is the right or wrong thing to do.
- *Should* is a modal verb. The only forms are *should* and *shouldn't*.
- You can also use *ought to* and *ought not to* instead of *should* / *shouldn't*.
  You should take an umbrella with you. You ought to take an umbrella with you.

3B   *must, may, might, can't* (deduction)

when you are sure something is true: *must*

> They **must** be out. There aren't any lights on.
> She **must** have a lot of money. She drives a Porsche.

when you think something is possibly true: *may* / *might*

> His phone's off. He **might** be on the plane now.
> She **might not** like that skirt. It's not her style.
> She's not at home. She **may** be working.
> He hasn't written. He **may not** have my address.

when you are sure something is impossible / not true: *can't*

> He **can't** be sick. I saw him at the gym.
> They **can't** be Italian. They're speaking to each other in Spanish.

- We often use *must*, *may* / *might*, and *can't* to say how sure or certain we are about something (based on the information we have).
- In this context, the opposite of *must* is *can't* NOT ~~must not~~.

3C   *can, could, be able to* (ability and possibility)

can / could

> I **can** speak Spanish very well.
> She **could** play the violin when she was three.
> She **can't** come tonight. She's sick.
> They **couldn't** wait because they were in a hurry.
> **Could** you open the door, please?

- *Can* is a modal verb. It only has a present, past, and conditional form (but can also be used with a future meaning).
- For other tenses and forms use *be able to*.

be able to + base form

> I **am able to** accept your invitation.
> They **weren't able to** come.
> I'**ll be able to** practice my English in the US.
> She **has been able to** speak French since she was a child.
> I'd like **to be able to** ski.
> I love **being able to** sleep late on weekends.

- You can use *be able to* in the present, past, future, present perfect, and as a gerund or infinitive.
- *be able to* in the present and past is more formal than *can* / *could*.

3A

a Circle the correct form.

You *don't have to* / (*must not*) drink that water. It's not safe.

1 We *must not* / *don't have to* hurry. We have plenty of time.
2 You *must* / *should* remember to write the report. The boss will be furious if you forget.
3 The exhibition was free so I *hadn't to* / *didn't have to* pay.
4 *Do you have to* / *Should you* wear a uniform at your school?
5 We *must* / *had to* wait two hours at security and nearly missed our flight.
6 *Had you to* / *Did you have to* do a lot of homework when you were at school?
7 I think people in apartments *must not* / *shouldn't* have dogs.
8 She's allergic to dairy products so she *can't* / *doesn't have to* eat anything made from milk.

b Complete the second sentence with **two** or **three** words so it means the same as the first.

Smoking is prohibited here.   You *must not smoke* here.

1 It isn't a good idea to go swimming after a big meal.
   You _____ swimming after a big meal.
2 Was it necessary for them to pay cash?
   Did _____ pay cash?
3 The meeting isn't obligatory.
   You _____ go to the meeting.
4 It's bad manners to talk loudly on a cell on a train.
   People _____ quietly on their cell phones on a train.
5 Trucks are not allowed to use this road.
   Trucks _____ this road.

3B

a Match the sentences.

1 He must be over 70. *I*
2 He can't be in college.
3 He may not remember me.
4 He might like this book.
5 He must be very shy.
6 He can't be serious.
7 He may be in bed already.
8 He might not be at home yet.
9 He must have a computer.
10 He can't be a good athlete.

A He hasn't seen me in a long time.
B He sends me lots of e-mails.
C He must be joking.
D He's interested in history.
E He sometimes works late.
F He gets up very early.
G He's only 16.
H He's not fit enough.
I He retired 10 years ago.
J He never opens his mouth.

b Complete with *might (not)*, *must*, or *can't*.

This sauce is really spicy. It ___*must*___ have chili in it.

1 **A** What music is this?
   B I'm not sure but it _____ be Mozart.
2 She looks very young. She _____ be more than 16.
3 I'm not sure why she hasn't called. She _____ have my new number.
4 They _____ have a lot of money. They live in a huge house.
5 He _____ be away. His car is outside his house.
6 I _____ be a size 44! I'm usually a 40 or 42.
7 It _____ be true! I saw it on the news.

3C

a Complete with the correct form of *be able to*.

[−] I've never *been able to* learn to swim.

1 [−] I _____ send any e-mails since lunchtime.
2 [+] She used to _____ speak German really well.
3 [−] I _____ do my homework until tomorrow.
4 [+] I'd really like _____ dance well.
5 [?] _____ you _____ come to our wedding? It's on May 10th.
6 [+] If I spoke better English, I _____ get a job in a hotel.
7 [+] When I've saved another $1,000, I _____ buy a new car.
8 [−] She hates _____ do what she wants.

b Complete with *can* / *can't*, or *could* / *couldn't* where possible. If not, use a form of *be able to*.

They told me that they *couldn't* do anything about the noise.

1 I _____ talk to you now. I'm too busy.
2 When I lived in Rome, I _____ speak Italian quite well.
3 I would love _____ play tennis very well.
4 If we don't hurry up, we _____ catch the last train.
5 My mother _____ see much better now with her new glasses.
6 To do this job you need _____ speak at least two languages.
7 I _____ help you tonight if you want.
8 They _____ find a house yet. They're still looking.

4A   first conditional and future time clauses + *when*, *until*, etc.

first conditional sentences: *if* (or *unless*) + simple present,
will / *won't* + base form

> If you **don't do** more work, you'll **fail** the exam.
> He'll **be** late for work if he **doesn't hurry up**.
> She won't get into college unless she **gets** good grades.

- Use the present tense (NOT the future) after *if* in first conditional sentences.
- *unless* = *if … not*
  I won't go unless she invites me. = *I won't go if she doesn't invite me.*
- You can also use an imperative instead of the *will* clause, e.g., *Come and see us next week if you have time.*

future time clauses

> As soon as you **get** your test results, **call** me.
> We'll **have** dinner when your father **gets** home.
> I **won't go** to bed until you **come** home.
> I'll **have** lunch before I **leave**.
> After I **graduate** from college, I'll probably **take** a year off and travel.

- Use the simple present (NOT the future) after *when*, *as soon as*, *until*, *before*, and *after* to talk about the future.
- *as soon as* = at the moment when, e.g. *I'll call you as soon as I arrive.*

4B   second conditional

second conditional sentences: *if* + past simple,
would / *wouldn't* + base form

> If I **had** more money, I **would buy** a bigger house.
> If he **spoke** English, he **could get** a job in a hotel.
> I'd **get along** better with my parents if I **didn't live** with them.
> I **wouldn't do** that job unless they **paid** me a really good salary.
> If I **were** you, I'd **buy** a new computer.

- Use the second conditional to talk about a hypothetical / imaginary situation in the present or future and its consequence. Compare:
  I don't have much money, so I can't buy a bigger house (real situation).
  If I had more money, I'd buy a bigger house (hypothetical / imaginary situation).
- Use *were* for all subjects if the second conditional *if* clause contains the verb *be*.
  If I were you …

would / wouldn't + base form

> My ideal vacation **would be** a week in the Bahamas.
> I'd never **buy** a car as big as yours.

- You can also use *would* / *wouldn't* + base form (without an *if* clause) when you talk about imaginary situations.
- The contraction of *would* is *'d*.

> ⚠ Remember the difference between first and second conditionals.
>
> *If I have time, I'll help you.*
> = a possible situation. I may have time.
>
> *If I had time, I'd help you.*
> = an imaginary / hypothetical situation.
> I don't / won't have time.

4C   *usually* and *used to*

present habits and states

> I usually **get up** at 8:00 on school days.
> I **don't** usually **go out** during the week.
> Houses in the suburbs usually **have** yards.
> **Do** you usually **walk** to work?

past habits and states

> We **used to be** close friends, but we don't see each other anymore.
> I **used to go out** with that girl when I was at school.
> **Did** you **use to wear** glasses?
> She **didn't use to have** blond hair. She had dark hair before.

- For present habits use *usually* or *normally* + simple present.
- For past habits use *used to* / *didn't use to* + base form. *Used to* does not exist in the present tense.
- We use *used to* for things that were true over a period of time in the past. It usually refers to something that is not true now.
  I used to live downtown. = I lived downtown for a period of time in the past, but now I don't.
- *Used to* / *didn't use to* can be used with action verbs (e.g., *wear*, *go out*) and non-action verbs (e.g., *be*, *have*).
- We often use *not … anymore* / *any longer* (= not now) with the simple present to contrast with *used to*.
  I used to go to the gym, but I don't anymore / any longer.

4A

a Complete with a word or expression from the list.

~~after~~   as soon as   before   if   unless   until   when

___After___ we have dinner, we could go for a walk.

1 I must write the date on my calendar _before_ I forget it.
2 Let's wait under the tree _when_ it stops raining.
3 This job is very urgent, so please do it _as soon as_ you can.
4 We won't get a table at the restaurant _____ we don't hurry.
5 I'll pay you back _____ I get my first paycheck.
6 I can't go _unless_ you pay for my ticket. I'm broke.
7 They'll be really happy _when_ they hear your news.
8 I want to go on working _____ I'm 65. Then I'll retire.
9 I must renew my passport _until_ I go to Mexico.
10 _before_ you work harder, you won't pass the final exam.

b Complete with the simple present or *will*.

I'll give him your message when I ___see___ him. (see)

1 Don't forget to turn off the lights before you _____. (leave)
2 Go to bed when the movie _____. (finish)
3 They _____ married until they find a place to live. (not get)
4 If I see Emma, I _____ her you are looking for her. (tell)
5 I'll call you as soon as I _____ at the hotel. (arrive)
6 You won't be able to park unless you _____ there early. (get)
7 As soon as it stops raining, we _____ out. (go)
8 She won't like curry if she _____ spicy food. (not like)
9 Don't write anything until I _____ you. (tell)
10 When she finds out what he's done, she _____ furious. (be)

4B

a Write second conditional sentences.

If you / speak to your boss, I'm sure he / understand.
If you spoke to your boss, I'm sure he would understand.

1 It / be better for me if we / meet tomorrow.
2 She / not treat him like that if she really / love him.
3 If I / can live anywhere in the world, I / live in New Zealand.
4 The kitchen / look bigger if we / paint it white.
5 I / not buy that house if I / be you.
6 He / be more attractive if he / wear nicer clothes.
7 If we / not have children, we / travel more.
8 What / you do in this situation if you / be me?

b First or second conditional? Complete the sentences.

If you tell her anything, she _'ll tell_ everybody in the office. (tell)
We'd have a dog if we _had_ a yard. (have)

1 It'll be quicker if we _____ a taxi to the airport. (take)
2 If you started exercising, you _____ better. (feel)
3 What would you do if you _____ your job? (lose)
4 If you buy the food, I _____ tonight. (cook)
5 I think he'd be happier if he _____ alone. (not live)
6 I'll be very surprised if Marina _____ coming here. (not get lost)
7 Where will he live if he _____ the job in Montreal? (get)
8 If she didn't have to work so hard, she _____ life more. (enjoy)

4C

a Correct the mistakes in the highlighted phrases.

She wasn't use to be so shy. *She didn't use to be*

1 I use to get up at 6:30, but I don't any more.
2 Did she always used to have long hair?
3 Do you use to have breakfast before you go to work?
4 They didn't used to have a car; they used to ride bikes everywhere.
5 He doesn't like coffee, so he use to drink tea in the morning.
6 He used be a teacher , but now he works for Greenpeace.
7 Do usually you wear pants or skirts?
8 Last year we used to go to Caracas in August.
9 Does she use to live near you when you were children?
10 At school we don't use to wear a uniform. We wore what we liked.

b Complete with *used to* in +, –, or ? and a verb from the list.

argue   be (x2)   ~~go~~   have (x2)   like   live   play   work

– I _didn't use to go_ to the theater much but now I go twice a month.

1 + Kirsty _____ in Boston but she moved to Orlando last year.
2 ? _____ you _____ a mustache? You look different.
3 – I _____ my boss but now we get along pretty well.
4 + We _____ really close, but now we hardly ever meet.
5 ? Where _____ you _____ before you started with this company?
6 + She _____ tennis professionally, but she retired last year.
7 + When I lived in Paris, I always _____ breakfast in a cafe.
8 ? _____ you _____ with your parents when you were a teenager?
9 – He _____ so thin. In fact, he was very overweight before.

5

5A   quantifiers

large quantities

> They have **a lot of money**.
> She has **lots of friends**.
> He eats **a lot**.
> There aren't **many cafes** near here.
> Do you watch **much TV**?
> Don't run. We have **plenty of time**.

- Use *a lot of / lots of* in ⊞ sentences.
- Use *a lot* when there is no noun, e.g., *He talks a lot*.
- *Much / many* are normally used in ⊟ sentences and ?, but *a lot of* can also be used.
- Use *plenty of* in ⊞ sentences to mean *as much as we need or more*.

small quantities

> A Do you want some ice cream? B Just **a little**.
> The town only has **a few banks**.
> Hurry up. We have **very little time**.
> I have **very few close friends**.

- Use *little* + uncountable nouns, *few* + plural countable nouns.
- *a little* and *a few* = some, but not a lot,
- *very little* and *very few* = not much / many.

zero quantity

> There **isn't any** room in the car.
> There**'s no** room in the car.
> A How much money do you have?
> B **None**.

- Use *any* for zero quantity with a ⊟ verb. Use *no* with a ⊞ verb.
- Use *none* (without a noun) in short answers.

more than you need or want

> I don't like this city. It's **too big**.
> There's **too much traffic**.
> There are **too many tourists**.

less than you need

> There aren't **enough parks**.
> The buses aren't **frequent enough**.

- Use *too* + adjective, *too much* + uncountable noun, *too many* + plural countable nouns.
- Use *enough* before a noun but after an adjective.

5B   articles: *a / an*, *the*, no article

Use *a / an* with singular countable nouns	
– the first time you mention a thing / person.	I saw **an old man** with **a dog**.
– when you say what something is.	It's **a nice house**.
– when you say what somebody does.	She's **a lawyer**.
– in exclamations with *What …!*	What **an awful day**!
– in expressions like …	three times **a week**

Use *the*	
– when we talk about something we've already mentioned.	I saw an old man with a dog, and **the dog** was barking.
– when there's only one of something.	**The moon** goes around **the sun**.
– when it's clear what you're referring to.	He opened **the door**.
– with places in a town, e.g., *bank* and *theater*.	I'm going to **the bank**.
– with superlatives.	It's **the best** restaurant in town.

Don't use *the*
– when you are speaking in general (with plural and uncountable nouns). **Women** often talk more about **money**.
– with some nouns (e.g., *home*, *work*, *school*) after *at / to / from*, She's not **at home** today.
– with **downtown** (no preposition). They went **downtown** today.
– before meals, days, and months. I never have **breakfast** on **Sunday**.
– before *next / last* + days, week, etc. See you **next Friday**.

5C   gerunds and infinitives

Use the gerund (verb + *-ing*)	
1 after prepositions and phrasal verbs.	I'm very good **at remembering** names. She **kept on talking**.
2 as the subject of a sentence.	**Eating out** is cheap here.
3 after some verbs, e.g., *dislike, enjoy*.	I **don't mind getting up** early.

Common verbs that take the gerund include: **Finish, mind, practice, quit, recommend, stop, suggest** and phrasal verbs, e.g., **give up, keep on**, etc.

Use the infinitive	
1 after adjectives.	My house is **easy to find**.
2 to express a reason or purpose.	He's saving money **to buy** a new car.
3 after some verbs, e.g., *want, need, learn*.	She's never **learned to drive**. **Try not to make** noise.

Common verbs that take the infinitive include: (**can't**) **afford, agree, decide, expect, forget, help, hope, learn, need, offer, plan, pretend, promise, refuse, remember, seem, try, want, would like**

⚠ Use the base form	
1 after most modal and auxiliary verbs	I **can't** drive. We **must** hurry.
2 after *make* and *let*.	My parents don't **let** me **go** out much. She always **makes** me **laugh**.

- Gerunds and infinitives form the negative with *not*, e.g., *not to be, not being*.
- These common verbs can take either the gerund or infinitive with no difference in meaning: **begin, continue, hate, like, love, prefer, start**.

⚠ Some verbs can take a gerund or an infinitive but the meaning is different, e.g.,

Try to be on time.
= make an effort to be on time.

Try doing yoga.
= do it to see if you like it.

Remember to call him.
= Don't forget to do it.

I remember meeting him years ago.
= I have a memory of it.

5A

a Circle the correct answer. Check (✔) if both are possible.

I think this restaurant is (too)/ *too much* expensive.

1 There are *too much* / *too many* people in my salsa class.
2 Nobody likes him. He has *very little* / *very few* friends.
3 We've had *a lot of* / *lots of* rain recently.
4 There aren't *enough parking lots* / *parking lots enough* downtown.
5 *I have no* / *I don't have any* time.
6 He works *a lot* / *much*. At least ten hours a day.
7 **A** Do you speak Japanese? **B** Yes, *a little* / *a few*.
8 I don't have *no time* / *any time* for myself.

b Right (✔) or wrong (✘). Correct the wrong sentences.

She drives too much fast . *too fast*

1 Slow down! We have plenty time .
2 We have too many work at the moment.
3 I think I made a few mistakes in the letter.
4 He isn't enough old to understand.
5 We can't go tomorrow. We're too busy .
6 We have very little time to do this.
7 **A** How many eggs are there? **B** Any .
8 He's retired so he has much free time .

5B

a Circle the correct answer.

Did you see *news* / (the news) on TV last night?

1 Did you lock *door* / *the door* when you left *a house* / *the house*?
2 My brother is married to *Russian* / *a Russian*. She's *lawyer* / *a lawyer*.
3 We go to *theater* / *the theater* about once *a month* / *the month*.
4 What *beautiful* / *a beautiful day*! Let's have breakfast on *a patio* / *the patio*.
5 I love *classical music* / *the classical music* and *Italian food* / *the Italian food*.
6 Who is *a girl* / *the girl* by *a window* / *the window*?
7 I leave *home* / *the home* at 8:00 and get to *work* / *the work* at 9:00.
8 *Men* / *The men* aren't normally as sensitive as *women* / *the women*.
9 We usually have *dinner* / *the dinner* at 8:00 and go to *bed* / *the bed* at about 11:30.
10 She has *a lovely face* / *the lovely face* and *the attractive eyes* / *attractive eyes*.

b Complete with *a* / *an*, *the*, or – (no article).

Can you give me __a__ ride to __the__ station? I want to catch __the__ 6:00 train.

1 We went to __a__ movies __at__ last night. We saw _____ great movie.
2 **A** Do you like _____ sports?
   B It depends. I hate _____ baseball. I think _____ players earn too much money.
3 He always wears _____ expensive clothes and drives _____ expensive car.
4 Jake's _____ musician and _____ artist.
5 They've changed _____ date of _____ meeting. It's _____ next Tuesday now.
6 We walked _____ downtown but we got _____ taxi back to _____ hotel.

5C

a Complete with the gerund or infinitive.

Smoking is banned in all public places. (smoke)

1 It's very expensive _renting_ an apartment downtown. (rent)
2 Are you afraid of _flying_? (fly)
3 I called the restaurant _reserve_ a table for tonight. (reserve)
4 Be careful _making_ noise when you come home tonight. (not make)
5 She's worried about _to fail_ the exam. (fail)
6 Everybody kept on _dancing_ until after midnight. (dance)
7 _____ an only child is a little boring. (be)
8 It's easy _____ the way if you look at the map. (find)
9 He's terrible at _____ languages. (learn)
10 **A** Why are you learning Spanish?
    B I want _to be_ talk to my in-laws. They're Argentinian, and they don't speak English. (be able to)

b Complete the sentences with *work*, *to work*, or *working*.

I regret not _working_ harder when I was at school.

1 I spent all weekend _work_ on the computer.
2 I've decided _to_ overseas next year.
3 You must _work_ harder if you want to get promoted.
4 My boss often makes me _work_ late.
5 He isn't very good at _working_ on a team.
6 I don't mind _working_ on Saturdays if I can have a day off during the week.
7 He's gone to the US _to work_ in his uncle's store.
8 _Working_ with members of your family can be pretty difficult.
9 My husband promised not _to work_ on my birthday.
10 I used _to work_ in a restaurant when I was a student.

6

6A reported speech: statements and questions

direct statements	reported statements
"**I like** shopping."	She said (that) **she liked** shopping.
"**I'm going tomorrow**."	He told her **he was** going **the next day**.
"**I'll** always love **you**."	He said **he would** always love **me**.
"**I passed** the exam!"	She told him **she had passed** the exam.
"**I've forgotten my** keys."	He said **he had forgotten his** keys.
"**I can't** come."	She said **she couldn't** come.
"**I may** be late."	He said **he might** be late.
"**I must** go."	She said **she had to** go.

- Tenses usually change like this: **present>past**; **will>would**; **simple past / present perfect>past perfect**
- Some modal verbs change, e.g., **can>could**, **may>might**, **must>had to**. Other modal verbs stay the same, e.g., *could, might, should*, etc.

direct questions	reported questions
"**Are you** married?"	She asked him **if he was** married.
"**Did she call**?"	He asked me **whether** she **had called**.
"**What's** your name?"	I asked him **what** his name **was**.
"**Where do you live**?"	They asked me **where I lived**.

⚠ • *Must* changes to *had to* BUT *must not* stays the same.
"*You must not touch it.*" *She said I must not touch it.*

- You usually have to change the pronouns.
"I like…">She said **she liked**…
- Using **that** after *said* and *told* is optional.
- If you report what someone said on a different day or in a different place, some time and place words can change, e.g., **tomorrow>the next day**, **here>there**, **this>that**, etc.
"I'll meet you here tomorrow.">He said he'd meet me there the next day.

⚠ After *said* don't use an object pronoun.
He said he was tired NOT ~~He said me…~~
After *told* you <u>must</u> use a person or pronoun.
He told me he was tired. NOT ~~He told he was…~~

- When you report a question, the tenses change as in reported statements.
- When a question begins with a verb (not a question word), add *if* (or *whether*).
- You also have to change the word order to subject + verb, and not use *do / did*.

reported speech: commands

direct speech	reported speech
"**Go** away."	She told him **to go** away.
"**Don't worry**."	The doctor told me **not to worry**.
"**Can / Could you help** me?"	I asked the salesperson **to help** me.

⚠ You can't use *said* in these sentences.
NOT ~~She said him to go away.~~

- To report an imperative or request, use *told* or *asked* + person + the infinitive.
- To report a negative imperative, use a negative infinitive (e.g., **not to do**).

6B the passive: *be* + past participle

A lot of films **are shot** on location.	My bike **has been stolen**.
My car **is being repaired** today.	You**'ll be picked up** at the airport.
Death in Venice **was directed by** Visconti.	This bill **has to be paid** tomorrow.
She died when **the film was being made**.	

- We often use the passive when it's not clear or important who does an action, e.g.,
My bike has been stolen.
(Somebody stole my bike. I don't know who.)
- If you want to say who did the action, use *by*.

6C relative clauses

defining relative clauses

Julia's the woman **who / that** works with me.
It's a book **that / which** tells you how to relax.
That's the house **where** I was born.
That's the boy **whose** father plays for the Lakers.
He's the man (**who / that**) I met on the plane.

- To give important information about a person, place, or thing use a relative clause = a relative pronoun + (subject +) verb.
- Use the relative pronouns *who / that* for people, *that / which* for things, and *where* for places. Use *whose* to mean "of who / of which."
- *That* is more common than *which* in defining clauses.
- *Who, which,* and *that* can be omitted when the relative pronoun is the object, not the subject, of the clause, e.g., *He's the man (that) I met on the plane.* (The subject of *met* is *I*, so it is not necessary to use *that*.)

non-defining relative clauses

This painting, **which** was painted in 1860, is worth $2 million.
Last week I visited my aunt, **who's** nearly 90 years old.
Stanford, **where** my mother was born, is a beautiful town.
My neighbor, **whose** son goes to my son's school, has just re-married.

- If a relative clause gives extra, non-essential information (the sentence makes sense without it), you must put it between commas (or a comma and a period).
- In these clauses, you can't leave out the relative pronoun (*who, which,* etc.).
- In these clauses, you **can't** use *that* instead of *who / which*.

6A

a Complete the sentences using reported speech.

"The hotel is full." The receptionist told me the hotel _was full_ .

1 "I'll call the manager." The waiter said _____.
2 "I've passed all my exams." Jack said _____.
3 "You should get to the airport early." They said that we _____.
4 "I may be late." Jack said _____.
5 "I didn't tell anybody!" Mary said _____.
6 "Can you help me?" She asked us _____.
7 "Do you want to dance?" He asked me _____.
8 "Have you been here before?" I asked her _____.
9 "What music do you like?" She asked me _____.
10 "Where's the nearest bank?" I asked her _____.

b Complete the reported imperatives and requests.

"Don't stop here." The traffic officer told us _not to stop there_.

1 "Be quiet!" The teacher told us _____.
2 "Please don't smoke!" I asked the taxi driver _____.
3 "Open your mouth." The dentist told me _____.
4 "Don't tell anyone!" Melinda told us _____.
5 "Could you show me your driver's license?" The police officer asked me _____.
6 "Please turn off your cell phones." The flight attendant told us _____.
7 "Don't eat with your mouth open!" I told my daughter _____.
8 "Can you bring me the check, please?" He asked the waiter _____.
9 "Get off at the next stop." The bus driver told me _____.
10 "Don't wait." Our friends told us _____.

6B

a Correct the mistakes in the highlighted phrases.

A lot of cars made in Brazil. _are made in Brazil._

1 A new highway is being build at the moment.
2 The movie based on a famous novel.
3 This program were watched by millions of people.
4 My suitcase was stole when I was in Florida.
5 The Harry Potter books were written for J.K. Rowling.
6 I couldn't send you an e-mail because my computer was repairing.
7 You will taken to your hotel by taxi.
8 Oh no! Our flight has being canceled.
9 English is spoke in this restaurant.
10 Seat belts must wear at all times.

b Rewrite the sentences with the passive.

They sell cold drinks here. Cold drinks _are sold here_ .

1 They subtitle a lot of foreign films.
A lot of foreign films _____.
2 Someone threw the letters away by mistake.
The letters _____.
3 Some people are painting my house.
My house _____.
4 They have sold all the tickets for the concert.
All the tickets for the concert _____.
5 They will play the game tomorrow.
The game _____.
6 Somebody must pay this bill tomorrow.
This bill _____.

6C

a Complete with *who, which, that, where,* or *whose.*

The man _whose_ car I crashed into is taking me to court.

1 We drove past the house _that_ we used to live.
2 The girl _that_ was talking to you is the boss's daughter.
3 Look! That's the man _whose_ son plays for the Red Sox.
4 The car was an invention _where_ changed the world.
5 That's the restaurant _where_ I told you about.
6 Is this the store _which_ you bought your camera?
7 What was the name of your friend _that_ wife is an actress?
8 The woman _whose_ called this morning didn't leave a message.
9 It's the movie _that_ won all the Oscars last year.
10 This is the book _which_ everybody is reading at the moment.

b Check (✔) the sentences in **a** where you could leave out the relative pronoun.

c Are the highlighted phrases right (✔) or wrong (✘)? Correct the wrong ones.

After Rome we went to Venice, that we loved . ✘
which we loved

1 Is that the girl you used to go out with ?
2 My brother, that you met at my wedding , is getting divorced.
3 It's a machine that makes candy .
4 He lives in Acapulco, that is on the west coast of Mexico .
5 Our neighbor, who yard is smaller than ours , has an enormous dog.
6 Jerry, who I work with , is completely bilingual.
7 The movie I saw last night was fantastic.
8 I met some people who they come from the same town as me .

7A third conditional

third conditional sentences: *if* + *had* + past participle, *would* + *have* + past participle.

> If I**'d known** about the meeting, I **would have gone**.
> If I **hadn't gone** to that party, I **wouldn't have met** my wife.
> You **wouldn't have been** late if you**'d gotten up** earlier.
> We **would have arrived** at 6:00 if we **hadn't gotten** lost.

- The contraction of *had* is *'d*.

- Use third conditional sentences to talk about a hypothetical / imaginary situation in the past (which didn't happen) and its consequence. Compare:
Yesterday I got up late and missed my train. (= the real situation)
If I hadn't gotten up late yesterday, I wouldn't have missed my train. (= the hypothetical / imaginary situation)
- To make a third conditional, use *if* + past perfect and *would have* + past participle.

7B tag questions, indirect questions

tag questions

affirmative verb, negative tag	negative verb, affirmative tag
It's cold today, **isn't it?**	She isn't here today, **is she?**
You're Peruvian, **aren't you?**	You aren't happy, **are you?**
They live in Kyoto, **don't they?**	They don't know, **do they?**
The game finishes at 8:00, **doesn't it?**	She doesn't eat meat, **does she?**
She worked in a bank, **didn't she?**	You didn't like the movie, **did you?**
We've met before, **haven't we?**	She hasn't been to Rome before, **has she?**
You'll be OK, **won't you?**	You won't tell anyone, **will you?**

- Tag questions are often used to check something you already think is true.
Your name's Maria, isn't it?
- To form a tag question use:
– the correct auxiliary verb, e.g., *do / does* for the present, *will / won't* for the future, etc.
– a pronoun, e.g., *he, it, they*, etc.
– a negative tag if the sentence is affirmative, and an affirmative tag if the sentence is negative.

indirect questions

direct question	indirect question
Where**'s the bank?**	Could you tell me where **the bank is?**
What time **do the stores close?**	Do you know what time **the stores close?**
Is there a bus stop near here?	Do you know **if there's a bus stop** near here?
Does this train go to Toronto?	Could you tell me **if this train goes** to Toronto?

- If the question doesn't start with a question word, add *if* (or *whether*) after *Could you tell me…? / Do you know…?*
- We also use this structure after *Can you remember…?*, e.g., *Can you remember where he lives?*

- To make a question more polite we often begin *Could you tell me…?* or *Do you know…?* The word order changes to subject + verb, e.g., *Do you know where the post office is?* NOT ~~Do you know where is the post office?~~

7C phrasal verbs

group 1: no object – verb + *up, on*, etc., can't be separated.
Come on! Hurry up! We're late.
The plane **took off** two hours late.
Go away and never **come back!**

- A phrasal verb is a verb combined with a particle (= an adverb or preposition).
- Sometimes the meaning of the phrasal verb is obvious from the verb and the particle, e.g., *sit down, come back*.
- Sometimes the meaning is not obvious, e.g. *give up, keep on talking* (= continue talking).
- In group 3, where the verb and particle can be separated, if the object is a pronoun, it must go between the verb and particle.
Turn it off. NOT ~~Turn off it.~~
Throw them away. NOT ~~Throw away them.~~

group 2: with object – verb + *up, on*, etc., can't be separated.
I'm **looking for** my keys. ~~NOT I'm looking my keys for.~~
I **asked for** chicken, not steak.
I don't **get along with** my sister.
I'm **looking forward to** the party.

group 3: with object – verb + *up, on*, etc., can be separated.
Please **turn off** your phone.   / Please **turn** your phone **off.**
Can you **fill out** this form, please? / Can you **fill** this form **out**, please?
They've **set up** a new company.   / They've **set** a new company **up.**
Don't **throw out** those papers.   / Don't **throw** those papers **out.**

> ⚠ Sometimes a phrasal verb has more than one meaning, e.g.,
> *The plane took off.*
> *He took off his shoes.*

7A

a Match the sentence halves.

1 If you hadn't reminded me, *I*
2 This wouldn't have happened *G*
3 If they hadn't worn their seat belts, *H*
4 We wouldn't have been late *K*
5 We would have gone to the beach
6 If you hadn't told me it was him, *J*
7 You would have laughed *A*
8 I wouldn't have bought it *E*
9 If you'd arrived two minutes earlier, *C*
10 If you hadn't forgotten the map, *B*
11 It would have been cheaper *F*

A if you'd seen what happened.
B we wouldn't have gotten lost.
C if it hadn't rained.
D you would have seen them.
E if I'd known you didn't like it.
F if we'd bought tickets on the Internet.
G if you'd been more careful.
H they would have been killed.
I I would have forgotten.
J I wouldn't have recognized him.
K if we hadn't missed the bus.

b Cover A–K. Look at 1–11 and try to remember the end of the sentence.

c Complete the third conditional sentences with the correct form of the verbs.

If you *hadn't helped* me, I *wouldn't have finished* on time. (not help, not finish)

1 We _____ if our best player _____ injured. (win, not be)
2 If she _____ he was so stingy, she _____ with him. (know, not go out)
3 I *would* _____ you some money if you _____ me. (lend, ask)
4 If we _____ more time, we _____ another day in Miami. (have, spend)
5 I _____ to help you if you _____ me about it earlier. (be able, tell)
6 If you _____ me yesterday, I _____ my plans. (ask, change)
7 You _____ the weekend if you _____ with us. (enjoy, come)

7B

a Complete with a tag question (*are you?, isn't it?*, etc.).

Your name's Mark, *isn't it* ?

1 You don't take sugar in your coffee, *Do you* ?
2 They're on vacation this week, *are they*?
3 He can't be serious, *He* ?
4 She eats meat, *Doesn't she*
5 You won't be late, *Do you*?
6 She was married to Tom Cruise, _____ ?
7 We've seen this movie before, _____ ?
8 You didn't tell anybody, *Did you* ?
9 You would like to come, *wouldn't* ?
10 It's hot today, *isn't it*?

b Make indirect questions.

Where's the station? Could you tell me *where the station is?*

1 Where do they live? Do you know *isn't it* ?
2 Is there a bank near here? Can you tell me _____ ?
3 Where can I buy some stamps? Do you know _____ ?
4 Does this bus go downtown? Could you tell me _____ ?
5 What time do the stores open? Do you know _____ ?
6 Where are the restrooms? Could you tell me _____ ?
7 Is Susan at work today? Do you know _____ ?
8 Did the Mets win last night? Do you know _____ ?
9 Where did we park the car? Can you remember _____ ?
10 What time is it? Could you tell me _____ ?

7C

a Complete with the right particle (*in, on*, etc.).

What time did you get *up* this morning?

1 Could you turn ___ the radio? I can't hear it.
2 I'm in a meeting. Could you call ___ later, say in half an hour?
3 Hurry ___! We'll be late.
4 The game is ___! Brazil won.
5 How long has she been going ___ with him?
6 Are we having dinner at home or are we eating ___?
7 Athletes always warm ___ before a race.
8 I didn't wake ___ until 8:30 this morning.
9 If you don't know the word, look it ___ in a dictionary.
10 I went online to find ___ what time the train left.

b Rewrite the sentences. Replace the *object* with a pronoun. Change the word order where necessary.

Turn on *the TV*. *Turn it on.*

1 Take off *your shoes*.
2 Could you fill out *this form*?
3 Do you get along with *your sister*?
4 Turn off *your cell phones*.
5 I'm looking for *my glasses*.
6 Please pick up *that towel*.
7 Turn down *the music*!
8 I'm really looking forward to *the trip*.
9 Can I try on *this dress*?
10 Don't throw away *that letter*!

Food and restaurants

1 Food

a Put two food words in each column. Use your dictionary to help you.

beans	duck	lettuce /'lɛtəs/	
peaches	shrimp /ʃrɪmp/	salmon /'sæmən/	
sausage /'sɔsɪdʒ/	strawberries /'strɔbɛriz/		

meat	fish / seafood	fruit	vegetables

b Add three more words to each column.

2 Food adjectives

Complete the adjective column with a word from the box.

fresh	frozen	homemade	low-fat	raw /rɔ/	spicy /'spaɪsi/	sweet	takeout

	Adjective
1 I love my mother's cooking. ▢ food is always the best.	_____
2 Mexican food can be very ▢.	_____
3 Sushi is made with ▢ fish.	_____
4 Food that is kept very cold is ▢.	_____
5 ▢ food is food you buy at a restaurant and take home to eat.	_____
6 People on a diet often try to eat ▢ food.	_____
7 These eggs are ▢. I bought them today.	_____
8 This tea's very ▢. You've put too much sugar in it!	_____

3 Restaurants and cooking

a Match the words and pictures.

- ▢ knife /naɪf/ pl knives /naɪvz/
- ▢ fork
- ▢ desserts /dɪ'zərts/
- ▢ spoon
- ▢ plate
- ▢ glass
- ▢ main courses /meɪn kɔrsɪz/
- ▢ napkin
- ▢ salt and pepper
- ▢ appetizers

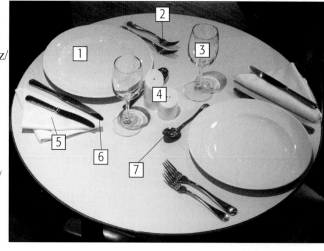

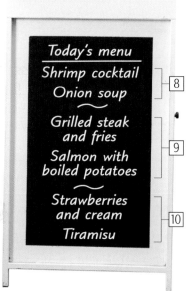

Today's menu
Shrimp cocktail
Onion soup ⎯⎯ 8
~
Grilled steak
and fries
Salmon with ⎯⎯ 9
boiled potatoes
~
Strawberries
and cream ⎯⎯ 10
Tiramisu

b Match the words and pictures.

- ▢ **boiled** rice
- ▢ **roast** chicken
- ▢ **baked** potatoes
- ▢ **grilled** fish
- ▢ **fried** eggs
- ▢ **steamed** vegetables

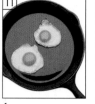

○ p.6

Can you remember the words on this page? Test yourself or a partner.

Study Link MultiROM www.oup.com/elt/americanenglishfile/3

Sports

1 People and places

a Match the words and pictures.

captain /'kæptən/	spectators
coach	team
fans	stadium
players	sports arena
referee	

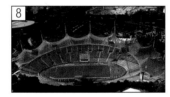

b Match the places and sports.

court /kɔrt/   course
field   pool   slope   track

1 tennis / basketball _____
2 soccer / baseball _____
3 swimming / diving _____
4 running / horse racing _____
5 golf _____
6 skiing _____

2 Verbs

a Complete with the past tense and past participles.

beat	_____	_____
win	_____	_____
lose	_____	_____
tie	_____	_____

b Complete the **Verb** column with the past tense of a verb from **a**.

	Verb
1 Costa Rica ___ US 3-0.	_____
2 The Chicago Bulls ___ 78-91 (to Celtics).	_____
3 Spain ___ with (Brazil) 2-2.	_____
4 Costa Rica ___ (the game) 3-0.	_____

⚠ You *win* a game, competition, medal, or trophy. You *beat* another team or person NOT Costa Rica ~~won~~ the US.

c Complete the **Verb** column.

do   get in shape   get injured /'ɪndʒərd/   go   play
score   train   warm up

	Verb
1 Players usually ___ before a game starts.	_____
2 Professional athletes have to ___ every day.	_____
3 It's dangerous to play tennis on a wet court. You might ___ .	_____
4 I've started going to the gym, because I want to ___ .	_____
5 He's a good player. I think he's going to ___ a lot of goals.	_____
6 Would you like to ___ swimming this afternoon?	_____
7 I ___ basketball twice a week.	_____
8 My brothers ___ yoga and tai chi.	_____

Can you remember the words on this page? Test yourself or a partner.

◀ **p.10**

Personality

1 What are they like?

a Complete the sentences with the personality adjectives.

affectionate /ə'fɛkʃənət/   aggressive   ambitious   bossy   charming   competitive   independent   jealous /'dʒɛləs/
manipulative   moody   reliable /rɪ'laɪəbl/   selfish   sensible   sensitive   sociable /'souʃəbl/   spoiled

1   _Spoiled_   children behave badly because they are given everything they want.
2   ambitious   people always want to win.
3   selfish   people think about themselves and not about other people.
4   aggressive   people use force to succeed and may fight or argue.
5   charming   people have an attractive personality that makes people like them.
6   _____   people have common sense and are practical.
7   sociable   people are friendly and enjoy being with other people.
8   _____   people get other people to do what they want cleverly or even unfairly.
9   moody   people are happy one minute and sad the next, and are often bad-tempered.
10   independent   people like doing things on their own, without help.
11   bossy   people like giving orders to other people.
12   affectionate   people show that they love or like people very much.
13   reliable   people are people you can trust or depend on.
14   sensitive   people understand other people's feelings or are easily hurt or offended.
15   _____   people want to be successful in life.
16   Jealous   people think that someone loves another person more than them or wants what other people have.

b With a partner, look at the adjectives again. Are they positive, negative, or neutral characteristics?

2 Opposite adjectives

Match the adjectives and their opposites.

outgoing   hardworking   self-confident
stingy   stupid   talkative

clever	stupid	lazy	Hardworking
generous	stingy	quiet	talkative
insecure	Self-confident	shy	outgoing

3 Negative prefixes

Which negative prefix do you use with these adjectives?
Put them in the correct column.

ambitious   friendly   honest /'ɑnəst/   imaginative
kind   organized   patient /'peɪʃnt/   reliable
responsible   selfish   sensitive   sociable

un-	dis-	in- / im- / ir-
unambitious	dishonest	
unfriendly		

Can you remember the words on this page?
Test yourself or a partner.

→ p.15

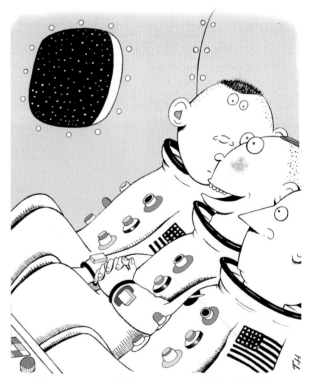

"Are we there yet? Are we there yet? Are we there yet?"

1 Verbs

Complete with a verb in the correct tense.

be worth /wərθ/	borrow	can't afford /əˈfɔrd/	charge	cost	earn
inherit	invest	lend	owe /oʊ/	save	take out
waste /weɪst/					

1 My uncle died and left me $2,000.　I _inherit_ $2,000 from my uncle.
2 I put some money aside every week for my next vacation.　I _save_ money every week.
3 I asked my brother to give me $10 until next week.　I _borrow_ $10 from him.
4 My brother gave me $10 until next week.　He _lend_ me $10.
5 I often spend money on stupid things.　I often _waste_ money.
6 I don't have enough money to buy that car.　I _can't affor_ to buy that car.
7 I had to pay the mechanic $500 to repair my car.　The mechanic _charge_ me $500.
8 I went to the ATM and got $200.　I _take out_ $200 from the ATM.
9 I bought a book. It was $25.　The book _cost_ (me) $25.
10 Jim gave me $100. I haven't paid it back yet.　I _owe_ Jim $100.
11 I bought some shares in the telephone company.　I _invest_ some money.
12 I work in a supermarket. They pay me $2,000 a month.　I _earn_ $2,000 a month.
13 I could sell my house for about $200,000.　My house _be worth_ about $200,000.

2 Prepositions

Complete the **Preposition** column.

	Preposition
1 I paid _the_ dinner last night.	_the_
2 Julia said she would pay me tomorrow.	_____
3 Would you like to pay _a_ cash or ____ credit card?	_a_ , _with_
4 I spent $50 ' ____ books yesterday.	_for_
5 I don't like to lend money _a_ friends.	_at_
6 I borrowed a lot of money ____ the bank.	_from_
7 They charged us $60 ____ a bottle of wine.	_for_

3 Nouns

Match the words and definitions.

ATM	bill	coin	loan
mortgage /ˈmɔrgɪdʒ/	salary	tax	

1 _coin_ A piece of money made of metal.
2 _bill_ A piece of paper money.
3 _salary_ Money a person gets for the work he / she does.
4 _tax_ Money that you pay to the government.
5 _loan_ Money that somebody (or a bank) lends you.
6 _mortgage_ Money that you borrow from a bank to buy a house.
7 _ATM_ A machine that you use to get money.

Can you remember the words on this page?
Test yourself or a partner.

⊙ p.21

Transportation and travel

1 Plane

Match the words and pictures.

☐ land (vb)	☐ take off (vb)
☐ check-in counter	☐ gate
☐ luggage /ˈlʌgɪdʒ/	☐ suitcase
☐ boarding card/pass	☐ aisle /aɪl/
☐ baggage claim	

2 Train

Match the words and pictures.

☐ train station
☐ platform
☐ (rail) car
☐ ticket office
☐ the subway

3 Road

a Match the words and pictures.

☐ bus	☐ bike
☐ truck	☐ car
☐ van	☐ taxi
☐ motorcycle	☐ streetcar
☐ helmet	☐ highway

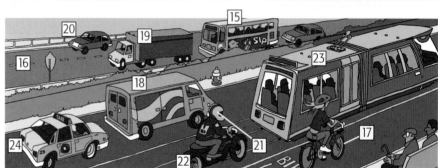

b Complete the compound nouns.

area   belt   crash   hour   jam   lane   light
limit   lot   stand   station   ticket   transportation

1	gas _____	a place where you can get gas, often with a shop or cafe
2	traffic _____	🚦
3	seat _____	➰
4	rush _____	the time of day when there is a lot of traffic
5	car _____	when two or more cars hit each other
6	parking _____	money you have to pay for parking illegally
7	traffic _____	when there is so much traffic that cars can't move
8	speed _____	55 MPH
9	public _____	buses, trains, etc.
10	pedestrian _____	a place where you can't drive
11	bike _____	a narrow part of the road for bicycles only
12	taxi _____	where taxis park when they are waiting for customers
13	parking _____	a place where you can leave your car

4 Travel

flight   journey /ˈdʒɜrni/
trip   travel

1 _____ means to go from one place to another.
2 A _____ is an occasion when a person travels from one place to another and back.
3 A long trip is sometimes called a _____.
4 A trip on an airplane is a _____.

Can you remember the words on this page? Test yourself or a partner.

↪ p.30

1 Age

Complete the phrases.

mid-	early	about	late	forties

1 He's _about_ 20.   = 19, 20, or 21
2 He's in his _forties_.   = between 41 and 49
3 She's in her _mid_ thirties. = between 34 and 36
4 She's in her _late_ sixties. = between 67 and 69
5 He's in his _early_ seventies. = between 71 and 73

2 Height and build

Match the sentences and pictures A–C.

1 A He's **tall** and **slim**.
2 C He's **short** and a little **overweight** /oʊvər'weɪt/.
3 B He's **medium height** /'midiəm haɪt/ and **well built**.

> ⚠ *Thin* and *slim* are both the opposite of *fat* and *heavy*, but *slim* = thin in an attractive way. *Heavy* is more polite than *fat*.

3 Hair

Match the sentences and pictures.

1 E She has **blond** hair and a **ponytail**.
2 A She has **long wavy** hair.
3 G He has **gray** hair and a **beard** /bɪrd/.
4 B She has **short brown curly** hair.
5 C She has **red shoulder-length** hair.
6 F He's **bald** /bɔld/ and has a **mustache** /mə'stæʃ/.
7 D She has **straight dark** hair and **bangs**.

4 General adjectives

Are these adjectives ⊞ or ⊟? Are they used for men, women, or both? Write M, W, or B.

	⊞ or ⊟	M, W, or B
attractive	+	B
beautiful	+	W
good-looking	+	B
handsome /'hænsəm/		M
plain	−	W
pretty /'prɪti/	+	W
ugly	−	B

> ⚠ *What does he / she look like?* = Can you describe his / her appearance?
> *What is he / she like?* = Can you describe his / her personality?

Can you remember the words on this page? Test yourself or a partner.

⬅ p.41

Education

1 Verbs

Complete the **Verb** column.

be<u>have</u>   cheat   do   fail   <u>gr</u>aduate   learn   leave   pass   re<u>view</u>   start   ~~study~~   take

	Verb
	study
1 When she was in school, she used to ☐ for hours every evening.	review
2 I must ☐ tonight. I have a test tomorrow.	learn
3 Our history teacher was terrible. We didn't ☐ anything.	do
4 If you don't ☐ your homework, you can't watch TV later.	cheat
5 The teacher was angry because some of the students had tried to ☐ on the test.	take (or *do*)
6 If you want to be a doctor, you have to ☐ a lot of exams.	star live
7 In the US, children ☐ school when they are five and can't ☐ before they are 16.	past faild
8 I hope I'm going to ☐ my exams. My parents will be furious if I ☐.	behave
9 He was a rebel at school. He used to ☐ very badly.	graduate
10 This is my last semester at the university. I'll ☐ in June.	

2 Places and people

Match the words and definitions.

<u>co</u>llege   ele<u>men</u>tary school   <u>gr</u>aduate   preschool   principal   <u>pri</u>vate school   professor   public school   secondary school   student

1	Public school	A school paid for by the government that gives free education.
2	Private	A non-government school where you have to pay.
3	Pre school	A school for very young children, e.g., 1–4.
4	elementare	A school for young children, e.g., 5–11.
5	Secondary	A school for older children, e.g., 12–18. (It includes junior high or middle school and high school.)
6	college	In the US, a general term for post-secondary education at the university level.
7	Principal	The "boss" of a school.
8	Professor	A senior university teacher.
9	Student	A person who is studying at a school, college, or university.
10	graduate	A person who has finished high school or university and has a degree (e.g., a bachelor's degree).

3 School life

Match the sentences and pictures.

1 [B] We have to wear a horrible **uniform**!
2 [A] The **discipline** here is very **strict**.
3 [E] My **schedule** is terrible this **semester**!
4 [C] I love **math**. It's my favorite **subject**.
5 [D] Look! I got my **test results** today!

Can you remember the words on this page?
Test yourself or a partner.

⬅ p.52

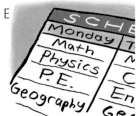

Houses

1 Types of houses

Match the words and pictures.

- 1 apartment building
- 4 cottage /ˈkɑtɪdʒ/
- 3 house
- 2 townhouse

2 Where people live

Match the sentences.

1 I live in the **country**. g
2 I live **downtown**. D
3 I live in the **suburbs**. E
4 I live in a **village** /ˈvɪlɪdʒ/. B
5 I live in a **small town**. A
6 I live in a **residential area**. C
7 I live on the **second floor**. f

a It has 20,000 inhabitants.
b It's very small, with only 800 inhabitants.
c There are a lot of houses but no offices or big stores.
d It's right in the middle of the city.
e It's the area outside the central part of town.
f There is one floor below me.
g There are fields and trees all around me.

3 Parts of a house

Match the words and pictures.

- 1 balcony
- 3 chimney
- 9 fence
- 8 garage /gəˈrɑdʒ/
- 6 garden
- 10 gate
- 11 patio
- 5 porch
- 2 roof
- 7 steps
- 4 yard

4 Furniture

a Put two words in each column. Use your dictionary to help you.

stove   toilet   shower
bedside table   dishwasher
coffee table   armchair
dresser

bathroom	kitchen	living room	bedroom
toilet shower	stove dishwasher	coffee table	dresser bedside table

b Add two more words to each column.

Can you remember the words on this page? Test yourself or a partner.

🔁 p.58

Study Link MultiROM www.oup.com/elt/americanenglishfile/3

151

Work

1 Describing your job

a Read the texts and match them to the pictures. What are the jobs?

1 I only work part-time – four mornings a week. And I sometimes work overtime on Saturday mornings. I don't earn a big salary. It's a temporary or "temp" job and I only have a six-month contract. But the working hours suit me as I have young children. When they go to school, I would like to find a permanent job and work full-time. What I like most about my job is working in complete silence! The only noise you can hear is people turning pages and whispering.

2 I took a six-month training course at a technical college to meet the qualifications for the job and then I worked for a local company to get some experience. I worked long hours for a low salary and so I quit last year and became self-employed. I prefer working for myself. I don't work regular hours (sometimes people call me in the middle of the night) but you can earn a lot of money in this job, especially in the winter. If I'm lucky, I'll be able to retire when I'm 60!

b Match the highlighted words in the texts and the definitions.

1	a written legal agreement	_contract_
2	the knowledge you get from doing a job	_____
3	a series of classes to learn to do a job	_____
4	the time you spend doing a job	_____
5	working for yourself, not for a company	_____
6	to stop working when you reach a certain age, e.g., 65	_____
7	left a job because you wanted to	_____
8	lasting for a short time	_____ (opposite _____)
9	for only a part of the day or the week	_____ (opposite _____)
10	the experience, skills, and knowledge you need for a job	_____

2 Saying what you do

Complete the **Prepositions** column.

	Prepositions
1 I **work** ▒ a multinational company.	_____
2 I **work** ▒ a manager.	_____
3 I'm ▒ **charge** ▒ the marketing department.	_____ , _____
4 I **work** ▒ a factory.	_____
5 I'm **responsible** ▒ customer loans.	_____
6 I'm ▒ **college**.	_____
7 I'm ▒ **my third year**.	_____

3 People

Write two more jobs in each column.

-er	-or	-ist	-ian	others
lawyer /ˈlɔyər/	actor	psychologist	electrician	accountant
plumber	conductor	scientist	librarian	chef /ʃɛf/

> ⚠ An **employer** is a person or company that employs other people. An **employee** is a person who works for somebody.

> **Can you remember the words on this page? Test yourself or a partner.**
>
> ⟲ p.76

1 Places

a Match the words and pictures.

- [ ] department store
- [ ] supermarket
- [ ] farmers' market
- [ ] shopping mall

b Match the shops and pictures of what you can buy there.

- [ ] bakery
- [ ] bookstore
- [ ] flower shop
- [ ] drugstore / pharmacy
- [ ] newsstand
- [ ] stationery store
- [ ] travel agency
- [ ] shoe store

2 In the store

Match the words and definitions or pictures.

bargain /ˈbɑrgən/   basket   cash register   customer   discount   manager
receipt /rɪˈsit/   refund   sale   salesperson   shopping cart   store window

1 _____ a time when stores sell things at lower prices than usual

2 _____ something that you buy for what you think is a good price

3 _____ a place at the front of a store where you can see the products

4 _____ a piece of paper which shows you have paid for something

5 _____ a reduction in the price

6 _____ a person who works in a store

7 _____ 🛒

8 _____ money that is paid back to you when you return something you bought

9 _____ 🧺

10 _____ a person who buys things in a store

11 _____ the person who is in charge of a store, hotel, etc.

12 _____ 🖩

3 Verbs and phrases

Match the sentences.

1 I often **buy** books **online**. [ ]
2 This store **sells** books. [ ]
3 I'm going to **buy** the dishwasher **on credit**. [ ]
4 I went back to the store to **complain**. [ ]
5 I had to **stand in line** for ages in the bank. [ ]
6 I want to **try on** this dress. [ ]
7 I'm **just looking**. [ ]
8 I had to **pay** 8% **sales tax**. [ ]

a I had to wait behind lots of other people.
b I don't need any help right now.
c I buy books on the Internet.
d I'm going to pay for it over 12 months.
e I want to see what I look like in it.
f I had to pay tax on it.
g You can buy books in this store.
h I went there to tell them I wasn't happy.

⟳ p.85

Can you remember the words on this page? Test yourself or a partner.

Movies

1 Kinds of movies

Match the movies and types.

- [ ] action movie
- [ ] comedy
- [ ] horror movie
- [ ] musical
- [ ] science fiction
- [ ] thriller
- [ ] western

2 People and things

Match the words and definitions.

audience /ˈɔdiəns/   cast   director   extra   plot   scene /sin/   script
sequel /ˈsikwəl/   soundtrack   special effects   star   subtitles

1	_cast_	all the people who act in a movie
2	_____	the most important actor or actress in a movie
3	_director_	the person who directs a movie
4	_soundtrack_	the music of a movie
5	_____	the story of a movie
6	_____	a part of a movie happening in one place
7	_____	the people who watch a movie in a theater
8	_____	a movie that continues the story of an earlier movie
9	_____	special images, often created by a computer
10	_____	the words of the movie
11	_____	person in a movie who has a small, unimportant part, e.g., in a crowd scene
12	_____	transcription (usually translation) of the dialogue of a movie that appears at the bottom of the screen

A Room with a View

3 Verbs and phrases

Match the sentences 1–6 with the sentences a–f.

1 The movie **was set** in 19th century Italy and England.
2 It **was based on** a novel by E.M. Forster.
3 It was **filmed / shot on location** in Florence, Italy.
4 It **was directed** by James Ivory.
5 Helena Bonham-Carter **played the part** of Lucy.
6 It **was dubbed** into other languages.

a He was the director.
b It was situated in that place at that time.
c This was her role in the movie.
d The actors originally spoke in English.
e It was an adaptation of the book.
f It was filmed in the real place, not in a studio.

Can you remember the words on this page? Test yourself or a partner.

🔄 p.90

Study Link MultiROM   www.oup.com/elt/americanenglishfile/3

a The phrasal verbs below are all from Files 1–7. Cover the **Particle** column and look at sentence 1. Try to remember the phrasal verb.

b Uncover to check. Then do the same for the other sentences.

		Particle
1	When I go to a restaurant I always **ask** ___ something low-fat.	for
2	I often **eat** ___ with friends at local restaurants.	out
3	Players usually **warm** ___ before a match starts.	up
4	When we have an argument, we always **make** ___ quickly.	up
5	How do you **get** ___ ___ your brothers and sisters?	along with
6	**Take** the camera ___ to the store and **get** your money ___ .	back, back
7	I **took** some money ___ of an ATM.	out
8	A German woman **gave** ___ all her money to charity.	away
9	I organized a school reunion but nobody **turned** ___ .	up
10	She had to **get** ___ very early every morning.	up
11	We **set** ___ early and caught the 6:00 a.m. train.	off
12	The plane **took** ___ and soon I was looking down on the ocean.	off
13	I **picked** ___ my suitcase and followed the "Exit" signs.	up
14	A taxi **picked** me ___ and took me to the airport.	up
15	I **checked** ___ at the airport and got my boarding pass.	in
16	We were talking on the phone, but suddenly she **hung** ___ .	up
17	If he's not at home, I'll **call** ___ later.	back
18	I think people should **turn** ___ their cell phones in restaurants.	off
19	I tried to learn to dance salsa but I **gave** ___ . I was terrible at it.	up
20	I want to **take** ___ a water sport like scuba diving.	up
21	If I like this course, I'll **keep** ___ studying next year.	on
22	Bethany has written a book which is going to be **made** ___ a movie.	into
23	The reporter decided to **find** ___ if school is easier than it used to be.	out
24	I have to **hand** ___ my story tomorrow.	in
25	Carol's parents didn't like her boyfriend so they **went** ___ together in secret.	out
26	After a year she **broke** ___ with her boyfriend.	up
27	If you have something you never use, **throw** it ___ .	away
28	**Slow** ___ ! You're driving too fast.	down
29	She worked, ran the house, and **brought** ___ the children.	up
30	My parents lived abroad, so they didn't see my children **grow** ___ .	up
31	Bill and Melinda Gates **set** ___ a foundation to provide vaccinations.	up
32	You're very nervous. You need to **calm** ___ .	down
33	I **bumped** ___ an old friend in the street yesterday.	into
34	He was **looking** ___ ___ having dinner with his friends.	forward to
35	**Look** ___ ! There's a car coming!	out
36	Her grandmother **passed** ___ last year at the age of 93.	away
37	We can't go to the concert. It's **sold** ___ .	out
38	**Turn** ___ the TV. There's a program I want to watch.	on
39	**Turn** ___ the radio. It's too loud.	down
40	Where can I **plug** ___ my computer?	in

Nobody turned up.

I broke up with him.

Look out!

> ⚠ Some phrasal verbs have more than one meaning:
> I was hot so I **took off** my jacket. The plane **took off**.

⊙ p.110   **Can you remember the words on this page? Test yourself or a partner.**

Irregular verbs

Base form	Simple past	Past participle
be	was	been
beat	beat	beaten
become	became	become
begin	began	begun
bite	bit	bitten
blow	blew /blu/	blown
break	broke	broken
bring	brought /brɔt/	brought
build	built /bɪlt/	built
buy	bought /bɔt/	bought
can	could /kʊd/ /kəd/	–
catch	caught /kɔt/	caught
choose	chose	chosen
come	came	come
cost	cost	cost
cut	cut	cut
do	did	done
draw	drew	drawn
drink	drank	drunk
drive	drove	driven
eat	ate	eaten
fall	fell	fallen
feel	felt	felt
fight	fought /fɔt/	fought
find	found	found
fly	flew /flu/	flown
forget	forgot	forgotten
get	got	gotten
give	gave	given
go	went	gone
grow	grew /gru/	grown
hang	hung	hung
have	had	had
hear	heard /hərd/	heard
hide	hid /hɪd/	hidden
hit	hit	hit
hold	held	held
hurt	hurt	hurt
keep	kept	kept
know	knew /nu/	known
leave	left	left
lend	lent	lent
let	let	let
lie	lay /leɪ/	lain /leɪn/
lose	lost	lost
make	made	made
mean	meant /mɛnt/	meant
meet	met	met
pay	paid	paid
put	put /pʊt/	put
read	read /rɛd/	read /rɛd/
ride	rode /roʊd/	ridden
ring	rang	rung
run	ran	run
say	said /sɛd/	said
see	saw /sɔ/	seen
sell	sold	sold
send	sent	sent
set	set	set
shine	shone /ʃoʊn/	shone
show	showed	shown /ʃoʊn/
shut	shut	shut
sing	sang	sung
sit	sat	sat
sleep	slept	slept
speak	spoke	spoken
spend	spent	spent
stand	stood /stʊd/	stood
steal	stole	stolen
swim	swam	swum
take	took /tʊk/	taken
teach	taught	taught
tell	told	told
think	thought /θɔt/	thought
throw	threw /θru/	thrown /θroʊn/
understand	understood	understood
wake	woke	woken
wear	wore	worn
win	won /wʌn/	won
write	wrote	written

Study Link MultiROM www.oup.com/elt/americanenglishfile/3

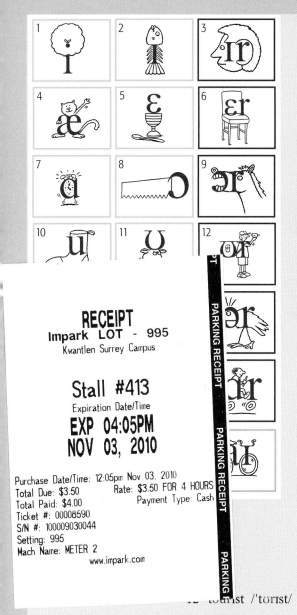

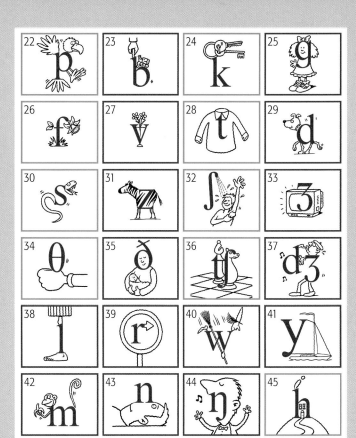

■ voiced
▨ unvoiced

12 tourist /ˈtʊrɪst/

2 fish /fɪʃ/

13 up /ʌp/

3 ear /ɪr/

14 computer /kəmˈpyutər/

4 cat /kæt/

15 bird /bərd/

5 egg /ɛg/

16 owl /aʊl/

6 chair /tʃɛr/

17 phone /foʊn/

7 clock /klɑk/

18 car /kɑr/

8 saw /sɔ/

19 train /treɪn/

9 horse /hɔrs/

20 boy /bɔɪ/

10 boot /but/

21 bike /baɪk/

11 bull /bʊl/

22 parrot /ˈpærət/

23 bag /bæg/

24 keys /kiz/

25 girl /gərl/

26 flower /ˈflaʊər/

27 vase /veɪs/

28 tie /taɪ/

29 dog /dɔg/

30 snake /sneɪk/

31 zebra /ˈzibrə/

32 shower /ˈʃaʊər/

33 television /ˈtɛləvɪʒn/

34 thumb /θʌm/

35 mother /ˈmʌðər/

36 chess /tʃɛs/

37 jazz /dʒæz/

38 leg /lɛg/

39 right /raɪt/

40 witch /wɪtʃ/

41 yacht /yɑt/

42 monkey /ˈmʌŋki/

43 nose /noʊz/

44 singer /ˈsɪŋər/

45 house /haʊs/

Sounds and spelling – vowels

		usual spelling	⚠ but also
tree	**ee** speed sweet **ea** peach team **e** refund medium	people magazine key niece receipt
fish	**i** dish bill trip fit ticket since	pretty women busy decided village physics
ear	**eer** beer engineer **ere** here we're **ear** beard appearance	serious
cat	**a** fan travel crash tax carry land	
egg	**e** menu lend text spend plenty cent	friendly already healthy many said
chair	**air** airport upstairs fair hair **are** rare careful	their there wear pear area
clock	**o** shop comedy plot shot cottage on	watch want calm
saw	**a** bald wall **aw** draw saw **al** talk walk	thought caught audience
horse	**or** sports floor **ore** bore score	warm course board
boot	**oo** pool moody **u*** true student	suitcase juice shoe move soup through

		usual spelling	⚠ but also
bull	**u** full **oo** cook book look good	could should would woman
tourist	A very unusual sound. sure plural	
up	**u** public subject ugly duck cup	money someone enough country tough
computer	Many different spellings, /ə/ is always unstressed. ab<u>ou</u>t compl<u>ai</u>n	
bird	**er** term prefer **ir** dirty third **ur** curly turn	learn work world worse journey
owl	**ou** hour lounge proud ground **ow** town brown	
phone	**o*** broke stone frozen stove **oa** roast coat	owe slow although shoulders
car	**ar** garden charge starter	heart
train	**a*** save gate **ai** railroad plain **ay** may say gray	break steak great weight they
boy	**oi** boiled noisy spoiled coin **oy** enjoy employer	
bike	**i** fine sign **y** shy motorcycle **igh** flight frightened	buy eyes height

***** especially before consonant + **e**

		usual spelling	⚠ but also
parrot	**p** **pp**	plate transport trip shopping apply	
bag	**b** **bb**	beans bill probably job rabbit dubbed	
keys	**c** **k** **ck**	court script kind basket track lucky	chemistry school mechanic sequel quit
girl	**g** **gg**	golf grilled burger forget aggressive luggage	
flower	**f** **ph** **ff**	food roof photo nephew traffic affectionate	enough laugh
vase	**v**	van vegetables travel invest private behave	of
tie	**t** **tt**	try tennis stupid strict attractive cottage	worked passed
dog	**d** **dd**	director afford comedy confident address middle	failed bored
snake	**s** **ss** **c** (before *e, i, y*)	steps likes boss assistant twice city cycle	science scene
zebra	**z** **s**	lazy freezing lose cosy loves cousins	
shower	**sh** **ti** (+ vowel) **ci** (+ vowel)	short dishwasher selfish cash ambitious station special sociable	sugar sure chef mustache
television		decision confusion usually	

		usual spelling	⚠ but also
thumb	**th**	thin thriller healthy path math both	
mother	**th**	the that farther whether	
chess	**ch** **tch** **t** (+**ure**)	change cheat watch match picture future	
jazz	**j** **g** **dge**	jealous just generous manager bridge judge	
leg	**l** **ll**	lettuce salary until reliable sell thriller	
right	**r** **rr**	result referee elementary fried borrow married	written wrong
witch	**w** **wh**	wear waste western highway white which	one once
yacht	**y** before **u**	yet year yogurt yourself university argue	
monkey	**m** **mm**	mean slim romantic charming summer swimming	lamb
nose	**n** **nn**	napkin honest none spoon tennis thinner	knife knew
singer	**ng**	cooking going spring bring	think bank
house	**h**	handsome helmet hard inherit unhappy perhaps	who whose whole

OXFORD
UNIVERSITY PRESS

198 Madison Avenue
New York, NY 10016 USA

Great Clarendon Street, Oxford OX2 6DP UK

Oxford University Press is a department of the University of
Oxford. It furthers the University's objective of excellence
in research, scholarship, and education by publishing
worldwide in

Oxford New York

Auckland Cape Town Dar es Salaam Hong Kong Karachi
Kuala Lumpur Madrid Melbourne Mexico City Nairobi New
Delhi Shanghai Taipei Toronto

With offices in

Argentina Austria Brazil Chile Czech Republic France
Greece Guatemala Hungary Italy Japan Poland Portugal
Singapore South Korea Switzerland Thailand Turkey
Ukraine Vietnam

OXFORD and OXFORD ENGLISH are registered trademarks of
Oxford University Press.

© Oxford University Press 2008

Database right Oxford University Press (maker)

Editorial Director: Sally Yagan
Publisher: Laura Pearson
Managing Editor: Anna Teevan
Project Editor: Maria A. Dalsenter
Design Director: Robert Carangelo
Project Leader: Bridget McGoldrick
Manufacturing Manager: Shanta Persaud
Manufacturing Controller: Eve Wong

ISBN: 978 0 19 477448 2

Printed in China

10 9 8 7 6 5 4 3 2

Acknowledgments

Design and composition by: Stephen Strong

Cover design by: Jaclyn Smith

*The authors would like to thank all the teachers and students
around the world whose feedback has helped us to shape this
series. We would also like to thank:* Kevin Poulter, Juan Antonio
Fernandez Marín, Karen Wade, Rafael Lloyd, and Dagmara
Walkowicz, for agreeing to be interviewed, and Qarie and
Victoria (Mark and Allie). The authors would also like to
thank Margaret Brooks and all those at Oxford University
Press (both in Oxford and around the world) who have
contributed their skills and ideas to producing this book.

Finally, very special thanks from Clive to María Angeles,
Lucia, and Eric, and from Christina to Cristina, for all their
help and encouragement. Christina would also like to thank
her children Joaquin, Marco, and Krysia for their constant
inspiration.

The authors would like to dedicate this book to Krzysztof
Dabrowski.

*The publisher and authors would also like to thank the following
for their invaluable feedback on the materials:* Beatriz Martín,
Michael O'Brien, Wendy Armstrong, Tim Banks, Brian
Brennan, Jane Hudson, Elena Ruiz, Maria Sonsoles de Haro
Brito, and Gaye Wilkinson.

*The authors and publisher are grateful to those who have given
permission to reproduce the following extracts and adaptations of
copyright material:* p. 19 adapted extracts from "Jam today…
tomorrow… yesterday… the day before that… the 11 years

before that" by Sam Coates from *The Times*, 23 June 2004 ©
Sam Coates/NI Syndication Limited 2004; p. 20 lyrics from
"Ka-ching!" by Shania Twain and Robert John Lange © 2002
Out of Pocket Prod. Ltd. and Loon Echo, Inc. All rights for
Out of Pocket Prod. Ltd. administered by Universal Music – Z
Tunes Llc. (ASCAP). All rights for Loon Echo, Inc. administered
by Universal Music – Z Songs (BMI). Used by permission. All
rights reserved; p. 22 translated and abridged extracts from
"Pobre por vocación" by Ana Alonso Montes from *El Mundo*,
24 March 2002. Reproduced by kind permission of El Mundo;
p. 26 adapted extracts from "A holiday can change your life"
by Mark Hodson from *The Sunday Times*, 27 April 2003 ©
Mark Hodson/NI Syndication Limited 2003; p. 35 adapted
extracts from "Why I didn't want to be a millionaire" by Kira
Cochrane from *The Sunday Times*, 11 January 2004. © Kira
Cochrane/NI Syndication Limited 2004; p. 38 adapted extracts
from "Grin and bear it" by Miranda Ingram from *The Times*,
16 June 2004 © Miranda Ingram/NI Syndication Limited 2004;
p. 40 adapted extracts from "A passport to embarrassment"
by John Crowley from *The Daily Telegraph*, 8 August 2003
© John Crowley/The Daily Telegraph Group Ltd. 2003; p. 43
abridged extracts from "Match the woman to the life" from
Marie Claire, June 2003 © Fanny Johnstone/Charlie Gray/
Neil Cooper/Marie Claire/ IPC+ Syndication; p. 53 abridged
extracts from "Homework… old habits die hard so I decide to
forget" by Damian Whitworth from *The Times* 30 November
2004 © Damian Whitworth/NI Syndication Limited 2004; p.
56 adapted extracts from "Getting personal – Joaquín Cortes"
by Carolyn Asome from *The Times*, 16 September 2004 ©
Carolyn Asome/NI Syndication Limited 2004; p. 56 adapted
extracts from "Getting personal – Isabella Rossellini" by
Carolyn Asome from *The Times*, 11 November 2004 © Carolyn
Asome/NI Syndication Limited 2004; p. 62 adapted extracts
from "Is it time to edit your friends?" by Julie Myerson taken
from the November 2001 issue of *Red Magazine*. Copyright
© 2001 Julie Myerson. Reproduced by permission of the
author c/o Rogers, Coleridge & White Ltd., 20 Powis Mews,
London W11; p. 67 adapted extracts from "All in all we want
education" by Adam Luck from *The Times*, 6 December 2004.
Reproduced by kind permission of the author; p. 73 adapted
extracts from "A gossip with the girls?" by Peter Markham
from The Daily Mail, 18 October 2001 © *The Daily Mail* 2001;
p. 83 adapted extracts from "Aimless sloth is secret to long
and happy life" by Roger Boyes from *The Times*, 21 April 2001
© Roger Boyes/NI Syndication Limited 2001; p. 99 adapted
extracts from "Designer brands are for monkeys" by Mary
Ann Sieghart from *The Times*, 28 April 2004 © Mary Ann
Sieghart/NI Syndication Limited 2004; p. 100 adapted extracts
from "Missed you!" from *The Daily Mail*, 26 July 2001 © The
Daily Mail 2001; p. 102 adapted extracts from "Cheat your
way to luck" by Richard Wiseman from *The Daily Mail*, 13
January 2003. Reproduced by kind permission of the author;
p. 106 extract from *A Venetian Reckoning* by Donna Leon,
1995. Copyright © Donna Leon, 1995. Used by permission of
Pan Macmillan, London; extract from Death and Judgement
by Donna Leon. Copyright © 1995 by Donna Leon. Used by
permission of Grove/Atlantic, Inc. Published under the title
Venetian Reckoning in the UK by Pan Macmillan and under
the title *Death and Judgement* in the US by Penguin Books; p.
115 adapted extracts from "The man who missed the lottery
bus" by Tim Woodward from *The Daily Mail*, 20 April 1999 ©
The Daily Mail 1999.

*The publisher would like to thank the following for their kind
permission to reproduce photographs and other copyright
material:* ABACA pp. 11 (McEnroe/Dubreul Corinne), 116
(Laila Ali/Olivier Douliery); Age Fotostock p. 75 (gym/Dennis
MacDonald); AKG pp. 15 (Archie Miles Collection), 154 (Star
Wars/Lucasfilm/20th Century Fox/Zuma Press); Alamy pp.
7 (trifle, cheese/Food Features), 20 (bills/Dennis Hallinan),
22—23 (coins/Bill Bachmann), 24 (woman/Jeff Greenberg,
tapestry/Petr Svarc), 81 (Moodboard), 116 (professor/
Ashley Cooper), 145 (referee/Jupiter Images/Brand X), 153
(magazines/Editorial Images LLC, farmers' market/Andre
Jenny); Albanpix p. 19 (Rob Howarth); Allstar p. 97 (Miramax);
Anthony Blake Photo Library p. 144 (chicken); Associated
Press p. 7 (kitchen/Bebeto Matthews), 11 (Ali/Gary Jones;
Jordan/Maddalone Minto; Beckenbauer/Bertil Ericson), 20
(sales/Susannah Ireland), 47 (Hamilton/Lucy Pemoni), 54
(results/Martin Rickett); Apex p. 115; Aviation Picture Library
p. 100/101 (plane); Bubbles p. 73 (women/Chris Rout); Camera
Press p. 56 (Rossellini/Gamma), 93 (Bernal/Chris Ashford);
Cartoonbank p. 39 (robot/Henry Martin); Catherine Blackie
pp. 38, 60 (graduation), 61; Geoff Cloake p. 89 (landscape);
Cittislow Ludlow p. 71 (logo); Corbis pp. 17 (Zefa/A. Inden),
52 (Tom Wagner), 54 (Carla/Zefa/K Mitchell, Ruben/Zefa/
John-Francis Bourke), 56 (Cortés/Reuters/Andrea Comas),
65 (house/Zefa/Theo Allofs), 70–71 (street/Bo Zanders), 88
(Di Caprio/Sygma), 93 (Aleidita Guevara/Howard Yanes), 94
(Koucher/Elvis Barukcic, Queen Rania/Stephanie Cardinale),

95 (Salvatore DiNolfi), 104 (misty scene/Hulton-Deutsch
Collection), 105 (Prince Albert/Bettmann, Sickert/Hulton);
Daily Telegraph pp. 40/41 (Winner/ Eddie Mulholland, Young/
John Taylor); Digital Vision p. 75 (man shopping/Dan Dalton);
Dorling Kindersley p. 144 (potatoes, vegetables); David
Elkington p. 60 (hockey); Easyjet p. 28; Everett Collection p.
92 (Motorcycle Diaries/© Focus Features), 104 (Depp/TM &
© 20th Century Fox Film Corp.), 108 (soap opera; Futurama/
TM and © 20th Century Fox Film Corp.), 154 (A Room with a
View/© Cinecom International); For Life Charity p. 35; Getty
Images pp. 4 (Image Bank), 14 (Wilson children/Time Life;
Wilson adults/DMI), 28 (car), 50 (Cheese Images/royalty free),
51 (Stockbite), 55, 60 (two women/Image Bank/Jason Homa,
students and teacher/Stone), 65 (New York/Photonica), 69
(woman/Taxi/David Oliver, man/Jasper James), 73 (men/Taxi/
John Booth), 79 (journalists), 102 (clover/Stone, horseshoe/
Iconica/Angelo Cavelli), 106 (Donna Leon/Sean Gallup), 108
(Who wants to be a Millionaire/Matt Stroshanel), 116 (Jon
Stewart/Peter Kramer, Danica Patrick/Ethan Miller), 145
(sports arena/Doug Pensinger), 151 (cottage/Photodisc), 153
(Macy's/Stephen Chemin); Nigel Hillier p. 74; Hunter House
Publishers p. 83; Icon Photo Media p. 67 (Robin Hammond);
The Independent p. 36 (Mark Chilvers); IndexStock p. 144
(eggs/Alamy); Inmagine p. 153 (flowers/Photodisc, books); IPC
p. 42; Kobal Collection pp. 88 (Streep/Universal), 89 (Woods/
New Line/Saul Zaentz/Wing Nut), 154 (High Noon/Stanley
Kramer/United, Indiana Jones/Lucasfilm Ltd/Paramount,
Chicago/Miramax, Dracula/Hammer, Dial M for Murder/
Warner Brothers, Laurel & Hardy/Hal Roach); Ben Lack p.
100 (Ian and Amy); Rafael Lloyd p. 43; Masons News Service
p. 111 (Duncan Miner); Masterfile p. 7 (egg/Masterfile RF);
Museo Anahuacalli p. 59 (museum); NHPA pp. 26 (oragutans/
Photoshot/Andy Rouse), 88 (giraffes/Photoshot); PA Photos
pp. 8 (Lorz), 9, 28 (Eurostar), 54 (results/Martin Rickett),
92 (Che flag), 93 (Rosario/Adam Davy), 145 (few players/
Sean Dempsey, fans/Phil Noble, spectators/Sean Dempsey,
captain/Adam Davy); PhotoEdit Inc. p. 147 (bills/Dennis
MacDonald), 151 (apartment building/Jeff Greenberg,
house/Dennis MacDonald), 153 (travel brochures/Spenser
Grant, supermarket/Mark Richards); Picture Alliance p. 8
(Onischenko/Sports Photo Agency); Kevin Poulter p. 7 (Kevin
Poulter and Frederick's); Punchstock pp. 5 (Digital Vision),
49, 90, 102 (dice/Westend61), 144 (fish/Stockbyte, rice, eggs),
145 (coach/Digital Vision, stadium/Author's Image), 153 (pills/
Photographer's Choice); Rex Features pp. 8 (Maradona), 40
(Ruth England), 94 (Henry/Ken McKay), 105 (James Maybrick,
letter), 116 (Nigel Kennedy/Karl Schoendorfer), Slow Food/
Fiona Richmond p. 70 (market/Maurizio Milanesio, logo);
Robert Harding Picture Library p. 28 (Avignon), 88 (Thailand);
Robertstock p. 23 (news reader/Color Blind Images), 153
(bandage/Simple Stock Shots.com); Sara Evans Picture Desk/
Sunday Times Travel p. 26 (Sally and Victoria); Sipa Press p.
93 (Korda/Angelo Vavalli), 94 (Bono), 99; Solo Syndication p.
101 (Dorothy Fletcher/Danny Howell); Take 3 Management
p. 41 (Ruth England); Terry Taylor Studio p. 41 (IDs), 58; The
Image Works pp. 7 (tennis/Professional Sport/Topham), 24
(Quito/Marcel Eva Malherbe), 33 (John Nordell), 145 (team/
James Marshall), 151 (townhouses/David Grossman), 153
(mall/Mike Greenlar/Syracuse Newspapers); Throckmorton
Fine Art p. 59 (Diego and Frida); The Times p. 47 (Du Toit/Gill
Allen); Dagmara Walkowicz p. 91, Matt Writtle p. 53; Zuma
Press p. 22 (Heidemarie Schwermer).

The painting on page 59 is *The Frame* © 2006 Banco de
México Diego Rivera & Frida Kahlo Museums Trust. Av. Cinco
de Mayo No. 2, Col. Centro, Del. Cuauhtémoc 06059, México,
D.F. Picture obtained from Agence Photographique de La
Réunion de Musées Nationaux, Paris.

Commissioned photography by: Gareth Boden pp. 78,
79 (Jessica), 144 (table); Rob Judges pp. 16, 32, 48, 52
(whiteboard), 64, 80 (meeting), 96, 112; Mark Mason pp. 68,
85, 102 (cat), 106 (book).

Illustrations by: Cartoonstock pp. 63 (Jerry King), 146
(astronauts/Mark Guthrie); Bob Dewar pp. 18, 34, 66, 82, 98,
113, 152; Phil Disley pp. 6, 7, 10 (couple), 12, 21, 25, 29, 30,
31, 37, 46, 62, 76, 107, 110, 149; Ellis Nadler pronunciation
symbols; Neil Gower pp. 28, 100; Ginna Magee p. 10
(penants), 109, 117, 120; Pete Miseredino pp. 148, 151; Andy
Parker pp. 41, 84; Phyllis Pollema-Cahill p. 58; Andy Smith pp.
150, 155 (boyfriend/girlfriend); Kath Walker pp. 9, 27, 39, 44,
54, 61, 72, 86, 87, 146 (presents), 155 (reunion, car); Annabel
Wright pp. 56, 57, 103.

Thanks to: Paul Seligson and Carmen Dolz for the English
Sounds chart.

*Although every effort has been made to trace and contact
copyright holders before publication, this has not been possible
in some cases. We apologize for any apparent infringement of
copyright and if notified, the publisher will be pleased to rectify
any errors or omission at the earliest opportunity.*